OXYMORON™

ANNUAL THEMATIC ANTHOLOGY OF THE
ARTS AND SCIENCES

"being only is

and nothing is altogether not."

parmenides

SERIOUS COMEDY

JUMBO shrimp

Long island eXPressway

PRAVDA

PHILISTINE CULTURE

Organized CHAOS

FRIendly FIRE

haPPiLy

Married

PARTIAI SEllOUT

BittersWeet

go LegaL ethics

IDIOT savant

URBAN CIVILIZATION

POLITICALly correct

gay DivOrcee

INTERNAL REVENUE SERVICE

TOUgh LOVE

publisher **PATRICIA HAGOOD**

editor **EDWARD BINKOWSKI**

design **KEN RABE   GERALD LEWIS**

editorial consultant **MELISSA MALOUF**

contributing editors **MARGARET BOE BIRNS**

JULIE TETEL

design consultant **PAMELA CANNON**

photography consultant **LINN SAGE**

ACKNOWLEDGMENT

henry pearson

THANKS TO:

helen tworkov TRICYCLE MAGAZINE **gini alhadeff** NORMAL MAGAZINE

FASHION INSTITUTE OF TECHNOLOGY FLYLEAF

CHANCE MEETINGS ©**duane michals**

WALKING ON AIR, TIGHTROPE WALKER ©**linn sage**

ISBN 0-9653852-0-5 • ISSN 1090-2236

©1997 Oxymoron Media, Inc.
150 Fifth Avenue, Suite 302
New York, NY 10011

VOLUME ONE

CHANCE

ES OF CHANCE

Last year, a truck driver in Las Vegas ate dinner at a casino and on his way out the door, played his pocket change in a slot machine. He won $10.9 million for his trouble. One lucky pull of the handle, and he was set for life. Adios Peterbilt.

He beat the odds, big ones, too. But in fact such miracles happen all the time, and it's just such possibilities, however fugitive, that bring the players into the casino in the first place. And it's just such possibilities that keep them there, spending their money. Thus their relationship with chance is probably rather more complicated than that of the house. Chance keeps the house on guard, but it gives players hope; chance makes the games fun and it keeps players coming back for more. Which keeps the casino in the chips.

Glenn Schaeffer

The casino operator knows that he and the players operate from the margins between what is most *likely* to happen and what can happen, united in a sort of *pas de deux* of possibilities. A player's hope springs forth from the gap between the likely and the possible. And it's from within this gap that the fundamental tension that underlies the business of chance arises, along with our culture's ambivalent relationship with the gaming business.

Who's got the edge? In gaming, the casino starts with it, and the players are after it. The edge is simple enough to understand, as a function of time and deep pockets, guaranteed by the mathematical probabilities of the games themselves. Plainly put, our pockets are deeper than yours. The casino generally sets table limits such as a $1,000 or $5,000 maximum bet, because any one-wager event can result in a lucky fluke, as the truck driver discovered. We want to encourage a lot of bets. Lots of bets flatten the statistical outliers: a craps player's hot streak, say, counterbalanced by the other players on any given night whose luck runs lukewarm. From the perspective of the house, to the degree you can control chance, then you do so through sheer duration, which we can afford. Over time, the casino's edge will win out.

High-budget players sometimes call the casino's math skills into service. When a certain foreign magnate comes to town, for example, it's not unusual for a math professor in California, on retainer to the big casinos, to get a telephone call and an assignment. The prof's an expert in probability theory, in calculating what happens in that gap between likely and possible.

His assignment will go as follows: Check the math for the amount of time—hours—that our customer must play, at prescribed stakes, to turn a profit for the house. The costs of this customer are no small issue. He requires that $75,000 be given him upon arrival (show-up money) as an inducement to his playing—plus $5,000 for his wife on the slot machines. When he loses, this customer wants a 10%-15% discount off the amount he drops. Then come the goodies. Complimentary room, food and beverage—this means multiple hotel suites, because our customer travels in

style with his entourage. He, or rather *they*, eat caviar and drink collector champagne at breakfast. Before long, our friend can knock through $50,000. Oh, and air-fare. Once our man got the urge for a fishing trip to Alaska—must have seen a documentary on a cable channel upstairs in his luxury suite—and the plane was ordered up forthwith, expenses covered.

Our professor's formula is:

average bet X hours X hands per hour X theoretical win percentage by game

= earning potential or house win.

From that result, you subtract all the costs, including rebates and discounts. That leaves the casino's expected profit from our high roller (assuming he loses), and a semblance of control over chance.

Of course, our guest can win, too. That's when he hauls back a trophy salmon from Ketchikan, contracts gout on our tab, and takes home a million bucks of our money to boot.

In a nutshell, then, that's the business of chance.

No wonder everyone wants an edge. For without it, you must rely on luck. The casino wants the customer's undivided attention at the games—*duration* is the key, remember, money at risk for a defined period. A truck driver can win millions off a one-time pull of a slot handle. But keep him at the machines long enough—maybe a very long time in this particular truck driver's case—and the house will eventually get it all back.

Every player recognizes that the house is always *slightly* more likely to win on any turn of the cards, roll of the dice, or pull of the handle, which is why there is a casino industry. Critics of our industry generally charge that players are victims of their own gullibility. But players in casinos are as smart as patrons elsewhere in the consumer economy. They expect to pay a price to receive value, and they're pretty adept at calibrating the relationship between the two. What's the value? Time having fun. Players want as much time as possible for their budget at the games, flirting with possibilities

The odds on the games determine how long the money lasts, and some odds favor the house more, or less, than others. Casinos possess these edges (or percentages) on the live games:

from .6–16.7 on craps, depending on odds given on the pass line
1.17–14.1 on baccarat
1.0 to 15.0 in twenty-one or blackjack, as it's also known
5.26 on roulette, assuming a double zero, and a 2.70 with a single zero.

The variations in odds in games such as craps or twenty-one have to do with player strategy; they're the result of dumb bets, simply put, or smart ones; the worst play in twenty-one gives the house an edge of 15%, the best play cuts that edge to 1% or sometimes even less. What all this means in terms of dollars and cents, is this: if you happen to be making bets at the rate of $100 every 20 minutes in double-zero roulette, for example, the house will likely end up with, on average, $5.26 of your money at the end of that period—the casino's "win" or "hold"—and you'd likely end up with $94.84, and so on through ensuing rounds of play. If you continue to play at this rate with your remaining money, it would take about six-and-a-half hours of play before all of your money was gone. You'd win some along the way, and lose some, but you'd lose just a bit more, assuming no hot streaks.

In all, close to $2,000 dollars would pass back and forth between you and the house during those six-and-a-half hours, a figure that's known in the business as the "handle," which is sometimes confused with revenue by lay observers, especially when governments start eyeing gaming as a source for more taxes. No matter what the handle, the casino's profit on all of this back-and-forth for six-and-a-half hours or so is that original $100, money turned into casino revenues, minus expenses for all of the things any other business spends money on such as labor, advertising, insurance, depreciation, maintenance, interest expenses, and taxes, plus a few things other businesses don't have to contend with, such as the occasional wealthy guest on a tear.

In slot machines, the house edge in the Las Vegas market ranges from 5%–10%—that is, if you were to drop $100 in a slot machine over the period of an hour, the slot machine would keep from $5–$10 of it—and this edge is completely controlled by the house. Inside a slot machine is a microchip that is programmed to dictate payoffs. At first glance, the temptation would seem to be to adjust for a stingy payback, but a casino's biggest earners are in fact the most generous slots. Players, naturally, are attracted to slots where their money lasts a little longer, and knowing this, the casinos keep the bigger denomination slots, like the dollar slots, "looser" than the smaller denomination slots, like quarters. Typically, 25% of a casino's slot "pieces" (gaming lingo for slot machines) might be dollar machines, but they produce about half of a casino's slot revenues.

Slot machines are increasingly the game of choice in casinos, accounting for more than 60% of casino revenues nationwide this past year. The lure of the machine, as opposed to live games, is twofold. First, there is no inhibition for the inexperienced player—and with the rise of the superstore in Las Vegas (which incorporates various attractions within the casino), more and more visitors are infrequent, even frosh players. At the tables, one's indecision or rash moves, which can worsen odds, are apparent to onlookers. At the machine by yourself, there are no bad moves; all players are equal before the algorithm. Anyone who can operate a VCR or automatic teller machine can be an expert. Second, you can get all-time lucky. Today you find slot machines electronically "linked" among numerous casinos, which boosts total jackpot sizes and spreads the risk away from any individual casino. Our truck driver hit it big on just such a machine.

In the end, no matter the game, the edge functions for the house—with time as an ally. Over the run of many bets, the numbers will true out, and the casino will beat most of the players most of the time (it's called probability theory). Play long enough, the casino triumphs.

Our wealthy player, like other players, understands all of this very well, understands that the house has the edge, particularly over time. For his part, he endeavors to be high maintenance, inflate the casino's cost structure, cut its margin, reduce its money. And have more fun while he loses by garnering as many comps, freebies, and trips to Alaska as possible. And in the meantime, his 15% discount on losses incurred at baccarat clips our theoretical edge per hand from 1.25% to almost 1%. He's attacking.

This is gambling in the big city today. But in the biggest city, Las Vegas, we've left the realm of gambling per se as entertainment superstores have come on the scene. Here, we've entered the realm of mainstream entertainment.

Entertainment has been the fastest-growing category of U.S. household spending since the late 1980s, moving up to third place overall, behind housing and food. Population statistics tell the story: the prosperous cohort of baby-boomers is now in middle-age, mostly beyond big-ticket purchases (college tuition being the prime exception); the golden grays, meanwhile, our post-55 generation that owns 60% of the financial and real assets in this country, have time, mobility, and, frequently, money on their hands. Together, these groups make up most of the new demand for travel and entertainment, driving the growth of that industry at a 30% premium to GDP. Travel and entertainment should become our largest industry in the next century.

The most popular "location-based" entertainment experience in 1995 in the U.S. was casino gaming, attracting visits from 30% of the American adult population. Las Vegas has done more than its share in driving the numbers. Since the introduction of entertainment superstores in the past half-decade, the visitor counts to the city have jumped nearly 50%, to approximately 30 million in 1995, making Las Vegas, Nevada the leading destination for entertainment in the U.S and the world.

Entertainment superstores in Las Vegas are a unique species. As recently as twenty years ago, a big casino and hotel on the Las Vegas Strip might contain 1,000 rooms and 40,000 square feet of casino space. Today, with companies like Circus Circus and Mirage Resorts at the fore, the superstores have won the day, typically featuring 3,000 rooms (or more) and 100,000 square feet of casino. The nine largest hotels in the country are all on the Las Vegas Strip, a literal stone's throw apart. Besides the standard offering of rooms and games, these superstores also present non-gaming attractions (ranging from *faux* volcanoes to pirate ship battles to dynamic-motion theaters to world-class roller coasters), along with inventive retail areas. You can spend a vacation inside a single superstore, whose themes are generally historic and grandiose. Luxor, a 32-story glass pyramid owned by Circus Circus, portrays ancient Egypt, complete with a replicated Tut's tomb.

Indeed, across the country, the rise of casinos has been a social phenomenon of the 1990s; eight states legalized casino gaming between 1990-94 at the same time that Las Vegas enjoyed its own boom. In 1995, casino revenues in the U.S. were approximately $19 billion. The casino sector of the total entertainment industry is substantial, especially when you compare casinos to, say, theme parks, or cinema box offices, or cruise ships—each less than one-third the size of the casino business. Master investor Peter Lynch, doubtless with a touch of hyperbole, has predicted that casinos *alone* will emerge as one of America's biggest industries in the twenty-first century. Automobiles, technology, biotech, casinos: an American parlay of millennial commercial might.

It's okay to play in America in the twenty-first century, though it hasn't always been so. The rise of the casino has bothered more than a few commentators, whose antipathy toward pleasure-seeking finds its locus in the casino, where money can be played for. This antipathy has religious roots harking back to a tension between our uptight Puritan culture, defined by its sober-faced work ethic, and our more freewheeling frontier culture, with its preference for escapism.

Though more than 80% of Americans in recent polls claim to regard gaming as legitimate recreation, it's the stiff-backed holdouts who get more press, especially through editorialists like William Safire, who like to sound notes that assert their "religious right–hood."

High-strung opponents to casinos frequently misread the facts of American history, replete as it is with risk-taking for money and the concomitant activity of gambling. What galls them today is what has bothered them clear back when they wore buckled shoes and tricorn hats: the notion that you can play a game with money, have fun, and get paid for it. This breaks the old-time Puritan covenant of hard work in exchange for the reward of grace. Money is sacramental to the arch-Protestant. Gambling, see, may be about money, but it can never be about profit, a distinction that demonizes gambling, for it falsely glorifies a kind of anti-profit that can be got without exertion, good character, or plan. For the arch-Protestant, you don't play with or for money; you must come by it piously.

Our most stringent Protestant inheritance is from John Calvin, the Protestant Reformation's main theorist, a theologian who was hostile to all forms of pleasure—in his spare time, he was known to burn a heretic (that is, a Catholic) now and then in the public square in Geneva—and he especially hated gambling, railing against pagan notions of chance or luck, "with whose significance the minds of the godly ought not to be occupied," he wrote. "For if every success is God's blessing, and calamity and adversity his curse, no place remains in human affairs for fortune and chance." A believer in determinism, Calvin perceived outright sacrilege in the very idea of gambling: given that chance itself couldn't exist outside divine law, the gambler by his hopeful wagers was, indeed, supplicating the Lord for an intervention in his favor. After all, in a pre-determined scheme of things, it would have to be God who set up your lucky number. God's no croupier and He's certainly no fixer. To gamble, by these strict lights, is to parody prayer.

For Calvin and his following, gambling violates the structure of blessed authority, which doles out reward in measure for dutiful behavior. And luck or chance, as a vector of reward, undercuts the Protestant theology of hard work. Money must be deserved. It isn't to be found or won, but earned.

So goes the controversy about casinos in America. They're places where money can be got without recourse to any moral framework. For the moralist, this money shouldn't count because it's neither reward nor profit. It doesn't reinforce obedient behavior. Funny money subverts the status quo. But this is a Puritan status quo, at bottom, based on historic, exigent circumstances as much as any theological text. The Bible, ironically enough, remains silent with respect to gambling.

What has changed markedly in the past three hundred years is the standard of affluence in America. In colonial America, you had to work hard to eat. Alone in the vast wilderness, the Puritans knew that slackers starved. But today, our economy is more bountiful and complex. Most of us in the 1990s possess resources for more than subsistence; we can afford discretionary consumption. Modern Americans' identities as consumers solidified, paradoxically, during the Depression when they were called upon to spend what money they had as a kind of patriotic duty. That's when the idea of the weekend finally took hold, a two-day period expressly oriented toward recreation, rest, and above all, shopping. Largely due to the weekend, our modern culture came to fully embrace the movie theater, professional spectator sports, amusement parks, department stores, museums, nightclubs, and the residential suburb as a preferred homesite. These places, in effect, are characterized by their being "away from work," created for the sheer spending of time and money. The social custom today is to consume 28% of our time (two days out of seven). The Puritans were right in their time and place, of course, but they were right 300 years ago in a hostile environment where the Devil really did take the hindmost. They couldn't afford to tolerate goof-offs back then. Now we can't afford not to have them.

With the shift from an industrial to an information economy, free time becomes an economic force. The social critic Jeremy Rifkin has argued in a recent book that we are on the verge of establishing an "after-work" society, where information professionals—workers—will have more control over their work schedules and sites. Suddenly, regimentation isn't the only way money's made.

Twenty-five years ago, the (late) futurist Herman Kahn was already predicting that leisure time would be a powerful force in the coming century, particularly among highly developed countries, thereby stimulating the tourism markets. An America with free time, for one thing, will ascribe positive values to experiences found outside of work. The pursuit of pleasure, escape, and the consumption of entertainment will be legitimized by their very market function. For these formerly taboo activities will now be vital growth sectors of our overall economy. As earnest a culture as Japan has recently arrived at the same port: their political rhetoric now urges their citizens to take time off and spend, in order to boost the consumer side of their flagging GDP. In our large, multifaceted economy, play has its purpose. By the year 2000, play (or leisure) will account for 15% of our national economy. And that 15% by itself is bigger than the GDPs of most other nations in the world.

Play has been gaining on us for years. Sixty years ago, in my mother's religious household, it was considered a sin to read funny papers on Sunday, to watch any movie whose theme wasn't uplifting, to dance, or to pipe up when one's parents were speaking. My grandmother, the daughter of a gospel singer (christened Perly Gates, if you can believe it), wasn't in her youth allowed to wear bright clothing of any kind, especially red. One day, in 1925, on duty as a cashier in the downstairs vault at Woolworth's in Los Angeles, she bought a jar of red shoe polish and painted up her white, sensible shoes. For a kick. By this gesture, I think, she called a time-out. Today, ninety and still devout, my grandmother admits no regret about that call.

Casinos, in their own fashion, are about time-outs. The visitor to an entertainment superstore casino in Las Vegas finds an environment dedicated to making money seem unreal. The pleasure proposition is straightforward: this isn't like work. It isn't life by the clock or the task. Here money becomes the stuff we play with rather than kill ourselves for. Yes, play: an alchemy that turns the most serious matter of workaday life, the getting of money, into a game of risking it to win more. And what our neo-Puritan critics conveniently

dismiss is that casino players, our consumers, know the deal. They're buying the environment, the privilege to goof off; they're paying a type of admission to a place where the rules of ordinary life don't control them. A fantasy. In principle, the casino resembles a movie theater, our culture's primary environment of unreality, where an admission price buys you two hours in the dark under the spell of celluloid images flickering on the screen. Time-out. The bonus, insofar as casinos go, is that in our environment you sometimes get your price of admission paid back to you, plus—when you're lucky—other people's as well.

In Las Vegas, we strive to build gargantuan stores for play. Besides big casinos, we develop monumental hotels (folks come to the Mojave Desert, mind you, to see these buildings; there's nothing else here), fine restaurants, elaborate shows, and novel shopping areas. In a word, the new casinos are theatrical. Entertainment superstores are supposed to be everything that home, office, factory, farm and Internet can never be: spaces defined solely by the rules of play.

With money to spend and time to spend it, the masses are looking for entertainment value. (Research shows that the average casino player's household income is above the national median. So is their level of education, by the way.) They don't have to look further than the contemporary casino. Luck itself is a kind of value, along with our moderate prices and variety of experiences. And so, in modern life, is play.

Calvinists, in our day and age, may still wish to deny or discount luck, yet here's a streak that's hard to condemn. A waiter we'll call Chad sat down at a twenty-one table at Circus Circus during the graveyard shift on New Year's Day a few years back. He walked in with $200 and bought into the game with $50, breaking it into $5 chips. His tiny stack began to grow. The shift manager, a senior colleague of mine today, knew Chad from a local coffee shop. Chad was easy to recognize because of his hairpiece and thick glasses. The manager said hello, surveyed the action on the other tables, and went into his office to finish some paperwork. When he came out, Chad was still going, his pile stacking higher. Night passed

into day and by 7:00 a.m., Chad had a crowd around him, a retinue, admirers, a rooting section. He was playing $500 on three spots per hand. This isn't tip money, $1,500 bets. Chad was now über-Chad. His hair looked like Samson's and his eyesight was X-ray. People were calling him "sir." Chad, you'd better believe, was encountering luck and winning the duel. It happens. The shift manager, by sight, could count down Chad's chip racks faster than Chad could.

Indeed, Chad thought he owned $30,000.

"It's fifty," the shift manager informed him.

The crowd beseeched Chad to quit. He wasn't having any. He had a single goal—a new Cadillac. The rest of the money was for fame. After he'd lost back enough to buy just his car, Chad got off his stool and went home. When the shift manager next met up with Chad a year or so later, he inquired about the Caddy.

"Best damn car I ever drove," Chad replied.

That car was like Cinderella's glass slipper saved from the ball.

In this world—a vale of tears as one literary Puritan called it—of work, rules, physics, and death, it's nice to allow for a little luck.

By the laws of science, luck may be a statistical outlier and certain not to prevail, but when you see it in action, it can flat amaze you.

In 1994, Kerry Packer, the Australian millionaire, had a big year. He beat the MGM in Las Vegas for $24 million, over numerous trips, at the twenty-one and baccarat tables. Packer's style is to go all six spots on the twenty-one layout at once, $75,000 a spot, $450,000 per hand. At baccarat, he shoots $250,000 per hand at you. It's only money. If you think chance is an easy business, then you play him.

EVERY HUMAN BEING HAS TO DECIDE IF LIFE IS WORTH LIVING
AND THAT HE IS WILLING TO "TAKE A CHANCE." IN THIS WAY THE GODDESS FORTUNA
IS THE REFLECTION OF OUR KIND OF TEMPERAMENT. HUMAN BEINGS WHO PERCEIVE THE VALIDITY OF LAW AND ORDER
WILL CHERISH FAITH IN AN ORDERED UNIVERSE.
THOSE...WHO FIND THAT ORDER SOMETIMES IMPOSES RESTRAINT
WILL REJOICE IN THE FREEDOM THAT BECKONS FROM UNCHARTED WAYS AND FOR THEM A UNIVERSE OF CHANCE
WILL MEAN A UNIVERSE OF OPPORTUNITY.

HOWARD PATCH [THE GODDESS FORTUNA IN MEDIAEVAL LITERATURE]

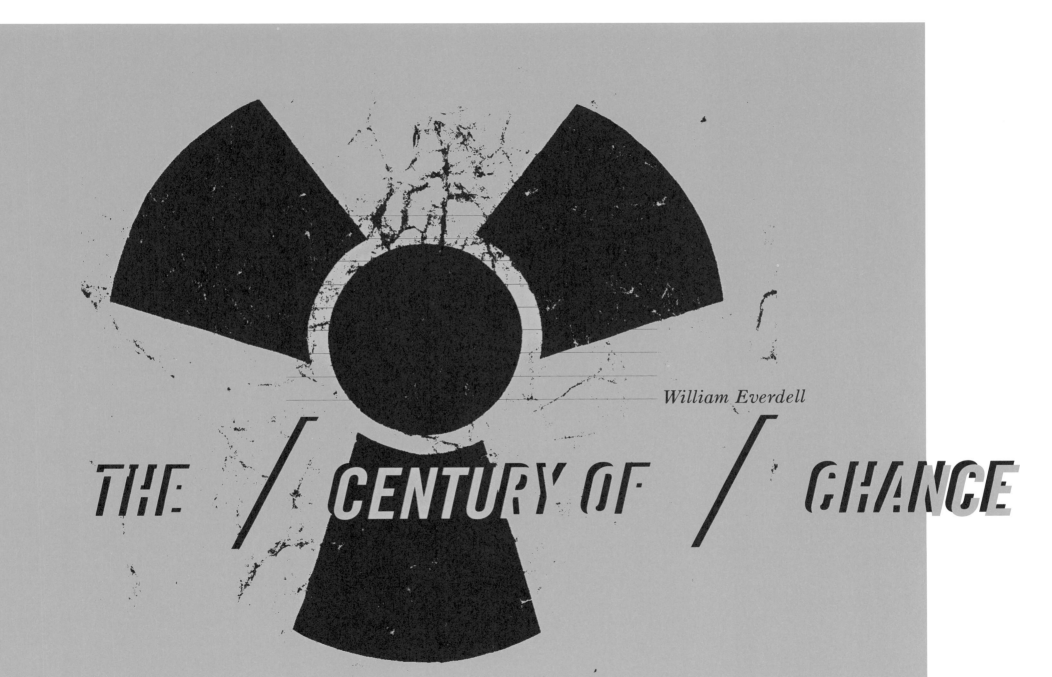

William Everdell

THE / CENTURY OF / CHANCE

When Caesar said "*Alea jacta est*" and gave the order to cross the Rubicon, dice were a Roman commonplace, but to Caesar they stood for the about-to-be-determined future, not the overall indeterminacy of truth. Times have changed. Two thousand years after Caesar, when Einstein said, "God does not play dice," his colleagues only shook their heads and said he was getting old. The Fates are as dead as the Great God Pan, and ours has become the century of chance. Stochastics and statistics are our everyday language of explanation. Our ancestors noticed the unpredictable, but our contemporaries assume it only for the future of individuals, confident that the future of aggregates is certain.

This distinction has not happened without reflection. In the seventeenth century Blaise Pascal and the Bernoulli brothers calculated odds, and in the eighteenth century Condorcet and Laplace turned the odds into laws of probability. Nineteenth-century minds discovered how to make those laws predict social behavior. But it is only in the last hundred years, on an earth so crowded as to virtually embody Jakob Bernoulli's Law of Large Numbers, that thinkers began to claim an unpredictable destiny not only for human individuals, but for the individual parts of the whole material universe. It is in our time that "law" has come to mean a statistical mean of a sample, and that "aleatory" or "dice-like" has come to describe the behavior of nearly everything there is.

This change was called the "Probabilistic Revolution" by the French mathematician Emile Borel in 1914. The revolution occurred between 1824 and 1930, or so it is generally agreed in a small academic suburb called the history of statistics. In 1987, a book in the form of a virtual conference among the historians of statistics appeared under the title The Probabilistic Revolution, *featuring the big six: Lorraine Daston of Brandeis, Ian Hacking of Toronto, Lorenz Krüger of Göttingen, Theodore M. Porter of Virginia, Stephen Stigler of Chicago, and Gerd Gigerenzer of the University of Constance, Switzerland. Thomas Kuhn led off by proposing that the rise of "probabilism" was a genuine example of one of his now-celebrated paradigm shifts. Kuhn had launched his academic career with a demonstration of how statistical thinking had led to Planck's energy quantum, and until his death in 1996 remained the leading science historian regularly teaching us how to distinguish an intellectual revolution from a mere change of heart.*

Probabilism may well be a revolution, but we don't know very much about it. Statistics and probability are not canonical in academic curricula. In mathematics they are an extra, and they are normally offered only as a practicum to physicists, epidemiologists, insurance underwriters, pollsters, and the composers of multiple-choice tests. The subject rarely invades the history of culture and, when it does, it is usually stolen from sociology or dragged in via the history of mathematics instead of the history of science, engineering, or social policy. This sidelong understanding leads to antinomies in thought and occasionally ridiculous bouts of public discourse—like the current American debate on relative risk. The U.S. national highway speed limit of 55 miles per hour has just been abandoned, apparently on the grounds of an all-but-constitutional right-to-drive. In the debate (such as it was), it proved impossible to convince American drivers of the tragically well-tested fact that highway deaths were certain to go up by a few thousand a year as the limit was raised to 60 miles per hour and beyond, and that each driver's risk of being one of them would go up commensurably. As a people, we found this baffling. How could the risk of a driver's dying on the road depend on anything but the driver's own skill and prudence? Perhaps it is American drivers who keep our proliferating state lotteries going, unable to grasp how very much less likely they are to win a million than they are to die on the highway. A prominent part of the American birthright is the most radically individualistic ethical tradition in the world. It often dictates, as it did in the time of Horatio Alger, that social policy could be based on a single life story. There are even some radical individualists who are prepared to argue that since so much social policy derives from statistics, we should make no social policy at all.

se public debates about risk and policy seem com-
ely uninformed by the commonplaces of late
ntieth-century physics. It remains hard to grasp, for
mple, that although there is virtual certainty that half
 radium atoms in a sample will break down sponta-
usly in 1,300 years, the future of any one atom is
rely unpredictable. The randomness of radioactive
ay, as this is called, has been known since the exper-
nts of Rutherford and Soddy at the turn of the
tury. Uncertainty about physical processes,
ever—or randomness in the laws that describe
n—had been known a generation or more before
oactivity was discovered. Between 1872 and 1877,
ennese physicist named Ludwig Boltzmann, with a
-looking beard, thick glasses, and a zest for contro-
y had proposed, and successfully defended, an
ation for the Second Law of Thermodynamics that
s more random than radioactive decay. It took the
n of the sum of the probabilities that all the six hun-
d sextillion speeding, colliding gas molecules in a
-mole (a standard gram-molecular weight of the
 container would be found in all of their possible
ngements or states. Previous physicists had
umed that the only way to do physics was the
vtonian way, to show how one state of a physical sys-
 was absolutely determined by the state that
ceded it in time. Boltzmann, who knew that the
d "gas" was Dutch for "chaos," gave up the idea of
ermining any one state of the system at all, arguing,
 that it was theoretically impossible, but simply that
vas not worth doing. Instead, the probability of a
e depended on the number of other, different states
 could lead to it. Boltzmann's equation for entropy,
 k log W, was beautiful, useful, and philosophically
llenging, for it led to reconceiving entropy, a func-
 of transferred heat and temperature, as the
vailability of energy, or simply, disorder. One of its
lications was that the direction of time itself was
 from states with lower probabilities to states with
er ones: whether in a one-mole container on earth
ver the entire universe, assuming it was finite. After
tzmann hanged himself in a fit of depression at an
iatic summer resort in 1906, $S = k \log W$ was en-
ved on his tombstone.

$$S = k \log W$$

Next came Max Planck, the patient, courtly German physicist who was the first to write Boltzmann's equation in the form S = k log W. Ironically, he had spent years trying to prove that Boltzmann's derivation of the Second Law from probabilities was wrong. Soon after Planck finally convinced himself it was right, he discovered that a derivation similar to Boltzmann's could be applied to the equation of radiation, solving the so-called Black-Body Problem that physicists had been working on for thirty years. To divide his first equations into statistics-like sums of terms, he had to assume a tiny unit of energy-time that, incidentally, turned up so deeply embedded in the final expression that he couldn't get it out again. This was the origin of the "quantum."

Planck's quantum appeared in the last month of the nineteenth century. Some twenty-five years later, Schrödinger, Heisenberg, and Dirac founded quantum mechanics. Indeterminacies emerged again, even more mind-boggling this time, making it more and more clear that for individual events, cause and effect had been almost completely disconnected. Bohr, Heisenberg's mentor, fathered an interpretation of all these results that suggested that any and all quantum-level events with any chance of happening actually were happening until a human being measured for one of those events and forced a choice on nature. What we can't know in some area of subatomic physics is only the complement—the missing half—of what we can know. Measure for waves and get waves; measure for particles and get particles. The waves and particles contradict each other, but since they're never on stage together, physics can survive a little longer.

Not long after, Schrödinger famously argued in letters to Einstein that if Bohr was right, a cat in a closed box which contained a cat killing mechanism triggered by a random radioactive decay, was not dead or alive, but both dead and alive, until the box was opened. This was where Einstein signed off with the famous dictum, "Gott würfelt nicht—God does not play dice." But even if no one was responsible, the dice kept being thrown. After World War II, Richard Feynman, with Schwinger, Tomonaga, and Dyson, found a new quantum theory by which one could compute the odds called the "vacuum potential"—the chance that "virtual pairs" of particles and antiparticles will arise at unpredictable times and in indeterminable locations in a space otherwise totally empty. Later physicists informed us of another precisely measurable chance, called the "tunneling potential": a quantum-level particle contained by a field can disappear and show up again in a different field in no time at all. More and more of the exact observations and certain events of past centuries dissolved into medians and resonances, central tendencies and potentials—the fabric of probability.

The submicroscopic world was a world of chance by mid-century, but only for physicists. As for the macroscopic world, it seemed as predictable as sunrise has always been. Actually, sunrise, too, was subject to chance perturbations. Ten years before Planck's quantum, the peerless French mathematician Henri Poincaré had turned his hand to the problem of completely describing and predicting the behavior of the solar system. After being supposedly "solved" in England by Newton, the problem had been almost completely taken over by the French. In Napoleon's time, Pierre-Simon Laplace had boiled down Newton's cosmology into such an elegant array of equations and polished off so many of the remaining difficulties, that when Napoleon asked him where the Creator might come into it, Laplace is famously said to have replied, "Sire, I have no need of that hypothesis." There was still one difficulty left, the Three-Body Problem of precisely predicting the behavior of three or more mutually orbiting, mutually gravitating, masses. Poincaré took it up in 1889, and in a few years he not only found it to be insoluble but managed to prove that it would always be insoluble. In fact, even the positions of the planets of our own solar system were impossible to predict exactly, by any conceivable law, no matter what their initial positions were and no matter how exactly they were known. There were, fortunately, regularities, and Poincaré provided a mathematics for them: the mathematics we now know as "chaos." There's that word again, Greek for "primeval disorder."

A century since Poincaré's discovery, the growing realization that most of physics is statistics has still not reached all the humanists. Sometimes, it is true, we hear a good deal about Heisenberg's "Uncertainty Principle," and how it has been seen to prove the existence of God or, at the very least, leave scope for what the nineteenth century called free will. In fact,

it does nothing of the kind. The principle only holds in the subatomic world, and doesn't seem to connect to macrocosmic events, as the radium atom was linked to Schrödinger's Cat. It simply states that if you multiply however much you don't know about the velocity of a subatomic particle by however much you don't know about its position, you will never get a figure less than h, Planck's tiny constant. So, the more you know about one, the less you are guaranteed to know about the other.

Surprising in its exactness, the Uncertainty Principle distances itself from the much more fuzzy probabilities of science. In those areas, the more measuring you do, the more the errors can be isolated and reduced and the less uncertain you become. It was the nineteenth century's first great statistical mathematician, Gauss, who discovered that the random part of a measuring error is inversely proportional to the square root of the number of measurements one makes. Because of Gauss, we often have the comfort of knowing that in the macro-world we can reduce error as often as we like even if we cannot eliminate it entirely. But in an exchange worthy of old Bohr himself, we are denied the assurance of knowing exactly what we mean by certainty or what the real status of a norm may be. Were the probabilities in the events or the particles themselves or in the mind that observed them? We know only that if probability were subjective instead of objective, no law could predict the behavior of objects (like dice) no matter how many trials were undergone.

These antinomies seem more solidly unresolvable when they arise in physics, the hard-nosed science par excellence, but they have arisen everywhere. Statistics was born in the same century as probability, and named for the effort of its pioneers to provide the emerging state bureacracies with accurate data about masses of citizen-subjects. Now those heady days are long gone. What began in the seventeenth century with amateurs poking about in parish bills of mortality and registers of birth had become a vast enterprise before the twentieth century began. New ways of thinking made it possible. Democracy made it necessary. (Mass marketing has privatized it and made it inescapable.) Seizing upon the measurements made by the British government of the chest diameters of 5,738 Scottish soldiers, an oddly obsessive Belgian named Adolphe Quételet began in 1835 to define something he called l'homme moyen, *"the average man." This creature, which he also called* l'homme type, *or the "typical man," was what every actual person would be and do were it not for random deviations (errors?) and what would later be called their "normal distribution." Quételet's book was called* On Man, *and later,* Social Physics. *It talked authoritatively of the average man's "penchant for crime" and the "tendency toward marriage." Every person, in Quételet's thinking, was capable on a percentage basis of doing whatever that percent of the whole citizenry did. If two percent of Englishmen murdered their wives, each Englishman must be said to harbor a two-percent tendency to murder his wife. Among the direct descendants of these two percent murderers, we recognize the 2.3 children each American family has today. (The Menendez brothers, perhaps?) Quételet's* l'homme moyen *was not at all what James*

Joyce would have called "sensuel." Nor, in this thicket of percentages, was there much maneuvering room for that great prize of nineteenth-century thought, free will. What has in our century deprived physicists of causation in quantum events gave the emerging sociologists of the nineteenth century their first taste of success in finding general causation in human events. Thus arose the time-honored moral argument about statistics that has continued for a century and a half.

The fact is that statistical regularities are not absolute. Taking them for laws as precise as gravity was the mistake Laplace made in his 1795 Philosophical Essay on Probabilities—*a mistake not wholly unexpected in the work of the man who had systematized Newton. They were not laws at all. No causal law underlies the probability of black or white balls being taken one-by-one from a jar; no predictive necessity dictates the stable percentage of men and women who get married or the ratio of girls to boys who get born.*

Such regularities, in fact, only seem absolute when viewed from the right distance, like the paintings Georges Seurat began to make in 1885. Franz Exner, Boltzmann's successor at the University of Vienna, was even so bold as to suggest in 1919 that microcosmic indeterminism adds up or averages out (as the phrase goes) to macrocosmic determinism. It's an attractive idea still, but it doesn't work. All it does is demonstrate once more the seductive magic of almost repeatable relationships and the smooth bell-shaped curves of normal distribution. Correlation of statistical norms may indeed result in pinning those norms to underlying events that we can call causes and effects, but the correlation itself, however elegant, is not sufficient. Stock prices have correlated inversely rather well with skirt lengths over time, but there does not seem to be any common cause.

In the decades between Quételet and 1900, the fate of statistics fell into the hands of the biologists. Francis Galton managed to show how to disengage two or more "bell" curves from one another, and Hugo De Vries showed how to use them to prove that Mendel had been right about the existence of genes. In the 1890s Galton's disciple Karl Pearson pioneered the "regression analysis" of data points to find the bell curves they concealed, and coined the term "standard deviation." Pearson's first thought was to apply his discoveries to the improvement of the human breed—a temptation that bell curves have been presenting to statisticians ever since. As the mathematical tools accumulated, the question of what, exactly, was being measured faded into the background; but it never died, and remains as problematical today as it ever did. We postulate that one sunrise is so comparable to another sunrise as to deserve the category and the name, but we do not prove it. The only possible proof is statistical. The question of identity leads to the question of number, which leads to the law of large numbers.

But the question of identity is also a statistical question. Ian Hacking tells the story of the formidable nineteenth-century Prussian statistician, Ernst Engel, who was asked by a court in 1850 to provide evidence of whether the new *Dresdener Journal* 1848-50 was the same newspaper as the old *Dresdener Tageblatt* of 1846-48. For 7,017 articles in 366 issues of the two papers, Engel made 84 subject categories, to which he added three article forms, several regional datelines, and five political tendencies. Having compared the newspapers in each category, he concluded they were not one but two.

It was in 1878 that the pioneering genius of Charles Sanders Peirce pointed out to the readers of *Popular Science Monthly* that the whole scientific effort to connect one sort of event with another rested necessarily on the inductive variety of logic, and was therefore utterly dependent on probability. That nature's behavior should be uniform was an assumption by no means guaranteed. The probability of the sun's rising could not be changed into certainty until more trials had been made of the event. Many more trials. An infinite number. The failure of strict induction is, in fact, a failure to find completed infinities. The incomplete is the child of the aleatory.

It gets worse. Some infinities are countable. Some are not. The ones that are, like the even numbers, have elements that can be picked out, one after another. They are well-ordered. The ones that are not countable are not well-ordered and do not contain elements that can be picked out. In a sense, we are unable to specify what we are doing when we distinguish an element in one of these latter infinities.

And life is open-ended, paradoxically, because it closes. In the long run, as Maynard Keynes remarked after he had published his *Treatise on Probability*, we are all dead. And a good thing, too, wrote Peirce in "The Doctrine of Chances," because in the longest run, all probabilities for individuals are negative:

All human affairs rest upon probabilities, and the same thing is true everywhere. If man were immortal he could be perfectly sure of seeing the day when everything in which *he had trusted should betray his trust, and, in short,* of coming eventually to hopeless misery. He would break down, at last, as every great fortune, as every dynasty, as every civilization does. *In place of this we have death.*

Like W. S. Gilbert's billiard sharp, we victims of the Probabilistic Revolution seem condemned to play "On a cloth untrue, with a twisted cue, and elliptical billiard balls." The difficulties for the scoffer, however, are as great as they are for the sharp. Repeated events, repeated inductions, correlations close to 1, all contribute to what Peirce called the Fixation of Belief. We act on what we believe, and we believe what has proved to be highly probable. Not for the probabilist is the hollow claim of the poststructuralist that history is unknowable and the writing of past history impossible. If history were indeed unknowable, the postmodernist would be excused from knowing it; and that would turn all of his démarches into discoveries and make all his discoveries original.

The more you know about the humanities, poststructuralists seem to think, the less you are guaranteed to know about the sciences. But it isn't true. Too many humanists mistakenly identify with "science" those relics of science's pre-probabilistic past that were taught to them in high-school courses without benefit of statistics. The humanities are thoroughly aleatory nowadays. John Cage's music is often randomized, and so is much of dance. True, most writers still prefer to think of themselves as being in control of words, and resist the loss of agency. Perhaps, in the end, it is literature that gives us our prejudice in favor of causation, and that when writing becomes obsolete the aleatory will explain everything. But then or now, as Poincaré's contemporary, Mallarmé, wrote in his last poem, "A throw of the dice will never abolish chance."

Black II
25″ x19″ Acrylic on canvas

Artists
24″ x18″ Mixed Media

Estelle Shay

15

DOCTOR:
 Now I am going to explain. The truth of life is—there is none.

MIRROR:
 Liar.

DOCTOR:
 Impossible. The truth about life isn't demonstrable.
What does this tell us about the word "truth"?
 It tells us that somewhere, on some level, there is a misuse of
the word "truth."

MIRROR:
 Or the word "life."

DOCTOR:
 No—that's not a word.

MIRROR:
 Of course it is.

DOCTOR:
 Sorry. That isn't a word.

MIRROR:
 "LIFE"—I just pronounced it.

DOCTOR:
 Did you?

MIRROR:
 I think so.

DOCTOR:
 You'd have to go back into the past to know for sure and one thing
I know for sure—you can't go back into the past.

MIRROR:
 I have a memory.

DOCTOR:
 Memory of the past?

MIRROR:
 Yes.

DOCTOR: (Pause)
 Hmm, I wonder if a memory about the past is really the past?

MIRROR:
 Let's let life give us the answer.

DOCTOR:
 Now you're talking.

MIRROR:
 Life always comes up with an
answer.

DOCTOR:
 Idiot—that's just talk.

MIRROR:
 That's just "Life"! This thing is called life
Doctor.

DOCTOR:
 This thing is called nothing.

MIRROR:
 Let's decide if this thing is called life
or this thing is called nothing.

DOCTOR:

This is nothing called life.

MIRROR:

How are we really going to decide?

DOCTOR:

You decide.

MIRROR:

I should decide how we are going to decide?

Or I should just decide between life and nothing?

DOCTOR:

Take your pick.

MIRROR: (Pause)

Nothing.

DOCTOR:

Ah—life!

MIRROR:
If you say so.

DOCTOR:
Brief but to the point.

MIRROR:
That's an anti-definition.

DOCTOR:
The criteria of any good definition.

MIRROR:
Except life is neither brief nor to the point.

DOCTOR:
What is?

MIRROR:
Nothing.

DOCTOR:
Let's argue that any description you give of life is incomplete?

MIRROR:
Exactly.

DOCTOR:
Then it's brief and to the point.

MIRROR:
Life? No. Life is the opposite.

DOCTOR:
If any definition you give of life is brief and to the point—it's not life.

MIRROR:
Then life is **not** describable.

DOCTOR:
Exactly.

MIRROR:
Well—that description is brief and to the point, isn't it?

DOCTOR:

Yes—but life isn't.

MIRROR:

What could life possibly be unless there's a way to describe it?

DOCTOR:

More than a description.

MIRROR:

Don't say "more" than a description—say "other" than a description.

DOCTOR:

OK.

MIRROR:

That's not right.

(P a u s e)

It would take a superior intelligence to figure this out.

DOCTOR:

Not really.

(Turning to the door.)

Oh great Duck, help us!

(Pause. The giant Duck enters.)

MIRROR:
It never says anything.

DOCTOR:
Except in Duck language.

MIRROR:
There is none.

DOCTOR:
Quacks.

OBJECTS IN MIRROR MAY B

MIRROR:
 That is not a language.

DOCTOR:
 Just quacks.

MIRROR:
 Right. Why are you always right?

DOCTOR:
 Wrong. It's you who's always right, my Friend.

MIRROR:
 How can that be?

DOCTOR:

Because.   You're a mirror.

MIRROR:

(Pause)

Right.

RICHARD FOREMAN

CLOSER THAN THEY APPEA

Chance

vs.

Causation & Chaos

Mario Bunge

Tell a small investor that the prices and earnings of all stocks are random, and he won't believe you. He is convinced that he, or at any rate his stockbroker, has a sure recipe for reading the future in the past. He believes that in every case "the writing is on the wall." All it takes to see the future is to find the right wall and to learn to decipher the inscriptions on it. He is a strict causalist. He suffers from chance-denial.

Yet, if economists agree on anything, it is precisely on the "random-walk" character of stock-price and earnings variations. Likewise, physicists agree that the behavior of electrons, photons, atomic nuclei, atoms and molecules is probabilistic. In other words, these things behave lawfully, but their very laws are probabilistic rather than the type of laws governing the motion of bullets or planets. They tell us not what will happen in all certainty, but only what is the probability of something's happening. Likewise, a geneticist may estimate the probability that a certain parental gene will occur in a newborn, but he cannot predict that the child will possess that gene. This is because, during the brief egg-fertilization process, the parental genes are shuffled randomly, like dice in a dice-box. These examples suggest that chance is not just a fancy name for ignorance or uncertainty, but a feature of the real world. This view is quite modern. In fact, it is no more than a century old, and it would have shocked Aristotle, though not Epicurus.

The traditional view was that chance was only an appearance. An omniscient being could predict every event, so that a probability was not a measure of objective possibility but a degree of uncertainty concerning the real, but occult, causal relations. Indeed, the traditional doctrine about the order of the world was strictly causal. Everything would unfold in accordance with rigid, causal patterns. The moral is obvious: always try to uncover the causal arrows underlying randomness. But, of course, this moral is not always pertinent. There are irreducibly random events, such as radioactive disintegrations and genetic mutations.

Many people believe that modern science has replaced causality with chance. Moreover, they believe that one can assign a probability to any possible event. Some even believe that the extremes of necessity and impossibility are just particular cases of randomness, that they have probabilities one and zero respectively. Both beliefs are widespread among mainstream economists, such as Milton Friedman and Gary Becker, and philosophers, such as Karl Popper and Patrick Suppes. Upon close examination, both beliefs turn out to be false. Let me explain.

To begin with, quantum physics has combined the ideas of causation and chance instead of reducing the first to the second. Indeed, the basic laws of the quantum theory involve forces, and every force is a special kind of cause. Thus, a typical quantum-theoretical calculation of the outcome of a collision between two particles results in a prediction such as this: the probability that the given field of force will deflect the incoming particle within a given solid angle is such and such. In other words, one calculates the probability that a fixed cause will produce one of several possible effects.

As for the belief that every event can be assigned a probability: in fact, only random events can legitimately be assigned probabilities. For example, the outcome of flipping an honest coin can, nay must, be stated in probabilistic terms. If, on the other hand, the coin has been manufactured by a professional gambler, there is no point in talking about probabilities. And, while the outcome of a game of chance is random, the expectations of the amateur gambler are biased, not probabilistic. For instance, he is likely to believe that, if a coin has fallen heads five times in a row, it is bound to fall tails in the next flip.

At the same time, opinions as to the likelihood of non-random events, such as deliberate actions, are not quantifiable. The same holds for propositions or statements. To assign them probabilities is just as preposterous as assigning them temperatures. A proposition can be more or less precise, plausible, or true, but not probable, for there is no randomness about it. We must, then, accept chance alongside causation. Both are objective modes of behavior. Hence, both categories are bound to occur side-by-side in scientific and technological theories.

But this is not the end of the story. Recently, a third character, namely chaos, has joined the party. Unfortunately, the word *chaos* has been the subject of a hype comparable to the one involved in advertising the yet-to-be-designed, intelligent computer. Hence, we had better introduce a modicum of precision and modesty.

First of all, the term *chaos* is ambiguous. In fact, until recently it denoted only formlessness, lawlessness, or orderlessness (like that on top of my desk). This concept is found in the book of *Genesis*, according to which God did not create the world but organized a chaotic jumble. But this is not the technical concept of chaos as it occurs in nonlinear dynamics. This field is dominated by perfectly definite, if complex, laws that are neither causal nor probabilistic.

Second, chaos is a sort of mock randomness. Indeed, a chaotic trajectory looks random to the naked eye until one uncovers its dynamics, which is at least partially causal. One characteristic of this dynamics is that small changes in the initial state of a system are followed by disproportionate changes in the final state. That is, two trajectories that are close at the beginning may end up being far apart—like the life histories of identical twins raised in different environments. In short, this is a case of "small causes, large effects."

Gamblers know that this is the case with roulette. A tiny deviation of the initial position of the ball may make th[e] difference between winning and losing. An academically more respectable example is provided by the following experiment that anyone can perform. Take a sheet of paper and drop it repeatedly from what you take to be the sa[me] height. The sheet will land in a different place every time.

A further characteristic of chaotic dynamics is that it is critically dependent upon the precise value of one or mor[e] parameters (sometimes called "knob variables") that occur in an algebraic or a differential equation. At first sight these parameters look just like the innocent constants. But, as the values of such parameters change ever so slightly, o[ne] is faced with unpredictable effects. It is not only that the response of a chaotic system to such a change can be huge[.] may also be that there are two possible responses instead of one. Worse, unlike the case of the forks of a random process, which can be assigned probabilities, those of chaotic processes cannot be so weighted.

The trajectories of a ball in a pinball board are chaotic. The heart, too, seems to become chaotic under certain circumstances. Here, the observable, but unpredictable, effect is arrhythmia. The reproduction of some insect population[s] seems to be chaotic. At times the population explodes, while at other times it crashes. Even local atmospheric disturbances may be chaotic. This is why local weather is much harder to forecast than global and long-term weather trend[s].

It has been suggested that the fluttering of a butterfly's wings in New York could cause a typhoon in the Sea of China. This "butterfly effect" would be an instance of chaotic dynamics. But this is sheer fantasy, because the shock waves generated by a butterfly's fluttering wings are soon dissipated in the surrounding air. Real storms involve huge energy transfers far beyond the power of even the largest swarm of Monarch butterflies flying from Canada to Mexico. Likewise, the radio waves emitted by the brain do not carry enough energy to move things around. Telekinesis is physically impossible.

In sum, chaos may be pervasive. However, one should not believe everything one reads these days about chaos. Much of it is sloppy, and some of it is just sensationalist hand waving. This warning applies, in particular, to the chaos-theory musings of the students of society who, without writing any equations, draw parallels between economic fluctuations or political turbulence, on the one hand, and chaotic dynamics on the other. Before buying any ware bearing the label *chaos*, ask the salesperson to display the equations and to compare their solutions with the corresponding social data, such as the time-series of prices.

Chaos dynamics is important and intriguing, but we must not allow ourselves to be carried away by propaganda. First, because not every irregularity is attributable to chaos dynamics. Second, because chaos "theory" is not yet such. So far it is only a collection of disconnected, if interesting, examples. Whether this jumble will eventually be turned into an orderly system of hypotheses (i.e., a theory) is still to be seen. "Chaos science," too, is still unborn. There are only a small number of interesting cases of chaos dynamics in several fields, from meteorology to medicine—only a few of them have been certified.

In short, chance and its companions, causation and chaos, are for real, and they should be treated as equals. In other words, our world has random, causal and chaotic features. It also satisfies laws that combine two or perhaps three of these basic categories.

As if this complexity were not enough, for good measure we must throw in a fourth category: namely, accident. Just think of the many accidents that punctuate anyone's life history, such as coincidences, mishaps, and opportunities, both taken or missed. True, some coincidences consist in the crossings of causal lines, and some accidents have a purely random root. Still, if comparatively rare, they are also likely to be unexpected.

Yes, life is rather messy. But we can often prevent a mess or at least clean it up. And sometimes we succeed in tacking our sailboat so as to take advantage of the changing winds—at least until the nearest whirlpool or the next freak storm. We must always count on chance, chaos, and accident. But we can also count on causality to counteract chance, chaos and accident, or at least to dampen their undesirable effects.

Although men flatter themselves with their great actions, They are not so often the result of a grand design as of chance

La Rochefoucauld.

Do we, holding that the gods exist,
deceive ourselves

with unsubstantial dreams and lies,

while random careless chance
and change alone control the world?

Euripides

CHANCES ARE

Melissa Malouf

Almost a year ago now: that first day out on the road in the early morning, mid-July. Out of the house I'd been holed up in for too long. Out across the San Bernardino Mountains. Out toward the rest of my life, and more or less out of my mind. There I was, on the way to my first stop—Las Vegas.

Outside of Barstow, I ran out of gas. Outside of Barstow: which is to say, on that stretch of highway that takes you into the Mojave Desert. Which is to say, not a good place to be reminded that you are alone, and that driving over the speed limit with a rock 'n' roll station blaring from the radio does not make you any younger, and that the maps and the bottled water and the chilled green apples there in the front seat do not mean that you are adequately prepared to drive long distances, do not mean that you can relax now and let your mind do what it most likes to do—remember, imagine, fret, remember, fret some more. (This does not include remembering to look at the gauges.)

The late morning sun got hotter as I sat there for a while, conducting a pointless, prideful struggle — because I didn't want to walk back toward where I'd started from. But forward, on foot, was out of the question. So. Damn. It had to be back. It had to be an image of ineptness and defeat.

We'll see about that, I told myself as I locked the car, took to the shoulder of the highway, and became, I thought, statuesque. So that if anyone passed by what they would see was an older woman in a white cotton dress, red canvas shoes, wearing dark, blind-man's sunglasses, carrying an overstuffed handbag, and holding her head up as if she'd planned this walk all along. Atta girl!

A trucker honked as he sped past me, as the false wind he created blew up a real dust. Does such honking always mean that you're "lookin' good"? Or can it just as well be derisive? Not both, surely—truckers' toots aren't designed to communicate "on the one hand, but then again on the other," right? I was pondering this matter, bucking myself up, when a car stopped, an old gas-eater of some American kind, then reversed until it caught up with me. The engine sputtered off. A car door opened. I kept walking.

"Hey, lady!" A man's voice yelled at me. "Do you need a lift?"

I turned. The man draped one arm over the open door, the other rested on the roof. Tap, tap, tap went his fingers on that roof. "No thanks," I said, and then kept on going.

"You run out of gas?"

He was still shouting, as though the distance between us were the size of a canyon, instead of a few yards. Perhaps he assumed, given my age, that I was hard of hearing.

I turned again, ready to offer a scolding. But he looked like the sort of man on whom a scolding fries to a crisp, then he'd pop the tasty tidbit into his remorseless mouth and grin. He was wearing a saggy pair of gray pants that might once have been part of a business suit, and a light pink golfer's t-shirt whose turned-up collar and unbuttoned buttons were supposed to look sharp but were stubbornly failing. A darkly tanned man of desert places, with thin black hair that needed a washing—he seemed to be neither young nor old. I couldn't see his eyes (he, too, was wearing sunglasses) but I remember wondering whether they were any match for his spooky lips, which resembled thick rubber bands that have lost their elasticity.

"Yes," I told him. "But you go on. I'm fine. I know the way back." (Too true by far.)

He stepped away from his car, shut the door.

Here's what I was thinking: I'm bigger than you are, mister. You don't want me to be knocking you in the head with this purse, believe me. Besides, this road isn't deserted, somebody drives by now and then. They'll wonder whether you're bothering me. So don't. Just watch your step, fella. And so on.

In other words, I was instantly afraid of him.

"I'd getcha there in fifteen, twenty minutes. An air-conditioned ride. On foot it'll take you an hour."

He walked up to me then, just as another car went by without any sign of slowing down. I guess there are times when a gal can be too statuesque.

"The walk will do me good." I smiled. "Thanks anyway. Bye now."

Good manners: what you resort to when you wish you had a handy can of mace in your purse, or a bodyguard at your side.

"It ain't right, ma'am."

"I'll be fine. Really."

"The whole world ain't right. I mean, isn't right."

A crazy, I thought. One who corrects his own grammar: does that make him more crazy than most? I fumbled out an "oh don't worry," managed an embarrassed—for both of us—little wave, and then did an about-face. But that didn't stop him. He spoke, loudly, to my walking-away back:

"It isn't right that everything's so wrong these days that a lady in distress can't accept the aid and assistance of a stranger—you hear me, ma'am?— lest that stranger be a priest or likewise a lady, and even then what happens is the question of whether the priest is really a priest or is in fact a raper and a rampager who is disguised as a priest. That question, which in olden times wouldn't have entered the pretty head of the lady in distress now enters it and sets there like a redwood stump, no budgin' it. Not only that, but she knows as well as she knows the dusty feel of sleep in her eyes that if it's another lady comes to her aid, she may be no lady at all, she may be just another self-con- gratulating, distress-loving female type of person who's in it for herself, wants to be able to tell the story of how she put her own needs aside, ruined her schedule, let dinner go to hell—but it's all bullshit, ain't it, ma'am? I mean, isn't it? These days, chances are real good that same so-called lady could even turn out to be a man dressed up as a woman, which used to be a phenom I scorned just as much as I did any other, but I have been forced to conclude that the man who dresses in a woman's clothes aims to disassociate himself because he has seen the same fact of the male condition that I have seen: and that is, the chivalrous man, the man of honor, has been outmoded, outvoted, and un-damn-done by men rich and poor alike, all colors and creeds of 'em, all ages, who inflict mistreatment upon each other and most especially upon the women they were once upon a time supposed to protect and provide for with all manner of courtesy and ceremony. And you can tell me 'til the cows come home that a woman can protect herself and provide for herself, but that doesn't change the basic and fundamental truth that it would be better for everybody if the mistreating men hadn't turned the pitiful, old-fashioned rest of us into darksome strangers that no good woman, no woman with any sense worth talking about, would trust any further than she could throw an anvil into a swamp. You hear?"

I heard. All of this was shouted. I'd kept walking, sort of, not wanting to offend, but also not wanting to be a captured audience. Then I heard his car door slam, the motor roar up. I was think- ing: he's crazy, all right. A Miniver Cheevy gone over the edge.

Soon it was clear that he hadn't kept going toward Mojave, that he'd made a u-turn, and I told myself that he wasn't, no he wasn't, no, he couldn't be crazy enough to run me down.

I was right. He wasn't. He flew by me, flooring it, picking up speed.

I walked back to my car. I needed to sit down, I needed some of that bottled water. Was I a wreck? You bet. But it wasn't only that encounter: it was that the whole thing—the whole coast-to-coast pursuit— felt like a mistake, an utter miscalculation of my abilities. I may as well have donned a spacesuit that morning, instead of a comfortable dress, and declared myself an astronaut.

I was still in the car, working myself up for the task at hand—which had become, not simply walking back toward Barstow for gas, but fighting off the you'll-never-make-it boogeyman—when the gas-eater pulled up behind me. I made sure, with my elbow, that my door was locked.

In the rearview mirror, I saw the man lug a five-gallon gas can from the back seat of his car. He saw me watching, signalled for me to pull the lever, open the lid of the gas tank. He was all business, no loosely grinning lips. I got a ten-dollar bill out of my purse, rolled down the window, half-way, and waited. Eventually, I heard the gas tank lid snap shut. Then he was there, at the window. "It ain't and it is not right," he said.

"But you are."

"Not very. And not often," he told me. "Put your money away, ma'am."

"I can't let you—"

"Yes, you can. This one's on me."

"I can't tell you how much I appreciate—"

"No, you can't." He had his hands on his hips, and he was moving as if he were rocking ever so lightly, ball-to-heel, ball-to-heel, back and forth.

"Then I suppose I'll be on my way. Are you sure—" I still had the ten-dollar bill in my hand.

"I'm sure."

"You're a genuine Galahad, sir."

"Keep that tank full. And get yourself a car phone."

"Many thanks."

"Yeah."

I pulled out onto the highway and looked back. My knight in shining armor was standing next to the empty gas can in the shoulder of the road, with his legs spread apart like a gunslinger. His right arm was raised above his head—there was his fist, and his stout middle finger pointing skyward, and then the redundant shout:

"Fuck you, lady! You hear me?"

SHAKESPEARE AND THE DISCOURSE OF CHAOS AND TIME

Robert Grudin

To begin with, a word about chaos.

For the contemporary scientific mind, *chaos* and *chaotic*, like *order* and *orderly*,
are relative terms, useful figuratively or
                    comparatively but of no precise denotative merit.

Just as nineteenth-century thought, with its discovery of entropy and probability,

invalidated theories of absolute order,

            twentieth-century thought, with its sensational formalist explanations

    of Brownian motion, quantum mechanics, DNA and the like, has more or less

        sounded the death-knell for the idea of absolute chaos.

                As Michael Polanyi put it at mid-century in *Personal Knowledge*,
                        "twentieth-century hard-science discoveries have gone far to
                                    restore the classical idea of a rational universe";
                recent developments in chaos and complexity theory have reinforced Polanyi's point.

        Chaos and complexity research, like all other rational inquiry, is a quest for order

                    in which chaos is one of a number of variables.

According to Field and Golubitsky, authors of *Symmetry in Chaos*,

            "the chaos in

                a given system is its degree of comparative

                        unpredictability and complexity."

For the Renaissance it was quite different. Chaos was a real phenomenon, not only verifiable by sensory data (Paracelsus, an early observer of Brownian motion, named gas after chaos) but also connected, via profound associations, with the political idea of anarchy and the psychology of human passion. And for Europe and Great Britain near the turn of the seventeenth century, chaos was not only a realistic designator but also a definite intellectual and social possibility. Indeed, notable commentators were asserting that chaos had already arrived: Montaigne, in "On vehicles," and in a particularly radical mood, sees the world as "a perpetual multiplication and variation of forms"; John Donne proclaims that the cosmos is "all in pieces, all coherence gone; /All just supply, and all relation."

Why was chaos such an urgent theme in the Renaissance? One might answer, without exaggeration, that the Renaissance and the Reformation (which are difficult to separate from each other as cultural phenomena) were innately chaotic events. By 1600, only eighty years after Luther nailed up his rebellious theses, Christianity was on the ropes, riven not only by the Protestant/Catholic struggle (which soon assumed the profile of competing international interests) but also by deep animosities between Protestant and Protestant, Catholic and Catholic. Free thought, though technically illegal, was nonetheless rampant in a bewildering variety of flavors: Averroistic, Hermetic, Anabaptist, Aristotelian, Platonist, Sceptic, Machiavellian, Epicurean, Nominalist, Pansophist. And perhaps worst of all, there were the scientists—figures like Copernicus, Paracelsus, William Harvey, John Dee, Giordano Bruno, Francis Bacon, and Galileo—who were figuratively tearing down the established universe and replacing it with a terrifying godless mechanism. With these developments in mind, it is not hard to see why, to a man of John Donne's sensibilities, chaos was not just a possibility but a reality.

But Renaissance chaos was not universally distressing. The Renaissance mind characteristically considered single subjects **in all of their possible ramifications,** and the subject of chaos was no exception. And looking at chaos in all of its possible ramifications, one observes (as did Boccaccio, Erasmus, Rabelais, and others) that chaos has its bright side. Though terrifying in its social and religious avatars, chaos is both promising and delightful in its relationship to humor, misrule, satire, Eros, and creativity. The bright side of chaos (which would later be lost in the serious proceedings of Bacon, Hobbes, and Locke) is indeed a kind of trademark of the Renaissance, a talisman whose deep meaning would not, in the end, be lost on Shakespeare.

SHAKESPEARE
1564–1984

The Renaissance attitude toward time was at once dynamic and disjunctive. On the one hand, there was a new understanding of time as a discrete, measurable, and uniform dimension of the natural world—an understanding that extended to fields as diverse as physics, poetry, and political science. Ricardo Quinones calls this, in effect, "The Renaissance Discovery of Time," a phrase I would interpret as implying that time, which had been for the Middle Ages a vague enveloping medium, became for the Renaissance an effective human tool. But this discovery was simultaneously an alienation. Time as tool was time divorced from the providential order that gave meaning to Christian life. Moreover, time as formidably rediscovered by Machiavelli was no longer a stable template for social transactions but rather a shimmering kaleidoscope of dangers and opportunities, based on a shifting foundation of power relationships, in which individuals had to look out for themselves. Time, in other words, had grown useful but also perilous. Implicit in its newly discovered face were corrosive turbulence and destructive chaos.

It is this latter, unsettling vision of time that occurs repeatedly in the earlier works of Shakespeare. Shakespeare's early work, up to and including the Sonnets and *Hamlet*, reflects a Tudor/humanist attitude regarding time: a world view in which time is chaotic and inimical to human institutions and values. The problem facing Prince Hamlet and the narrator of the Sonnets is not how to integrate the idea of time into a dynamic perspective, but rather how to construct a human edifice that resists, or at least lessens, time's influence. And this problem is not merely moral and speculative but psychologically deep-rooted: again and again *Shakespeare connects time's effects—change, opportunity—to uncomfortable thoughts about women and sexuality.*

In his Lancastrian history plays, however, Shakespeare takes a different tack. Here he views time as a precious commodity, a delicate structure that can be preserved only through personal and political wisdom but which otherwise crumbles into chaos. Richard II's tearful comment, **"I wasted time, and now doth time waste me,"** is borne out by a detailed list of his political errors and their fearsome consequences, concluding with his assassination by an agent of Bolingbroke, the future Henry IV. And when Henry takes the throne, he encounters comparable difficulties with the ordering and preservation of time: "So shaken as we are, so wan with care,/Find we a time for frighted Peace to pant." Henry deserves what he gets. Just as Richard had corrupted time by wasting it, Henry has polluted time by destroying its political supports.

33

This view of disordered time is backed up by a set of allusions to the Fall of Man. As all literate Christians knew from St. Augustine, Adam's fall had in effect "started the clock," since falling from God's grace meant falling out of eternity and into temporality. In the Lancastrian tetralogy, Shakespeare forcefully suggests that there has been a second fall, out of temporality (honorable human transactions) and into chaos. Richard II's Queen rails against the Gardener for breaking the news of the King's capture:

Thou old Adam's likeness, set to dress this garden,
How dares thy harsh rude tongue sound this unpleasing news?
What Eve, what serpent, hath suggested thee
To make a second fall of cursed man?
(Richard II, III.iv.73-77)

King Henry V reproves the traitor Scroop:

I will weep for thee;
For this revolt of thine, methinks, is like
Another fall of man.
(Henry V, II.ii.140-142)

And Falstaff claims an ancient precedent for his own moral collapse:

Thou knowest in the state of innocency Adam fell, and
what should poor Jack Falstaff do in the days of villainy?
(Henry IV, Part 1, III.iii.164-166)

These comments suggest that for Shakespeare, the "second fall" is a linear extension of the first. Humanity, originally fallen from grace into traditional politics, now falls from traditional politics into apolitical chaos.

The original fall from grace is a descent from eternity into time, from innocence into morality. The fallen counterpart of grace is honor: honesty in negotiation, respect for tradition, acknowledgment of virtue. The fallen counterpart of Eden is the Queen's "garden." A distinctly postlapsarian order, vulnerable to weeds and dependent on vigilant human care, the Queen's garden is an image of politics. Defect of vigilance tempts the second fall, a descent from orderly politics into depravity. Richard's fall from power brings with it the loss of the second garden, the defeat of the ordered polity. But (unlike Eden) the second garden may be won back again. Henry IV's continual efforts to reinstate "frighted Peace," Hotspur's monomaniacal pursuit of honor, and Hal's project of redeeming time all speak to this goal. But only Hal will achieve it.

Hal's success is brought about by what might be called the Machiavellian paradox, or cheating the cheaters:

I'll so offend, to make offense a skill,
Redeeming time when men think least I will.
(*Henry IV*, Part 1, I.ii.216ff.)

Prince Hal's "offenses" amount to a series of bluffs and thefts. Distancing himself from his father's compromised government, he feigns indifference to politics and spends his time carousing with the aged and infamous libertine, Sir John Falstaff. With Falstaff he robs a group of Canterbury pilgrims; then in disguise he robs Falstaff and gives the money back to the pilgrims. He robs his rival Hotspur of his military titles by defeating him in combat.

O Harry, thou hast robb'd me of my youth!
I better brook the loss of brittle life
Than those proud titles thou hast won of me.
(*Henry IV*, Part I, V.iv, 77-79)

And finally, as king, he commits the grandest larceny of all, grabbing power from France at the Battle of Agincourt. Yet after all these offenses he comes out smelling like roses, because each of them has helped to seduce and galvanize the British people.

Significantly, Hal's progress or lack of progress toward this political redemption is characterized repeatedly in terms of time. At home he confides to Poins,

Well, thus we play the fools with the time, and the
spirits of the wise sit in the clouds and mock us.
(*Henry IV*, Part 1, II.ii.142ff.)

And later, after extended frivolities at the Boar's Head Tavern, he tells Poins that he feels "much to blame,/So idly to profane the precious time." In *Henry IV*, Part 2, Warwick (a counselor skilled in the interpretation of time) predicts that "in the perfectness of time" the young prince will cast off his idle followers and make good; and, once Hal as king has done so, Exeter characterizes him to the French court as one who "weighs time/ Even to the utmost grain." The Epilogue of *Henry V*, eulogizing the King as an achiever of gardens, throws him into a broader relationship to time:

Small time, but in that small most greatly liv'd
This star of England. Fortune made his sword;
By which the world's best garden he achieved,
And of it left his son imperial lord.
Henry the Sixth, in infant bands crown'd King
Of France and England, did this King succeed;
Whose state so many had the managing,
That they lost France, and made his England bleed...
(*Epilogue*, 5-12)

While acknowledging the magnitude of Henry's achievement, these words suggest the limitations of his political philosophy. Service to time, however heroic, is but servitude to it; the fortune that makes swords breaks them in unpredictable ways.

After the great tragedies, which like the histories focus on the catastrophic consequences of disordered time, Shakespeare turns his attention again to the reclamation of time. But here, instead of addressing the issue politically, as in the Lancastrian plays, he confronts it philosophically and psychologically. In his late play *The Winter's Tale* (drawn from Robert Greene's romance *Pandosto, or the Triumph of Time*), he presents time as a universal but morally neutral force. Time itself, embodied allegorically as Chorus in Act IV, asserts its capacity for good as well as ill:

> *I, that please some, try all, both joy and terror*
> *Of good and bad, that makes and unfolds error....*
> (IV.i.1-2)

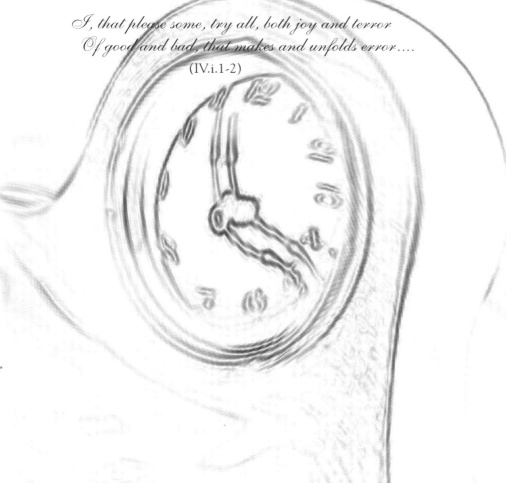

Shakespeare suggests, moreover, that time's power, like any other natural force, can be harnessed for human good.

The Winter's Tale begins like a boilerplate domestic tragedy, vaguely reminiscent of the London tabloids. Leontes, King of Sicilia, suspects that his wife, Queen Hermione, is having an affair. Although he is completely mistaken and has no evidence to support his belief, he humiliates her publicly and imprisons her. Their son, Mamillius, dies of shame and grief. Perdita, Hermione's newborn baby daughter, is banished, to be abandoned on a distant shore, and Hermione herself collapses at her trial and is presumed dead. In fact, she has been spirited off by a friend, Paulina, who hides her away for sixteen long years, until Paulina judges (in her own words) that "'T'is time." Time has made a new man, humbler, more self-aware, of Leontes, while Paulina's enlightened trickery and Hermione's reappearance "as a statue"—i.e., an art-figure—conveys the message that time can be spiritually renewing when it is in the service of art.

A somewhat different reconciliation with time is suggested by another late Shakespearean play, *Antony and Cleopatra*. Time, with its dazzling variety of events and its constant revolution from one opposite pole to another (adversity/prosperity, assertion/denial, embodiment/disembodiment, love/hate, approval/contempt), is a primary theme in the play. No character in the play is more closely connected with time than Cleopatra, the Egyptian seductress-politician whose chief ploys are reversal and surprise. Cleopatra is praised for her "becomings," a strange noun whose double meaning implies that, if used artfully, change can be delightful and seductive. She is also praised for her "infinite variety," an attribute often associated with time. In Cleopatra we find Shakespeare, once time's enemy, making peace with the chaos, unpredictability, and passion that are time's indivisible companions. You might say that while the younger Shakespeare rejected time as entropic chaos, the older

Shakespeare accepts time as creative disorder.

Edmund Spenser, Shakespeare's contemporary, took an equally interesting line when he avowed in *The Fairie Queene* that time "dilates"—that is, expands and varies—the things we know in life. Spenser's term, "dilate" (*dilatare* in Cicero and Quintilian) comes straight out of a humanistic rhetorical tradition, known as *copia* (abundance, variety), whose chief advocate in the Renaissance had been Erasmus. In his textbook, *De Copia*, Erasmus asserted that we should think abundantly and variously and express ourselves abundantly and variously because **that is how God made the world.** *De Copia*, which was taught in many humanist schools, became a major influence on Renaissance thought. In the hands of some writers—Rabelais, Montaigne, Spenser, Shakespeare—*copia* became the stylistic template for large-scale literary structures of creative disorder dilating out from a central theme. By the same token, *copia* suggested a kind of pansophic philosophy that accepted disorder, even chaos, as elements in a continuum that also included symmetry and harmony.

Shakespeare, who had used *copia* as a stylistic device from the earliest days of his career, grew more and more cognizant of its philosophical implications as he matured. In his late plays he was able to bring this subtle perspective to the understanding of time, and thus to achieve an appreciation of chaos as a necessary component in a rational universe.

Such a sophisticated view of time would not have been unknown among Shakespeare's contemporaries. Michel de Montaigne, in the essay "Of experience" from which Shakespeare took the phrase "infinite variety" for *Antony and Cleopatra*, had developed a subtle view of experience in which chaotic interactions played an important role:

> Our life is composed, like the harmony of the world, of contrary things, also of different tones, sweet and harsh, sharp and flat, soft and loud. If a musician liked only one kind, what would he have to say? He must know how to use them together and blend them. And so must we do with good and evil, which are consubstantial with our life. Our existence is impossible without this mixture, and one element is no less necessary for it than the other.

ARTICLE DESIGN BY PAMELA CANNON

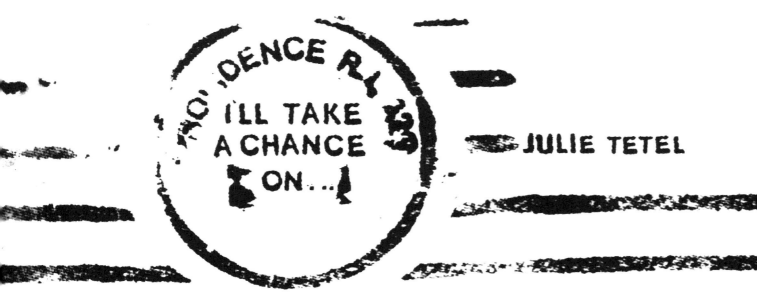

PROVIDENCE R.I.
I'LL TAKE
A CHANCE
ON...

JULIE TETEL

Two pairs of eyes

meet across a crowded room. Click and
hook. Trials and tribulations. Eventual happy end.
War rages. Two lovers meet. Danger, deception, desire,
then the many-layered conflicts are resolved. Two
strangers find themselves alone together in an
elevator/in a foreign embassy/on a boat. It stops/is
bombed/is cast adrift. They survive with nothing but
their own resourcefulness and one another. Not only do
they live to tell whatever tale there is to be told, they also
fall in love.

What are the chances that these pairs of people--just these
very pairs--are perfect for the situation and one another?
What are the chances that the person on the other end of a
wrong number will turn out to be The One? That the travelers
whose two suitcases are mistakenly switched, producing
complications either disastrous or hilarious, are meant for
one another? That the frog, once kissed, is restored to
his princely form? That the Damsel in Distress is not just
a damsel in this dress? Well, really, what are the chances?

     Add to the mix the well-known jinx that if you're
looking for love, the magic can't happen. You have to be
otherwise engaged in life. Upon meeting that possible
perfect other, you should be: worrying about your aging
parents, working through your wayward brother's problems,
struggling with your child's disability, chasing the crook,
arguing the case, solving the mystery, averting the hostile
take-over, saving the world, or possibly all of the above.
But whatever you're doing, you can't be thinking: what if
s/he's The One? You can't be expecting to find True Love.

     So now what are the chances? A million to one? A zillion
to one? No, surely that's too optimistic. The real chances,
the statistical chances are more likely to hover in the
neighborhood of: zip, zero, zilch. Nada, nolla, null.

     Face it. The odds stink if you're committed to
finding True Love within the particular illusion commonly
called the real world. That's why I don't hang out there
much. In the world I tend to inhabit--romance writing--
the odds of romantic encounter are terrific because the
chances are overdetermined and the possibilities are
endless. And speaking of possibilities, the odds really
stink if you're going to get picky and require your perfect
other to be of the same evolutionary kind. Remember that
Frog Prince. Or Beauty and the Beast. Which reminds me of
Leda and the Swan--and every other mythological romantic
who shifted shape to get the guy or the girl. But even
Zeus was never so inventive to have transformed himself
into a murderously elegant, blood-suckingly suave
Transylvanian who could get both the guy and the girl.
Yum. Oh, and while we're on the subject, let's not
forget Batman and that interspecies stuff he has going
with Catwoman. Or is the real action with the
androgynous Robin? That's what I thought.

Notice that we haven't even left the realm of vertebrates, and save for the occasional amphibian or bird here and there, we're still dealing mostly with mammals, including flying ones. So, clearly, the possibilities are only just opening up. Now, things don't get really interesting until we overcome not only our species-ism but also our carbon-chain-ism. I mean, if we're not going to restrict the possibilities to our own evolutionary kind, why restrict the possibilities to an evolutionarily-produced creature at all? Especially when there are such good silicon others out there these days--to the third and fourth generations already. And just think of the galaxies, the universes, and the parallel universes where any, all, or some combination of these creatures could live! It's enough to keep anyone with half an imagination busy for a lifetime. Several lifetimes, in fact.

Oh my. We still have all the reincarnation romances to factor into the possibilities. Time-travel, too. Forwards or backwards in linear fashion or looped into the reincarnation cycle where interspecies romances can take on entirely new dimensions. Say, just what is it about that frog?

I don't have time to answer that question. The UPS man just came to my door with a misdirected package, and it happens to contain the names of the terrorists who have bought weapons-grade plutonium from the secret nuclear sites in the former Soviet Union. A suspicious car has just cruised by, and the UPS man recognizes it as one that has been following him all morning. It looks as though he and I are going to be busy for a while...

EXCEPT FOR THE CRAZY OR THOSE IN LOVE,
THERE ARE TWO PSYCHOLOGICAL DOMAINS, PERFECTLY NORMAL, WHERE THE NOTIONS OF CHANCE AND PROBABILITY ARE STRANGERS:

THE WORLDS OF THE PRIMITIVE AND THE INFANT.

PIAGET

Sans parler des états psycho-pathologiques ... et sans parler non plus des états passionnels de l'amoureux ... c'est deux sortes de terrains psychologiques parfaitement normaux auxquels les notions de hasard et de probabilités paraissent plus ou moins étrangers: la mentalité primitive et celle du petit enfant.

Jean Piaget

Take a chance. Don't have a platitude
For your attitude.
lucky numbers: 2,7,15,21,37,42

☺ Constance Brock

The person who loves
Never grows old ☺

The wheel of Fortune
Always turns.

52 8 44 29 47 21

Watching Wallenpaupack. Rosalee Isaly 22″ x 30″, Monoprint

INCURSION I

The way to Truro is by chance,
Adrift in pine the native Trace extends;
The far place.
Gulls veer in, scattering cries,
The black duck skims its pool.
Hills green slowly in the Spring:
Salt cast ridge
Laced through with light,
A spark of cricket wings, and sand
In flight to new design.

In the far place sound is but encampment;
Voice of iron, clashing wheel rude guests
From some mechanic race and mind,
The way to Truro?
"We find but one." No questions intersect,
So sure the route.

The bridge of passage stands in half,
Rails undone, timbers in the tidal strait.
The rest a clutch of bramble chaff.
Dark, this roadway gone to thicket runs,
By chance emerging
In the scrub of grasses on the sand.

—Xenia Argon

would think that it is not even within God's power to know what events will happen by accident or

by chance. If he does know, then obviously the event must happen. But if it

must happen, chance does not exist. Yet chance does exist. There is

therefore no foreknowledge of things that happen by chance. Cicero

THE ORDERLY WORLD OF CHANCES

LAWRENCE SKLAR

Our ordinary life is pervaded by chance. Chance encounters with other people or with microbes determine our social and medical fates. Chances in the market make us wealthy or impoverished. Chances in the weather turn our picnics and vacations into joys or miseries.

We are inclined, on the other hand, to think of the world as seen by the scientist as one of order and predictability, seemingly the very opposites of chance. The astronomical bodies provide a heavenly clockwork whose regular progression was already charted by several independent ancient civilizations. Science is the discipline that produces, after all, "laws" of nature. What is a law if not an exceptionless generalization that informs us that, appearances to the contrary, all is regularity and order and nothing is left to chance?

Doesn't science, then, find the order hiding under the surface appearance of a world governed merely by chances? Well, yes, it does. But it also goes on to find that, concealed under many of the apparently lawlike regularities of nature described by its profound generalizations, there is a realm that is itself governed by chance. But the discovery of such a realm of chance, chance unsuspected by and not apparent to our surface acquaintance with the world, does not mean that the scientific search for order and regularity comes to a screeching halt. Scientists are persistent and imaginative. Apparently unable to eliminate chance from the world, they develop wholly novel ways of bringing order and regularity to their descriptions of the world. They find new ways of comprehending and controlling the world, even if that world is chancy at its most fundamental level.

Mathematics is often the language of science. The more fundamental our theories of the world are, the more likely they are to be framed by the formalism of mathematics. Mathematics has its very origin in the need to find appropriate ways in which to characterize our physical, scientific insights. Geometry, algebra, analysis and topology found much of their inspiration in the attempts of scientists to find the right concepts with which to frame their characterizations of the world of observation and experiment. The full development of these concepts, however, at the hands of the "pure" mathematicians, then took leave of their origins in scientific applications.

final normalization of a mathematical theory of probability didn't happen until the twentieth century. This is even more remarkable in that the final theory, at least as applied to the cases where the number of basic outcomes is finite, is almost mathematically trivial in its axioms. It is highly non-trivial, though, in the wealth of fascinating and non-intuitive results that follow from these axioms.

The laws of probability theory are simple and uncontroversial. But the interpretation of probability, the answers given to the question, "What are the laws of probability about?," is a matter of interminable controversy. Probability has been said to be mere relative frequency, the limit of relative frequency in the "long run"; the pure dispositional propensity of a single experiment to have a given outcome; a property of things defined by its place in an overall theory; the degree of logical entailment one proposition has to another; or the degree of subjective belief in a claim held by an individual agent. Despite its unquestionable applicability to the world, what probability is remains an open question.

Statistics, the science of inferring from observed outcomes to probabilistic laws and to other inferable outcomes, had its early development at the hands of those concerned with the social realm. Such topics as rates of birth and death, the spread of disease, the relative merits of various agricultural seeds, and the behavior of juries and of voters were the subjects under examination by the inventors of theories of statistical inference. Only later did it become evident that statistical inference had a role to play in our fundamental physical theories of the world.

The mathematical concepts and rules needed to understand chance, as it is dealt with in our scientific comprehension of the world, are those of probability theory and statistics. Curiously, though, it wasn't the physical scientists whose needs first inspired these branches of mathematics.

Probability theory first arose in the practical context of trying to compute appropriate odds in gambling situations. The brilliant insights of Pascal and others allowed the gambler to calculate the chances of any complex outcome by simply knowing the chances of certain basic outcomes. Thus knowing that the odds of picking any card at random from an ordinary deck are one in fifty-two, we can calculate the chances of a straight or flush. It is a remarkable fact that the

Probability and statistics have much to tell us about chances as they play a role in the biological and social realm. But I will focus my attention on the roles they play in describing and explaining the most basic physical facts about the world. One of the dominant threads of the physics of the last one-hundred-and-fifty years has been the continual discovery of a greater and greater domain in the universe for chance.

The first place in which chances and probabilities forced themselves into our description of the world was in kinetic theory and statistical mechanics. In the late-eighteenth and early-nineteenth centuries, the phenomena of heat and its transformations to and from mechanical energy were described by the elegant theory of thermodynamics. Several brilliant investigators realized that one could understand the laws governing heat and its dynamics if one thought of macroscopic objects as being made up of tiny pieces too small to see, components whose motions were governed by the ordinary dynamical laws. Clausius talks of "the kind of motion that we call heat," hot objects being those whose tiny constituents moved quickly, and cold objects those whose constituents moved slowly.

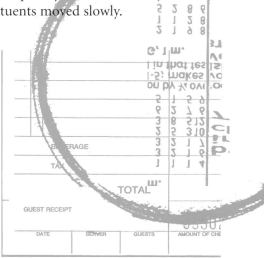

At the hands of James Clerk Maxwell, Ludwig Boltzmann, and Josiah Gibbs this theory gradually developed into another, statistical mechanics, that remains one of the fundamental theories of contemporary physics. But it is a peculiar theory. It presupposes the facts about how large objects are made up out of their tiny constituents (which we now, of course, call molecules and atoms). It takes from basic physics the dynamical laws governing the motion of these small constituents. But then it adds a crucial additional assumption of its own. To make the theory work, we must assume that at any time the various possible ways in which the small constituents may be arranged (in position and in their speeds) have definite probabilities. It is from the positing of these appropriate probabilities, the chances of the various situations, that the laws of the thermodynamics of macroscopic objects can be derived.

But just why these probabilistic assertions hold true of the world remains a deep mystery. Their source has been sought in the large number of constituents in a macroscopic object, in the fundamental dynamic laws governing the microscopic objects, in the random disturbances these internal systems feel from the outside world, in cosmology and even in our subjective appraisal of likelihoods.

How a physical system evolves depends upon its initial state and upon the laws governing its dynamics. In ordinary physics we think of the laws as given by the nature of "initial conditions." A pendulum, for example, will have its swinging motion determined in part by the initial state. In statistical mechanics, however, it is the probability distribution over these initial conditions, somehow given to us by nature, that determines the most fundamental consequences of the theory. The reason behind this special condition on initial states remains one of the most controversial areas of statistical mechanics.

There is an interesting argument to the effect that the appearance of order at the macroscopic level, the order summarized in the laws of thermodynamics, is the result of a fundamental kind of disorder at the microscopic level. For many dynamical systems we can show that there is an extraordinary sensitivity in the future behavior of one of the microscopic systems to the details of its initial state. Two systems with their initial states very close together will show rapidly diverging behavior in a short period of time. This would make predicting the future behavior of the system from a microscopic perspective impossible, even if we could know, to arbitrarily high degrees of accuracy, its initial microscopic disposition. Curiously, it is this very high degree of "randomness" at the microscopic level that makes for such regularity and order at the macroscopic level of the ordinary things of our world.

Deep mysteries still abound in the world described by statistical mechanics. One of the most intractable is that of time asymmetry. In the world of macroscopic objects, the past and future are radically different from one another. We can stir cream into our coffee; we can't stir it out. But the laws governing the dynamics of the microscopic parts seem to allow that for each possible process in time, the reverse of that process is possible as well. So where does the irreversibility we experience come from? There are probably more distinct answers to that question than there are persons who have thought seriously about it, since some of the thinkers have held several, incompatible views over their lifetimes (and sometimes even at one time). Merely invoking "chances" doesn't answer the question. We remain mystified as to why the chances seem to run one way into the future and quite a different way into the past.

As we have seen, statistical mechanics argues that it is chaotic disorder at the microscopic level that is responsible for at least some of the apparently lawlike order we find at the macroscopic level. It is only because the states of the microscopic components taken collectively are sufficiently random that we experience the stability and order familiar to us in ordinary-sized objects composed of these microscopic components. Curiously, however, the same sensitivity to initial conditions that gives rise to microscopic randomness, and hence to macroscopic order (for the systems describable by thermodynamics and statistical mechanics), can give rise to chaotic unpredictability for a different kind of macroscopic system. This is the subject of chaos theory.

This theory has a peculiar history. Its basic precepts were first discovered by Henri Poincaré at the turn of the century. His findings were then pretty much ignored for half a century. Attention was redirected to his discoveries when computers came into vogue as a means of displaying the solutions of equations that can't be represented by analytical formulas. Extremely simple equations were used to represent grossly simplified models of the motion of the atmosphere. Despite their simplicity, the equations couldn't be analytically solved. So the solutions were displayed on a computer using approximation algorithms. What appeared in the display was the representation of a system whose macroscopic features over time varied radically with infinitesimal changes in its initial state. Once again, we witness the sensitivity to initial conditions, but this time for the macroscopic system itself.

Such systems are "in principle" unpredictable. If the tiniest change in initial condition leads to radical variation as time goes on, the most accurate determination of that initial condition won't be accurate enough for even gross predictions over a long enough time. What comes as something of a surprise is that the overwhelming majority of simple systems turns out to be "chaotic." The misleading impression given by the standard physics textbooks—that systems are generally predictable in detail—is the result of a highly selective choice of examples. In general, only members of that limited class of non-chaotic, predictable systems are chosen for examination and illustration.

Hopes for unlimited predictability, then, have been dashed. Even an extensive network of data collectors and even the most advanced super-computers of the future won't let us predict our local weather years in advance. If the atmosphere is a chaotic system, a tiny disturbance now can result in a radical change in the future. This leads to the so-called "butterfly wing" effect, in which the twitch of an insect's wing in the Brazilian rain forest today might lead to the formation of a massive storm in the United States in the distant future. But this doesn't mean that science is at a loss in finding order in this chaos. The predictability of individual systems is given up, but the orderly characterization of the large-scale, qualitative features of systems becomes the focus of investigation. Insights are obtained into such questions as the long-term, average behavior of chaotic systems, their qualitative features, the nature of the boundary between the predictable realm and the chaotic realm, and so on. But "chanciness" of a sort is now seen to be an ineliminable part of our macroscopic world as well as of its microscopic underpinnings.

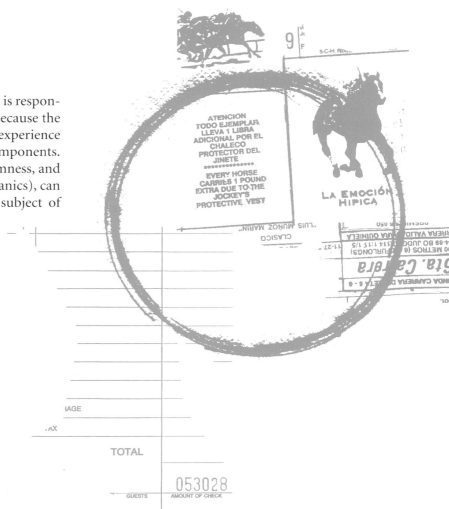

There is one more place where chance plays a crucial role in our fundamental picture of the world. And this is the most mysterious and controversial place of all. With respect to the two theories discussed above, the general opinion is to take chances as measures solely of our ignorance of the world. The physical systems, from this point of view, have definite non-chancy states. But the sensitivity of the systems to even the smallest variation in their initial states makes these initial states inaccessible to us as something we could know and, therefore, use to predict the future behavior of the system. So we must resort, it is argued, to probabilities over the possible initial states. But this invocation of probability is only a reflection of the limits of our knowledge of the world, not some indicator of a true randomness in the states themselves. At least that is the "orthodox" opinion. There are those who think that statistical mechanics and chaos theory, by themselves, do indicate real randomness in the basic states of things.

It is usually in quantum mechanics, however, that the proponents of real chance in the world find their favorite arguments. Quantum theory describes features of the world of a far more radical and bizarre sort than do the other fundamental theories of modern physics—strange as the world may be from their point of view. The experiments behind quantum mechanics show us that particles have wave-like aspects and that waves have particle-like features. Use a Geiger counter to locate an electron, and it appears as a point-like particle, localizable in as small a volume of space as one likes. But reflect a beam of electrons off a crystal lattice and the pattern of the scattered electrons looks like a wave that is distributed over a large volume of space. Worse yet, the theory seems to tell us that events far separated from one another are connected by lawlike correlations that can't be thought of as causal in any ordinary sense.

Where does chance play a role in the quantum description of things? In the standard version of the theory, the so-called "Copenhagen Interpretation" developed by Niels Bohr, there are two distinct processes in the world: dynamic evolution and measurement. Prepare a system in a given state. It then undergoes dynamic evolution, an evolution determined by the forces to which the system is subject. This evolution is just as deterministic, and unchancy, as that described in the non-quantum theories. But then, if we wish to determine the value of some quantity possessed by the system, say its position or its momentum or its spin, we must measure it. The state that the system is in determines a class of possible outcomes only upon measurement. And it assigns to each possible outcome the probability that the particular outcome will be observed. But, in the general case, there is no assurance from the state of the system that one particular outcome will be the one observed.

Now one might try to understand this situation by thinking that the state of the system described by quantum theory is only an "incomplete" state. Couldn't there be other features of the system, not described by the quantum state, that fully determine which outcome of the measurement will result? Many interpreters of quantum mechanics deny that such "hidden variables" can exist. Their reason for this denial is not mere dogmatism. It rests on a variety of proofs to the effect that if such hidden variables exist, then the predicted statistical outcomes of quantum theory could not be the case. So, the argument goes, either there are no hidden variables "behind" quantum theory, or else quantum theory is just plain wrong.

But the situation isn't that simple. What the proofs of "no hidden variables" actually show is that there could not be hidden variables that obeyed certain plausible conditions. The most important of these are "non-contextuality" and "locality." It turns out that one can generate the probabilities predicted by quantum theory out of an underlying hidden variable theory if one will tolerate two things. First of all, the outcome of a measurement may depend upon what other, compatible measurements one chooses to perform at the same time. Second, the outcome of a measurement at one place may depend upon the outcome of a measurement performed at some spatially distant place, even though no causal signal can connect the two measurements in question.

Hidden variables that are peculiar in the second way, non-local hidden variables, are strange indeed. Determinism has been saved for the world, but only at a great cost. If there are non-local hidden variables, then it is in principle impossible to think of any system as being really isolated from the rest of the world. No matter how independent it may be of its environment in the causal ways, a quantum, non-causal correlation may instantaneously change its nature if an action is performed arbitrarily far away from the system in question.

The prevalent interpretation of quantum mechanics—the one in which the quantum state is declared to be a "complete" description of the state of a system—posits chance as a component of the world in as radical a way as possible. From this perspective, there really is no fact of the world that will determine whether or not a radioactive nucleus will decay in the next hour. Some of the given kind will; some won't. But no fact of the world determines which will decay and which will not. Real chance, then, rules the world.

Even many of the theories that would supplement the quantum state by hidden variables still posit a strong degree of chanciness to the world. Many of these hidden variable theories declare that it is impossible in principle for observers to determine the values of the hidden variables. Whereas the world would now be deterministic and not chancy in the sense noted above, it would still be radically chancy in the sense that we could never go beyond probabilistic prediction to make deterministic predictions. For the determinism rests on hidden variables forever inaccessible to our knowledge. Other hidden variable accounts, though, allow for the possibility of knowing the hidden variable values, taking the purely probabilistic prediction of quantum mechanics to be limited only because of our, in principle eliminable, ignorance of the deeper structures of the world.

No matter how one interprets quantum theory, it should be noted, we are once again in the typical scientific situation with regard to chance. Even if the chance nature of things provides some limitations on our ability to predict and control the world, the whole point of the scientific enterprise is to offer a theory in which chances play a controllable role. The laws of the theory give us a great deal of knowledge of what the chances are and how they are related to one another. This structural knowledge of chances bears much in common with the lawlike grasp of the structure of chances provided by statistical mechanics and by chaos theory.

Let me end with a plea for caution. The appearance of chances in the fundamental level of the scientific description of the world has led a number of people to think that they can find here the clue to various aspects of unpredictability as it plays a role in our ordinary affairs. What is free will, after all, if it isn't the unpredictabilty of human decision-making and human action? What is creativity if it isn't the unpredictability of human inventiveness? Isn't it easier for us to find a place for free will and for genuine creativity in a world of chances than it was for us to find a spot for them in the older, deterministic world picture?

Indeed, some go beyond this. There have been numerous attempts to actually explain what free will is or to explain what creativity is by using the resources of contemporary physics. And these projects are not always the feeble efforts of amateurs who don't understand the physics. It is top professionals in physics who dare these speculative ventures. David Bohm finds mind and meaning arising, perhaps, out of the "implicate order" (essentially the non-locality) of quantum theory. And Roger Penrose suggests that the source of free will and creativity might be found in the quantum account of gravity.

Well, I doubt it. Freedom of thought and action are indeed puzzles. There is a serious task to be done in fitting our conceptual analysis of decision-making and choice into the world described by lawlike physics. And creativity is, indeed, an aspect of mind that remains elusive to our understanding. But it is hard to see why the kind of chance introduced into the physicists' world picture is relevant to our understanding of free will or creativity. A mind driven by microscopic roulette wheels in the brain is no more congenial to our notions of conscious free choice or mental creativity than is a mind driven by a brain held in the lockstep of exceptionless laws. If we want to understand the place of free will or of creativity in the world, I think we need to look elsewhere than in the realm of chance as described by physics.

When chance impinges on our ordinary life in the ways familiar from gambling (the randomness of tosses in a dice game, for example), physics can tell us a great deal about what is going on. But the pretensions of some physicists to account for our freedom or our creative novelty strike me as just one more example of disciplinary overreach. What physics does show us, though, is something wonderful in its own right. The aim of physical science is now, as it has always been, to subsume the richly varied phenomena of the physical world under a set of general principles that, for all their subtlety, are unified and of elegant simplicity. What statistical mechanics, chaos theory, and quantum mechanics show us is that this perennial aim of physics can be fulfilled even in a world whose fundamental nature is governed by chance.

OCCURRENCE

In memoriam, Robert Frost

I saw a dark and momentary bird
Sail in a twilit emptiness of sky
Across the apex inexplicably
To etch the moon's face like a written word
So quick that I might doubt it had occurred,
But for the image graven in my eye
Of two black eyebrows arched malignantly
Upon an eggshell, lofty and absurd.
What brought the dark thing twixt the moon and me?
Was it a demon with an hour to kill,
Or Fate, in its capacity to chill,
Or blind chance, with an eye to irony?
A grim design aping coincidence?
Or just a gross refinement of the sense?

--Robert Grudin

Scratch the play area in

the **g**ambler's **go**d

John Boe

Scratch the play area

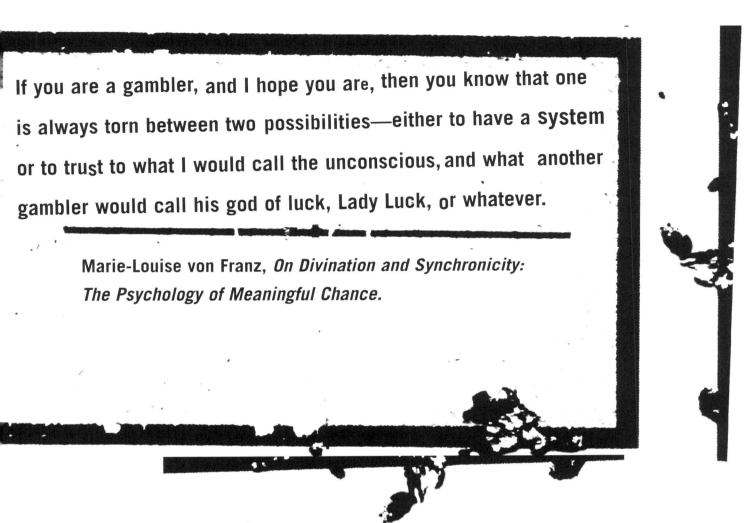

> If you are a gambler, and I hope you are, then you know that one is always torn between two possibilities—either to have a system or to trust to what I would call the unconscious, and what another gambler would call his god of luck, Lady Luck, or whatever.
>
> Marie-Louise von Franz, *On Divination and Synchronicity: The Psychology of Meaningful Chance.*

Einstein refused to accept the claims of quantum mechanics that subatomic events are governed by uncertainty and chance. He famously insisted to Niels Bohr: "God does not play dice with the universe." As von Franz remarks, Einstein "must have had the God of law in the *Old Testament* in mind. For dice-throwing is a very ancient symbol, used in earlier times to illustrate the creative activities of the deity." She points, for example, to the god Krishna, who in the *Bhagavad-Gita* says of himself, "I am the game of dice," and to Heraclitus: "The Aion [eternal duration] is a boy who plays, placing the counters here and there. To a child belongs the cosmic mastery."

Because the rolling dice represent the randomness of future events, we can easily imagine God's playing dice. Players of such games (gamblers and children) try through cleverness or luck to foretell or influence the future. When you are on a lucky streak, when you win and win, it is easy to feel that God is on your side or even that you are a little like a god. For a gambler, such an inflation can be dangerous. Consider the Grimm's fairy tale "Gambling Hansel":

When Gambling Hansel had lost all his money and was about to be evicted from his home, God and St. Peter happened to drop by and ask for an evening's shelter. Although God had paid twice for the food—the first time Hansel had gambled away the money—and had miraculously supplied the wine, God told Hansel that as a reward for his hospitality Hansel could have three wishes. God assumed that one of these wishes would be a ticket to Heaven, but Hansel instead asked for a never-losing pack of cards, a never-losing pair of dice, and a tree with all kinds of fruit from which no one who had climbed up could climb down unless Hansel said so.

So Hansel set out to gamble and soon won half the world. St. Peter and God, understandably bothered, sent Death to Hansel. Hansel was at the card table and asked to be allowed to finish that game. Death, in the meantime, could climb his fruit tree so they might have a snack on their journey.

And so Death was stuck in the fruit tree for another seven years, during which time no one died and Hansel won control of the whole world. St. Peter complained to God about this situation, so God himself went to Hansel and commanded him to let Death down. Death then took Hansel to Hell, and Hansel soon began to gamble there, winning Hell and all its devils from Lucifer. Looking for more action, Hansel went to a high hill with his devils and began to bang on the floor of Heaven with a long hop-pole, so that Heaven itself began to crack. St. Peter ran to God and told him that Heaven would be overthrown unless Hansel were let in. God had no choice but to let Hansel in, and Hansel began to gamble in Heaven until there was such noise and confusion that God couldn't even hear himself think. So St. Peter advised God to throw Hansel down lest he make all Heaven rebellious. So Hansel was thrown down from Heaven to earth, and his soul broke into many pieces, pieces that went into the souls of all gamblers, even the souls of those gamblers who are living today.

Gambling Hansel wins all the time because of God's gifts; he has some of God's power. Hansel takes this power and instead of using it for religious purposes, he secularizes it into gambling; once he tries to be like God, to win all the time and to control the world, he becomes, from the Christian perspective of the tale, a new Lucifer. So the fairy tale is on the surface a cautionary tale about the dangers of trying to be like God (to win all the time), about the evils of gambling, and the misuse of a divine gift—luck.

While Gambling Hansel is like Lucifer, winning control of Hell then challenging Heaven in open rebellion, he is at the end of the story also like the Orphic Dionysus. As an infant, Dionysus was devoured by the Titans, but since his sister Minerva saved his heart, he was able to be reborn. Zeus, angry at the Titans, struck them with a thunder bolt, reducing them to ashes that fell onto the earth and generated the first human beings. According to the Orphic interpretation, our earthly evil side is our Titanic nature, but the divine spark within us comes from Dionysus. And gamblers do feel

such a spark in themselves, a connection with divine or demonic energy. Since my father was a gambler, and I am a bit of a gambler, I can't help but admire Hansel: even if a gambler is more like Lucifer than God, at least he is, in his own rebellious way, aspiring to Heaven. Still, I understand the lesson of the folk tale: as a religious path, gambling is limited.

My friend Kevin tells a story about how his father tried to discourage him and his siblings from gambling. His family was driving through Nevada and stopped for lunch at a restaurant that, typically, was full of slot machines. Throughout lunch, the father lectured the children on the evils of gambling, explaining that only suckers gambled, that gambling was in fact nothing but throwing away money. As they were leaving, to illustrate his point, he made all the children watch while he demonstrated the irrationality of gambling, throwing a quarter away for their edification. He ceremoniously put a quarter in one of the slot machines, pulled the handle, and suddenly quarters were pouring out, bells were ringing, people were gathering. The father sheepishly collected his several-hundred dollar jackpot and the family drove on in silence. The father had taken for granted that he could control chance, that he could be sure of losing. He wanted to teach a patriarchal good-sense lesson about gambling, but the gambler's god had other ideas.

Etymologically, the word "chance" descends from the Latin root *cadere*, "to fall." Chance is what happens to fall, what befalls us. The English word "chance" is furthermore specifically connected with falling dice, for it is probably taken from the Old French, *cheance*, meaning "accident" or, from the image of falling dice, "luck, chance." So gambling—throwing dice—is an archetypal, original way to understand chance.

Lewis Carroll, in *Alice in Wonderland*, used cards to represent our hierarchical social world. Dmitri Mendeleyev used them to represent all the world's elements. Mendeleyev, frustrated in his attempt to classify the elements, had taken a break to play solitaire when he hit upon the idea of making cards of the elements and playing with them instead of the regular cards. Thus he formed a system (subsequently reversed on the basis of a dream) that became the periodic table of the elements. In modified form, this table, the product of playing with cards, is still used today.

Before the Renaissance, it was difficult to separate gambling from divination. Ancient Egypt and the classical world used astragals (knucklebones, frequently of sheep) for both fortune telling and gambling. (And today dice are still called "bones.") The winning throws of the dice game were, as you might expect, also propitious throws of the oracle. For the Romans, the best was the "Venus" throw, when all four astragals showed a different face.

In the fourteenth century, when playing cards became popular throughout Europe, the tarot trump cards were dropped from the deck (with the Fool retained as the Joker), so that the fifty-two-card deck was used for gambling and the ninety-seven-card or seventy-eight-card tarot deck for divination. Similarly, until the later Renaissance, lots were drawn only as an appeal to Providence. In England it wasn't until 1566 that Queen Elizabeth I authorized the first official lottery (to finance harbor improvements). Then in the seventeenth century, the Virginia Company used lotteries on a larger scale to finance the colonization of America.

The birth of a modern attitude toward gambling (connecting it to mathematics as well as to divination) can be seen in the life and work of one of the founders of modern mathematics, Jerome Cardan (1501-1576). Cardan was primarily a physician (thus an astrologer), but he was also a mathematician, in part because mathematics helped him understand two of his passions: music and gambling. His mathematical masterpiece, *Artis Magnae Sive de Regulis Algebraicis (The Great Art, or Algebraic Rules)*, is a cornerstone of modern algebra, offering the first attempts at a systematic theory of equations (including calculations with imaginary numbers) and containing the first published account of the solution for equations of the third and fourth degree. His contribution to the mathematics of gambling was *De Ludo Alea (On Games of Chance)*, which for the first time gave the correct odds on the throws of dice. This study of gambling games was somewhat disreputable in its time, but because of it Cardan can be seen as the father of the calculus of probability.

Cardan discovered what is now called "the law of large numbers." The modern scientific method depends on this law, which suggests that if you throw a coin a large enough number of times, you will get an equal number of heads and tails. (This statement understandably simplifies the story, and ignores the experience, for example, of the statistician who began his lecture on probability by flipping a coin only to have it land, this one time, on its edge.) Chance is the enemy of science, so scientists replicate experiments.

Scratch the play area in

GAME 2

While Cardan used his mathematical understanding of probability to improve his own chances of winning, he admitted that, over his lifetime, gambling had cost him money (as well as time and reputation). Cardan knew that having a rational system helped, but his gambling experience convinced him that winning was more often a function of being in touch with the god of luck, what Cardan called his "genius." Cardan, like his father before him, felt that he was watched over throughout his life by a protective personal spirit who occasionally directly communicated to him (tapping on walls, knocking on doors, shaking walls) and who occasionally brought him gambling luck. In *On Games of Chance*, Cardan describes his greatest gambling victory. In 1526 a Venetian senator, Thomas Lezius, had invited Cardan to play at cards, and because the cards were marked, Lezius won. But on returning home, Cardan used some sort of geomantic divination in order to see future winning card plays. He then returned to Lezius's residence, where he won so much that Lezius suggested that Cardan was being advised by a demon. Cardan did not dispute this suggestion.

That some occult force was at work is suggested by the bizarre conclusion of the story, narrated in Cardan's autobiography. In order to leave with his winnings, Cardan drew a dagger, wounded Lezius in the face, and fled with the money, clothes, and rings. But since Cardan had wounded a senator, he needed to hide from the police. After dark he wandered down by the docks with his dagger under his cloak. Unfortunately, he slipped, fell into the water, and was carried out to sea. He floated adrift in the dark, prepared to die, but by chance a boat came by in the darkness. Cardan grabbed onto the side of it and was saved by the passengers. Once on board, Cardan discovered among the passengers Thomas Lezius, who (perhaps struck by the meaningfulness of this chance occurrence) gave Cardan warm clothes and traveled in his company to Padua.

While Cardan developed accurate methods for determining the probable results in gambling games, his experience taught him the importance of luck in any single gambling game. The law of large numbers can't accurately predict one throw of the dice or even what kinds of cards you will get over a long evening. Cardan understood that luck depended on what the Greeks called *kairos*, which means "the right time for action" and was associated with the Goddess of Fate.

While science and the calculus of probability depend on the law of large numbers, gambling, like divination, depends on the singular moment. You are supposed to ask the *I Ching* your question only one time. And at the racetrack, you can hear gamblers shout the magical plea "One time!" as their horses come down the stretch. Whatever the odds, the gambler seizes on the possibility that the horse can win this one time.

As a gambler and a scientist, Cardan was understandably interested in time: one of his astronomical contributions was a very accurate calculation of the length of the year. The connection of gambling with time is suggested both by the fifty-two cards in the deck and the thirty-six numbers on the roulette wheel. Fifty-two is of course the number of weeks in a year, and just as we round off the degrees in a circle to 360 in imitation of the days in the year, the roulette wheel correspondingly gives thirty-six numbers (with the zero perhaps representing the extra five days). Any gambling game teaches the importance of time, and any gambler knows that to ride a lucky streak is an experience of synchronicity. When you act at just the right moment, you feel in touch with your genius.

Cardan saw that business, like gambling, depended on luck as well as skill: "For it is agreed by all that one man may be more fortunate than another, or even than himself at another time of life, not only in games but also in business, and with one man more than another and on one day more than another." Capitalism is a kind of institutional gambling, a gambling increasingly secularized away from its religious and divinatory roots. In the modern world, business

comes the respectable way to gamble, so playing the stock market then becomes advisable (as everyone seems to think these days). While industry and skill are important in business as they are in cards, you can't beat luck. It is crucial in almost any success.

Max Weber made famous the idea that Protestantism, which was born out of the Renaissance, gave birth to the spirit of capitalism. So it makes sense that John Calvin's stern Protestant God is a kind of gambler. After all, the most important theological factor is God's grace. You are chosen as one of the elect only by God's grace—indeed He has already chosen you from before the beginning of time. You don't get to heaven by virtue of good works (the old Catholic idea), but rather by grace—that is, by being lucky. For Calvin, the gambling God is not throwing dice but rather conducting a lottery, where, before time begins, He picks the winning numbers. Grace from Him is luck for us.

The Protestant devotion to business is sometimes explained on the basis of "evidence": one doesn't earn election by being virtuous and working hard (by being a moral and successful businessman), but rather this status is evidence that God has elected you as one of the blessed. Your success is due to God's grace: "Can't help it if I'm lucky." In a kind of knock-on-wood move, you deflect the negative

consequences of your success because it is really God's success. And God, through you, can keep winning forever. The lucky Protestant never thinks, as Gambling Hansel does, that *he* is winning, that *he* can challenge God. No wonder the Protestants put so much energy into business (a kind of gambling): success there proves that they are eternally lucky.

Protestantism is an almost absurdist modern theology. What an irrational God, to randomly pick the elect without consideration for their merit! Protestantism co-opts the spirit of gambling, transforming the gambler's good-luck feeling into a theological experience of God's grace.

Cardan said of gambling that "in times of great anxiety and grief, it is considered to be not only allowable, but even beneficial." That the appropriate time to gamble is when you are unlucky in life is suggested by the old saying "Lucky in cards, unlucky in love." Certainly poor people who gamble aren't poor because they gamble, but rather they gamble because they are poor. We superstitious humans always expect fortune's wheel to turn (even if it doesn't always—see *King Lear*). If too many good things happen to us, we worry, for we expect a certain amount of bad luck. When life goes badly, we often think that we are owed some good luck—so we gamble.

The onset of Feodor Dostoevsky's famous gambling mania came about at such a time of bad luck, especially of bad luck in love. In the early 1860s Dostoevsky was frequently separated from his ill-tempered wife Marya, who was dying of tuberculosis. Sometime in the winter of 1862-3, the forty-two-year old Dostoevsky began an affair with the twenty-three-year old Apollonaria ("Polina") Suslova. Polina was the daughter of a serf who had bought his freedom and educated his daughters. She was a writer, she was beautiful, and she was thoroughly "modern" (her younger sister was the first Russian woman to get a medical degree).

By summer 1863, the journal *Time*, owned and edited by Dostoevsky and his brother, was banned by the government, so Dostoevsky lost his main source of income. He found himself subject to increasingly frequent and severe epileptic seizures (followed by periods of depression). In order to finance his trip to Paris to meet Polina, Dostoevsky borrowed 1500 rubles. In August 1863, he departed for Paris, anticipating a kind of European honeymoon.

Because he was desperately short of money, Dostoevsky decided to make a four-day roulette stopover in Wiesbaden. He had won 11,000 francs the previous year on his first try at roulette—the gambler's god usually lets you win the first time. And this time, too, he left the tables a winner (10,400 francs ahead), but then returned to lose half his winnings. He sent some money to his brother for safekeeping and some to his wife, then hurried to Paris to meet his lover.

When he arrived on August 14, he was given a letter from Polina that told him, "You are coming too late…everything has changed within a few days." Just a few days before (when Dostoevsky had been gambling at Wiesbaden), she had allowed herself to be seduced by a Spanish medical student, in her own words to Dostoevsky, "without a struggle, without assurance, almost without hope that I was being loved." Nonetheless, Dostoevsky and Polina didn't separate. Instead, unlucky-in-love Dostoevsky spent his time calling on Polina, consoling her on being jilted by her Spanish lover, and playing roulette. At this time, he wrote a friend that he had discovered the secret of how to win at roulette: "I really do know the secret—it is terribly silly and simple, merely a matter of keeping oneself under constant control and never getting excited, no matter how the game shifts." He would return to this idea again in his subsequent years of roulette mania, but even here, at the first mention, he sees the fatal flaw: "But the difficulty is not in finding this out, but in being able to put it into practice once you do. You may be wise as a serpent and have a will of iron, but you will still succumb."

Dostoevsky was facing the classic gambler's choice: system or luck. This choice was a special problem for Dostoevsky, for one of his constant literary themes was that reason is limited, that contact with the irrational is the redemption from the deadness of systematized modern life. He describes the hero of his novel *The Gambler* as follows:

e essential is that all his vital powers of life, his violence, his audacity are devoted to roulette. He is a gambler, but t an ordinary gambler.... He is a poet in his fashion, but he is ashamed of that poetry because he profoundly feels baseness, although the need of risk ennobles him in his own eyes.

stoevsky the gambler is like the classic Petrarchan lover: disdained and tortured by the woman loves, he turns his frustration into poetry, in this case the poetry of roulette. Part of the poetry gambling comes from the gambler's ambivalent attitude toward money. The important thing is game, and losing is better than not playing at all. To gamble you have to have a contempt for ney, a willingness to lose it all (as Dostoevsky did again and again). Throwing his money away he roulette tables even when he was in desperate need of money was a poetic gesture express- Dostoevsky's admirable contempt for money, his admirable contempt for the materialistic dern world.

e *Gambler* is a first-person confessional novel, the story of Aleksey Ivanovich, a brilliant, alien- d twenty-two-year-old expatriate Russian. Except for his age, Aleksy's situation explicitly allels Dostoevsky's own recent life: at the beginning of the novel, Aleksey is frustrated in his e for a fascinating young woman named Polina, and by the end of the novel he is still hope- sly in love with her and with the game of roulette.

ly in the novel, Aleksey explains that Russians love roulette because they are interested in tting rich quickly, in a couple of hours without working," which he finds no worse than "the man capacity for making a pile by honest toil." Touring the German city of "Roulettenburg," is horrified by those moralizing little German picture-books: "...every house has its *Vater*, adfully virtuous and exceedingly honest. So honest, in fact, that it's terrible to go near him."

ksey is one of Dostoevsky's most appealing "underground" men; cynical and witty, he elegantly omplishes the trick of both caring deeply about life and seeming not to care at all. He believes t gambling allows you to live life passionately in the present moment. Dostoevsky's novel shows energy in such gambling.

g offers an intriguing comment on the gambler's energy: "In emotional intensity, game and bler coincide." Von Franz explains this remark:

It is because of the passionate, emotional intensity with which one is gripped in gam- bling that one becomes, so to speak, the game. Every true and decent gambler is right in it, his mind is occupied with it, he just waits and prays that the die will fall a certain way. That is the great pleasure in it. One lives when one gambles. One is right in it and involved. . . .If there is such a passion, then we know an archetype is at work.

Such emotional intensity is found both in gambling and in love, a combination of intensities *The Gambler* explores. Being in a gambling game, like being in love, concentrates the mind. The moments when the ball is spinning, like the moments with the beloved, are supremely important. The gambler, like the lover, is not planning for the future, is not acting like the good father living a provisional life. Gamblers and lovers, alive in the present moment with everything at stake, can grow used to, even addicted to, the intensity. As Aleksey admits near the end of the novel, "I had got used to staking everything on a single throw of the dice."

The Gambler has my all-time favorite "Lady or the Tiger?" ending. Aleksey wins a fortune gambling, but he loses Polina. He then pointlessly throws away his money on Blanche (a manipulative courtesan) and is subsequently humiliated by having to work as a servant. Finally, he is told by the Englishman Mr. Astley (also in love with Polina) that Polina really does love him, Aleksey. Astley is sure Aleksey nonetheless has no hope, that he is so addicted to roulette that he will never reunite with Polina.

Aleksey feels that if he can only win enough money to be worthy of Polina, he will return to her and give up roulette forever. The novel ends with a soliloquy that vacillates between hope and despair:

Let Polina know that I can still be a man. I need only...but now it is too late, but tomorrow.... Surely I can understand that I am done for! But why can't I rise again? Yes! I have only to be prudent and patient for once in my life—and that's all. I have only to stand firm once, and I can change the whole course of my destiny in an hour! The chief thing is strength of will. I need only remember the incident of this sort seven months ago in Roulettenburg. There really is something special in the feeling when alone, in a strange country, far away from home and friends and not knowing what you will eat that day, you stake your last gulden, your very, very last! I won, and twenty minutes later I left the station with 170 gulden in my pocket. That is a fact! You see what one's last gulden may sometimes mean! And what if I had lost courage then, if I had not dared to decide.

Tomorrow, tomorrow it will all come to an end!

Most critics read this ending as if Mr. Astley is definitely right, that Aleksey is "a lost soul" who will lose his money and Polina. But the critics are usually middle-aged academics, not gamblers or lovers. I first read the novel when I was twenty-five or so (and hadn't read any of the critics), when I still believed in the hope of gambling, and I remember believing with crazy Aleksey that, yes, he can win it all back, if not by sticking with a system then maybe by pure luck. The end of the novel is almost like the spinning of the roulette wheel—tomorrow the number will come up, and it will all be decided. Whatever the odds, Aleksey doesn't *have* to lose. A gambler can win, no matter what the critical fatherworld thinks.

Rereading the novel at fifty-one, I sympathize a little more with the critics' weary pessimism. Still, when Dostoevsky wrote the novel (and for some years afterwards), he was a gambler who did believe that if he had the strength of will to play his system and not get caught up in emotional intensity, he could win. The novel leaves us with the world of chance, the ball spinning around, love and money waiting to be determined by the wheel of fortune: "What am I now? Zero. What may I be tomorrow? Tomorrow I may rise from the dead and begin to live again!" Ah, to keep alive a gambler's hope, that the wheel can turn, that you have a chance to be reborn, to believe in the gambler's god despite the critical voices of reason! To end *The Gambler* with fortune's wheel spinning is to insist that we live in a world of chance—that, like Aleksey, we all need luck.

Despite Dostoevsky's gambling, these were productive artistic years. Joseph Frank, Dostoevsky's greatest biographer, titles his volume on Dostoevsky's life from 1865-1871, *The Miraculous Years*. While he was hopelessly unlucky in gambling, he was very lucky in his second marriage and, most of all, lucky in his work. There is something called "writer's luck"—the gift that lets inspiration come, the work go well, the words be right. These days I increasingly feel about writing the way I used to feel about gambling. Writing is like having a ticket on a horse.

Freud claimed Dostoevsky was driven by masochism to lose at gambling, that Dostoevsky enjoyed losing as well as the humiliation of having *lost*. It's even been claimed, by Alan Wykes, that Dostoevsky once had an orgasm when he lost a big bet at roulette. But Dostoevsky's "masochism" could also be explained as part of a writer/gambler's psychology. As John Cohen points out, "A common way of gaining luck is by courting contempt." The king's fool drives away the king's bad luck by abusing the king, the "roast" is a ceremony of tribute and respect, and Dostoevsky's "masochistic" gambling coincided with his most miraculous writing years: *Notes from the Underground* (1864), *Crime and Punishment* (1866), *The Gambler* (1866), *The Idiot* (1868), *The Eternal Husband* (1869), *The Devils* (1871). Perhaps the masochism of his gambling was a way of gaining literary luck, both in the magical manner of "courting contempt" and in the more practical way of putting himself in a situation where his only economic chance was writing.

Even today, when scientists or mathematicians explain probability (that is, chance), they talk about gambling. After all, probability theory was invented in a correspondence between Pascal and Fermat, a correspondence occasioned by gambling problems for dice posed by Antoine Gombaud, the Chevalier de Méré. (Because of Pascal's various ball and wheel experiments regarding the theory of probability, folklore makes him the inventor of the roulette wheel.)

No wonder "Monte Carlo" has become the accepted term for algorithmic methods employing random numbers. As Newman and Odell explain in *The Generation of Random Variates*, these methods were developed in the 1940s as sampling techniques applied "to non-probabilistic problems to gain answers to very difficult problems primarily arising in nuclear physics." In 1947, in order to apply Monte Carlo methods to the analysis of the effects of random errors on the trajectory of rockets, the Rand Corporation (working for the U. S. Air Force) used an IBM model 856 Cardatype to produce a million random digits. In 1955, The Rand Corporation published these tables in a book, *A Million Random Digits with 100,000 Normal Deviates*. In the introduction to this one-of-a-kind work, the corporate authors make a charming admission: "Because of the very nature of the table, it did not seem necessary to proofread every page of the final manuscript in order to catch random errors of the Cardatype."

It is not easy to generate a series of random, truly unpredictable numbers. For one thing, the results of the most well-known methods of generating a random sequence, such as flipping a coin or spinning a roulette wheel, are obviously determined by the laws of physics. Thus gamblers with computers have been successful in detecting the biases of roulette wheels, and there are machines that will throw heads 95% percent of the time.

The Rand numbers were (and are) used, but they cannot truly be called random. After all, they were determined, produced according to a program to control the computer's arithmetical operations. And once a random variable has been observed, it's not random any more. (This statistical, mathematical observation has its philosophical corollary: Chance is defined by verb tense. Until the time "has come," the future is a matter of chance, but once the time "has come," the event is history, perhaps was even "fated.") Because I can look up the first or the

500,000th number in the Rand book (both are "1" and always will be), we can at best consider the Rand million digits a "pseudo-random" series. But as Donald Knuth writes, "Being 'apparently random' is perhaps all that can be said about any random sequence anyway." The best we can say about *any* "random" number series is that it behaves as if it could have been generated randomly.

Pi, the number that expresses the ratio of the circle's circumference to its diameter, behaves as if it could have been generated randomly. Mathematicians have for a long time found this distressing. After all, the circle is perhaps our most perfect symbol of order, and so it is something of an oxymoron to have its eternal mathematical basis turn out to be an infinite *random* number series. It is as if chance is the secret heart of order.

The quest to find order in pi has made this number an object of much study. Pi is an irrational number (that is, it cannot be expressed as the ratio of two integers, like, for example, the square root of 2). When you look at the decimal form of rational and irrational numbers, you appreciate the poetry of these mathematical terms. Only the "rational" shows completion (as a whole integer) or pattern (as ratio).

By the eighteenth century, as Peter Beckman points out in his *History of Pi*, "people began to suspect that there were 'worse' numbers than irrational ones." These are "transcendental" numbers, numbers that cannot be the solution to any algebraic equation such as $X^2-2=0$ (whose solution is the square root of 2). Such numbers "transcend" algebra. While there are infinite numbers of rational, of irrational, and of transcendental numbers, it is perhaps distressing that the greater infinity by far is that of the transcendental numbers, which are not only irrational but are also algebraically unsatisfactory. Pi is also such a transcendental number.

Because pi is the mathematical secret to the circle, it has received far more attention than the infinity of other transcendental numbers. Throughout history the number of decimal places calculated for pi has steadily increased—recently, a team at the University of Tokyo calculated it to three and a half billion places. Many people have memorized pi to a number of decimal places. One of those who can recite the most digits is Rajan Mahadevan, who at one time held the pi-digit world record of 31,812. Mahadevan stopped there because he "just forgot." As he explained to T. R. Reid in the *Washinton Post*, "The 31,812th digit, I don't know why, I am always stumbling over that one."

Mahadevan says that he enjoys memorizing the digits in the random walk of pi and that he especially enjoys certain series. His favorite is the 100-number series

from 2,901 to 3,000. "I just love those hundred digits," he

plained before passionately reciting them:

"81911979399520614196634287544051437
451237181921799983910159195618414675
142691239748940907186494231961."

is hard for anyone to justify aesthetic judgment, but Mahadevan did say, "I don't know why I love those digits so much. It's like seeing a woman and you just like her

m the first for no reason. That series, it is like an old, old friend I will never forget."

aditionally we think of beauty, if not in terms of symmetry, at least in terms of order or pattern. But it is a mistake to think, as most people seem to, that ndom means disordered. As Donald Knuth says, "A truly random sequence will exhibit local nonrandomness." Experience suggests that this rule is true for sequence of events in life as well as for a sequence of numbers: every so often, things happen that make sense.

people are asked to write down a series of random numbers, they do a bad job, Knuth points out, for they "tend to avoid things which seem nonrandom, ch as pairs of equal adjacent digits (although about one out of every ten digits should equal its predecessor). And if we would show someone a table of truly ndom digits, he would quite probably tell us they are not random at all; his eye would spot certain apparent regularities." Chip Denman, a reporter for the ashington Post, recently asked readers to send him numbers chosen in various specified "random" ways, including out of their heads. The results demonstrated that most people mistakenly think that random means "without pattern." Thus, people avoided multiples of ten and generally picked too many prime numbers, thinking that numbers like 37 and 13 were somehow especially random.

The "pseudo-random" sequence of pi *of course* has patches of order, patches someone sensitive to a number series (like Mahadevan) could find beautiful. Indeed, since pi goes on to infinity, it has every conceivable numerical order in it. If you could look far enough into pi, you would find patches of a million straight zeroes, all the batting averages in the history of baseball listed in chronological order, the numbers in the current Manhattan telephone directory. Within an infinite random series there are patches of *extreme* order. While we have only started looking at the beginning of pi's infinite series of numbers, we have already seen "88888888" around the three-hundred-millionth digit, "6666666666" a little time later, and at around a half-billion good old "123456789." There are, by chance, patches of order.

Perhaps the greatest mathematician who has spent the most time looking at pi is Gregory Chudnovsky, who, with his brother David, has at various times held the world record for calculating pi to the most digits, a record achieved with a super-computer they built in Gregory's apartment. They claim "that the digits of pi form the most nearly perfect random sequence of digits that has ever been discovered," that while pi can't be seen as a random number (after all, it is determined by the nature of the circle), it is certainly "a damned good fake of a random number," as quoted by Richard Preston in *The New Yorker.* In trying to find an ordering principle in pi, the Chudnovsky brothers are investigating a philosophical as well as a mathematical problem. They are trying to find out what "random" means.

The decimal expansion of pi is the longest "pseudo-random" number series ever calculated—it puts to shame the Rand Corporation's meager million. The Chudnovskys have found no statistically significant order in the first few billion digits of pi,

but they feel there might be a hint of order in the "running average of the digits." As the series approach infinity the average of the digits 0 to 9 should approach 4.5, but the Chudnovskys have noticed that average of the digits in pi's first billion digits seems to be a little high, and the average of the digits in second billion digits seems to be a little low. "It's not statistically significant," Gregory admits, but, " close to the edge of significance." The brothers think that with a trillion digits they will be able to tel there is a statistically significant "wave" that runs through pi.

Finding order in pi is in part a function of how we look at pi. G. W. Leibniz, the co-inventor with Newton the calculus, discovered an elegant and orderly way of representing pi as an infinite series of fractions. Leibniz series is one of mathematics' most beautiful patterns: $pi=4/1-4/3+4/5-4/7+4/9-4/11+4/$ $4/15+4/17. . .$ and so on forever. In the Leibniz series, pi is the undulating dance that the number f does with the infinite series of odd integers. (That the number four should be the infinitely repeated in ger in Leibniz's equation for pi coincidentally offers support for one of Jung's least understood ideas: connection between the number four and the circle; both symbols of psychic wholeness are unified in Jun central symbol of the mandala, the cross in the circle). Perhaps the undulating dance of the number f with the odd integers (pi in the Leibniz series) has a parallel in waves that will become apparent when analyze a trillion digits of pi.

If the Leibniz series offers a comforting glimpse of order, the decimal series still shows only chance. A so some mathematicians think the Chudnovskys have gone crazy. "For all we know," Gregory Chudnov admits, "we may never find a rule in pi." But the random series of pi can be looked at in various ways. *The Amazing Dr. Matrix*, Martin Gardner quotes the greatest numerologist who ever lived, Irving Mat "Mathematicians consider the decimal expansion of pi a random series, but to a modern numerologist rich with remarkable patterns." Matrix points out a pattern in the first thirty-three digits. Twenty-six is first repeated two-digit number, and symmetrically arranged on each side of the second 26 are match pairs: 79, 32, and 38 on the left balanced by 38, 32, and 79 on the right. This striking symmetry in p of course by chance. But any random series will at some time show chance symmetries.

I myself have found an order in pi through music. I took the number one to equal middle C and mov straight up the scale in the key of C according to the progression of the integers (0 became the B belo middle C). With this musical translation, I transcribed the first forty-one integers of pi (the forty-first integer is a one,

and it made for a nice sense of tonality and closure to end on C). I like it played as if it were a Mozart dance or canon

written by Bach reincarnated as Eric Satie. I include my translation here. There are, of course, numerous possible phras-

ings for these first forty-one notes of the Song of Pi.

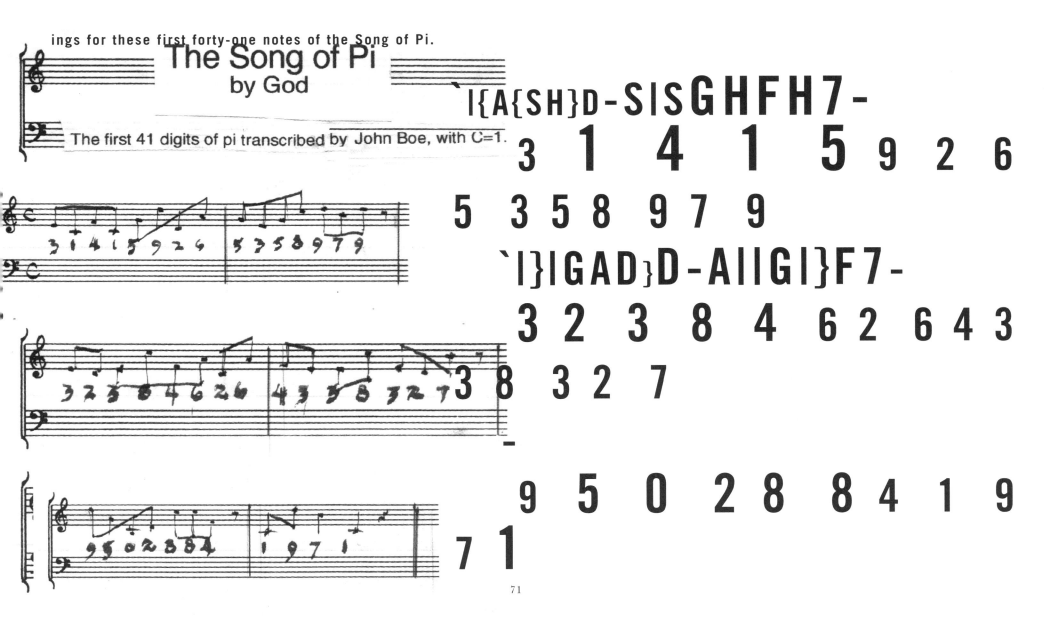

The Song of Pi
by God

The first 41 digits of pi transcribed by John Boe, with C=1.

Translated into music, the first forty-one digits of pi's random sequence make musical sense, indeed sound beautiful, classical. Not all sequences in pi's random walk are equally beautiful. The music found in the first forty-one digits is an example of what Jung called "synchronicity," a meaningful coincidence, acausal order.

Synchronicities are the patches of order that inevitably appear in any random series. Most people underestimate the frequency of such synchronicities in life, just as they underestimate the order that will be found in an extended random number series. Some people (perhaps especially those with a strong aesthetic sense) more frequently notice such moments of synchronicity, pick out shape in the random stream, find beauty and order. Through aesthetic judgment, we find order and meaning in the random. While there are 190,899,322 different rhyme schemes for a fourteen-line sonnet, the Petrarchan and Shakespearean variations seem most pleasing. And the designer of a Zen rock garden (like the designer of the Sierra Mountains) is able to find the beauty in random order.

To some degree, artists have always had to trust to chance, but in the modern era some have even embraced it. The Brazilian composer Hector Villa-Lobos found the shape for some of his most beautiful melodies by drawing the outline of a mountain range or a city skyline on a musical staff and then putting notes on that line. Jackson Pollack made beauty by randomly dripping or throwing paint. And John Cage most obviously of all let the random generate art. In his famous piece 4'33," the performer sits at the piano but doesn't play for four minutes and thirty-three seconds. The goal is to get the listener to hear the random sounds in whatever space the performance is taking place, to listen for the music in the random sounds of the everyday.

We live in a contingent universe where what is, often seems to have been randomly chosen. We fall in love with someone we meet by chance, and most events, important and trivial, seem unpredictable. We can find meaning in the flow of events in two ways: either through systems like science and mathematics by which we statistically look at events in the long run; or through special moments of synchronicity, when we find a patch of order in the random stream, and, like a gambler on a roll, feel one with the flow of the universe.

We have to accept much of physical reality as a "just so" story. The velocity of light is 186,300 miles per second—the absolute speed limit, Avogadro's number is 6.02×10^{23}, and the fine structure constant is 1/137.

There's an old story Dr. Matrix liked to tell "about how the physicist Wolfgang Pauli, after he had died, asked God why he had picked 137. God handed him some papers covered with formulas and said, 'It's all here.' Pauli studied the formulas carefully, frowned, looked up, and said, 'Das ist falsch.'" Perhaps even our greatest geniuses will never fully understand God's seemingly random methods.

When God threw the dice to define the circle, the pseudo-random series we call pi came up, and it will come up eternally and infinitely. God does seem to play dice with the universe, but there is consolation: even Einstein at his most pessimistic assumes that it is God throwing the dice. And if the numbers on God's dice are sometimes irrational and transcendental, still there are such miracles of order as circles.

The Fate of Fortuna

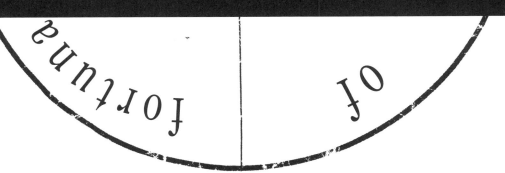

The late Jimmy (the Greek) Snyder was associated with football, a bizarre theory of athletic eugenics, and Las Vegas—a desert city that conjures up the mirage of Caesar's Palace. Jimmy the Greek and his wife also lived in Durham, North Carolina, a Piedmont and pedantic city which, with its university, tobacco warehouses, and insurance companies and their actuarial tables, can hardly be described as Las Vegas without the glitter. Demetrios Georgios Synodios was a second-generation Greek born in Ohio. His last name, which means a coming together or coincidence in Greek, became Snyder, the tailor. There is nothing Greek in the odds he cut throughout a long career managing probabilities, handicaps, chance, and the goddess Fortuna. Nor is there anything Roman in Caesar's Palace.

Diskin Clay

Greek Tyche and Roman Fortuna were powerful divinities, too powerful for any mere human to calculate or manipulate. Greek philosophers and Aristotle in particular were interested in probability and the logical value of statements about the future. But Greek mathematics developed neither a theory of probability nor a stochastic calculus nor a model for chaos theory. The Greeks were wise and cautious enough to see the past laid out clearly before them. As for the future, this stretched behind them and they backed cautiously into it. In Greek, *eis topisthen* meant both moving backwards and moving into the future. The ancient Greeks made careful calculations about the uncertainties of the future, and they expressed these in all four moods of their delicate and precise verb system (indicative, subjunctive, optative, and even imperative). The Greek system of conditions regarding the future is the despair of any beginning Greek student. Unlike the Romans, the Greeks were wary of using a future perfect: "When I shall have become king of Greece, I will have...." In Attic Greek, only two verbs allowed this tense in the active voice: "I shall have taken a stand," and "I shall have died."

For both the Roman goddess Fortuna and the remoter Greek Tyche, the emblem of fate is the wheel. In Medieval times the stages in the revolution of her wheel were: REGNO, **REGNABAM, SUM SINE REGNO, REGNABO.** I AM KING, I WAS KING, I HAVE LOST MY KINGDOM, I WILL BE KING AGAIN.

Fortune's wheel once stood upright. Now it lies horizontally in the prostrate form of the game of roulette. Both wheels rotate, but the fortunes of the roulette wheel in Las Vegas are determined as a percentage of the wagers by the Gaming Commission of the State of Nevada.

For Americans, fortune is a vast sum of money gained by buying a lottery ticket or betting on the horses at the Sierra Turf Club off Douglas Alley in Reno; or earned by parsimony and thrift; or realized by investing prudently in the stock market, or by inventing a product like Microsoft. If asked, "Is this a game of chance?," most votaries of the American goddess Fortuna (also know as Pecunia) would reply with W. C. Fields, "Not the way I play it." We know what fortune is and how it is made from *Fortune Magazine* and its "*Fortune's 500.*"

But in ancient Italy even a crude character like Trimalchio and his wife Fortunata recognized divine help in gaining their staggeringly vulgar wealth. They would have enjoyed Caesar's Palace immensely. In their own palace, according to the *Satyricon*, guests could admire a wall painting showing Fortuna with her cornucopia and

Mercury lifting Trimalchio on high by his chin. The ancients were more pious and cautious than we are. We know the story of the Lydian King who thought that he was a fortunate man (*olbios*) because of his vast wealth (*olbos*). Croesus came to understand, with the help of a Greek named Solon, that his wealth was not happiness, when his empire was overthrown by Cyrus the Great. Herodotus tells us that as Cyrus, at the height of his power, planned more and more elusive conquests, Croesus came to offer him a piece of advice:

> " If you fancy that you are immortal and command an army of immortals, I do not need to take the trouble to tell you what I think of your expedition [into Scythia]. But, if you realize that you and all those you command are mere mortals, learn first this lesson: all human endeavors rotate on a wheel. As it turns, this wheel does not allow the same people to be forever fortunate."

Croesus's word for being fortunate connects with the Greek word for fortune: tyche. If you translate from Greek into Latin, the most available equivalent for tyche is fortuna. But the match is far from perfect. Greek *tyche* and the Greek goddess Tyche derive from the verb *tynghano*. This verb has a range of meanings that stretches our imagination. It can describe whatever happens by chance as opposed to human design; or, it can describe human designs: to hit what you are aiming at, to get what you want. Latin fortuna belongs to a different world. Roman speakers connected this name with the Latin verb *ferre*, to bring or to bear. The cult of Fortuna had clear associations with the fertility goddess, Mater Matuta. There is even a Fortuna Mammosa worshipped in Rome (Fortuna of the generous breasts). Roman coins show Fortuna with a rudder in one hand, which is her emblem in Greek, and a cornucopia in the other. In Praeneste (Palestrina) to the southeast of Rome, there was a vast temple to Fortuna Primigenita, Fortune the first born.

Bellini, Giovanni. Allegory of Fortune. Accademia, Venice, Italy.

But, if they differed in their etymologies, the Greeks and Romans agreed on the power of Fortuna. In both the Greek and Roman worlds, Tyche and Fortuna represented a powerful divine force that moved human lives and human events. It was prudent only to propitiate such a force. Tyche and Fortuna operated in two spheres of influence. In the smaller, they affected the lives and careers of individuals; in the larger and concentric sphere, they affected the prosperity and fate of cities. One example of Tyche's smaller sphere comes from Demosthenes's famous speech on the civic crown his rival Aeschines had attempted to deprive him of. Aeschines had spoken of *tyche*, and Demosthenes responded by speaking of the fortune (we would say "lot") divinity distributes to each individual. This conception of divine dispensation is the platform for Demosthenes's devastating contrast between his life and fortune and that of the low-life Aeschines. His term for divinity is *daimon*. His manner of reviewing his life is completely alien to our way of seeing the world. If we are farmers on the plains of Kansas or Oklahoma, we can recognize and accept God's will in the drought that is now scorching the Midwest and raising prices everywhere. But we cannot at the same time hold Fortune responsible for the success or failure of our crops. The Greeks were capable of speaking of a *daimon* and *tyche* as they did because they recognized forces surpassing human calculation. Their *daimones* are divine forces influencing human life that cannot be located within the sphere of influence of the gods recognized by cult.

In Homer, speakers recognize this divine power over human life as they address anyone who acts out of character as *daimonie*. This expression embarrasses translators. It can best be captured by "What's got into you?" Heraclitus uttered a curt and oracular correction to this manner of recognizing the divine in the extraordinary events of human life: *ethos anthropoi daimon:* "Your inner character is your outer *daimon*."

Just as the Greeks were reluctant to demarcate clear boundaries between one state and another but left a no-man's-land strip between, they recognized divine powers that cannot readily be defined. Tyche is one of these. In a speech at the beginning of the Peloponnesian War, Pericles warns the Athenian assembly of the fact that their best-laid plans can go awry:

"There is often no more logic in the course of events than there is in the plans of men, and this is why we blame our luck when things don't turn out the way we expect." This is a secular view of *tyche*. Sophocles finds a more religious way of putting this contemporary insight when he has Oedipus, who is on the verge of discovering who his true parents are, proclaim that he is the son of Fortune (Tyche), "the giver of good." And he speaks of the months as "brothers who shaped him when he was small and when he was great." His conception of the waxing months as his brothers is a religious attempt to reassert a rational control over his life. The phases of the moon are variable, but predictable. (In a late astrological text, the moon is called Tyche.)

Oedipus's Tyche is his personal fate. The Romans, too, recognized a personal Fortuna. Just as every Roman male had *Genius* and every Roman female had her *Juno*, each Roman had his or her *fortuna*. The most striking example I know the combination of Genius and Fortuna comes from a Greek source. In his *Life of Antony*, Plutarch speaks of the cooperation and fiercely competitive relation between Antony and the young Octavian (later dignified as Augustus). An Egyptian expert in casting horoscopes was impressed by Antony's brilliant Fortuna, but saw it eclipsed by Octavian's Genius: "Your Genius," he said, "fears the Genius of Octavian. When it is by itself, it stands tall and proud; but when the Genius of Octavian comes near, yours shrinks and is obscured." Plutarch's Greek is just what we would expect. He speaks Antony's *tyche* and *daimon*.

Cities, too, had their presiding Tyche or Fortuna. In Athens, Tyche had a temple overlooking the stadium to the west. chance, the sculptor who created the famous Tyche of Antioch was named Eutychides, son of Luck. But in Rome the worship of Fortuna was astounding. No ancient city was so devoted to Fortuna. The early king Servius Tullius was associated with establishing her cult in Rome. (There was a Fortuna Tulliana.) A walking tour of Lawrence Richardson, Jr.'s *New Topographical Dictionary of Rome* reveals thirty-two sites at which a Roman could worship Fortuna in her many uses. This worship brings home the meaning of the Latin Proverb *Fortuna adiuvat fortes:* Fortune helps the strong. Indeed, the virtue of bravery, *fortitudo* actually seems to be implicated in the name *Fortuna*.

When in Rome, where to worship? Among the many choices, I would recommend the cult of Fortuna Huiusce Diei— Fortune of this present day. She can still be worshiped in the Largo Argentina. (The cats will tell you that you have found your destination.) For the incurable optimist there is also the altar of Mala Fortuna. Plutarch notes a Fortuna calcata, Fortuna daubed with lime or the Fowler's Fortuna. For the individual there is Fortuna Privata. For women there Fortuna Virgo and, despite her name, Fortuna Virilis. Fortuna Virilis was worshiped with Venus Verticordia on April 1. Venus turned the heart; Fortuna Virilis turned a man's eye and mind away from blemishes on a woman's body. She was especially important in baths. Ovid explains the reason why women offer her incense at the baths:

> The baths witness every blemish of the naked body,
>
> Once the lady is undressed.
>
> Don't be distressed. This is the moment
>
> to offer a peck of incense on the altar of Fortuna Virilis.
>
> She will respond by covering every blemish from men's eyes.

In *On the Fortune of the Romans*, Plutarch wondered whether their fortune or their virtue were responsible for their rise to world dominion. He decided that in the case of the Romans alone these two antagonistic forces worked hand-in-hand. So he would not have been surprised by the exquisite mirror that Benvenuto Cellini's father made for his Medici patrons. Its hub was a looking glass; its spokes the wheel of Fortune; on top of the wheel stood representations of the seven virtues. As the wheel revolved around the stationary looking glass a new virtue ascended to its top. Giovanni Cellini gave his conceit a Latin inscription:

ROTA SUM: SEMPER QUOQUO ME VERTO, STAT VIRTUS
"I am a Wheel. Wherever I turn stands Virtue."

Greeks before the age of Plutarch and the Pax Romana were less optimistic about the relation between virtue (and the virtue of wisdom, especially) and the goddess Tyche. Beginning in the fourth century B.C., the Athenians invoked the powerful protection of Tyche by inscribing over their decrees the words ΑΓΑΘΗΙ ΤΥΧΗΙ, "with Tyche prospering." At the top of a decree from Tegea in the Peloponnese we find a representation of Tyche holding a rudder. The meaning of this emblem is that Tyche—not the human calculations of political assemblies—directed the course of the ship of state. A rationalist like Democritus could protest: "Humans have fashioned the image of Tyche as a cover for their own lack of deliberation. Tyche and intelligence are seldom at war. Sharp-sighted and quick comprehension steer the course of most of life." His was not quite a voice in the wilderness. Epicurus reinforced his conception of the control of intelligence over human life in *Master Saying* XVI.

When Greek Tyche was overwhelmed by Roman Fortuna, Greeks adopted the word Fortuna. In modern Greek, *fortouna* is a sudden storm at sea. And the Turks, who learned about the sea from the Greeks, call such a storm *fırtın*. Such is the fate of Fortuna.

. . . I consider that it is better to be adventurous than cautious, because Fortune is a woman, and if you wish to keep her under it is necessary to beat and ill-use her, and it is seen that she allows herself to be mastered by the adventurous. . . She is, therefore, always woman-like, a lover of young men. . .

MACHIAVELLI

...THERE IS NO SUCH THING AS FORTUNE IN THE WORLD;
NOR DOES ANYTHING THAT HAPPENS HERE BELOW OF GOOD OR ILL COME BY CHANCE,
BUT BY THE PARTICULAR PROVIDENCE OF HEAVEN;

AND THIS MAKES GOOD THE PROVERB,
THAT EVERY MAN MAY THANK HIMSELF FOR HIS

OWN FORTUNE. FOR MY PART, I HAVE BEEN THE MAKER OF MINE,
BUT FOR WANT OF USING THE DISCRETION I OUGHT TO HAVE USED,
ALL MY PRESUMPTIOUS EDIFICE SUNK, AND TUMBLED DOWN AT ONCE.

DON QUIXOTE

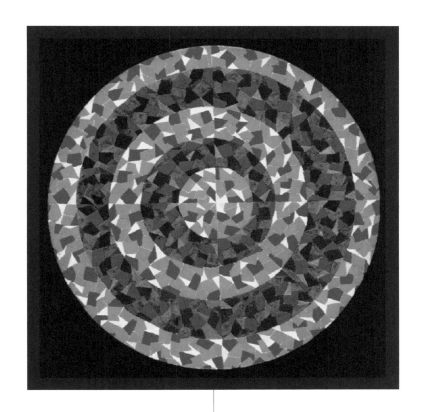

Wheel of Darkness
12″ round. Acrylic on canvas

Wheel of Light
12″ round. Acrylic on canvas

Patricia Hagood

TAROT SUITE: THE MAJOR ARCANA

Card: 10 THE WHEEL OF FORTUNE

You give the circle a tiny twist, a rap, a
shake.
   The pattern changes
   as it always does.
   Minute modification:
     the pieces swing and shift -
     new light, new reflection, new
combination.
They rise and settle down, back or forth they
dance -
   divergence, convergence, variation -
   Always the same pieces.

           --Barbara Ardinger

THE   KORAN   INCULCATES,

IN   THE   MOST   ABSOLUTE

SENSE, THE TENETS OF FATE AND PREDESTINATION, WHICH WOULD EXTINGUISH

BOTH INDUSTRY AND VIRTUE. YET THEIR INFLUENCE IN EVERY AGE HAS EXALTED

THE   COURAGE   OF   THE   SARACENS   AND   TURKS.   THE   FIRST   COMPANIONS   OF

MOHAMMED ADVANCED TO BATTLE WITH A FEARLESS CONFIDENCE: THERE IS NO

DANGER WHERE THERE IS NO CHANCE; THEY WERE ORDAINED TO PERISH IN THEIR

BEDS; OR THEY WERE SAFE

AND   INVULNERABLE   AMIDST

THE DARTS OF THE ENEMY.

GIBBON

IT IS UNIVERSALLY ALLOWED
THAT NOTHING EXISTS WITHOUT A CAUSE OF ITS EXISTENCE, AND THAT CHANCE, WHEN STRICTLY EXAMINED IS A MERE NEGATIVE
WORD, AND MEANS NOT ANY REAL POWER WHICH HAS ANYWHERE A BEING IN NATURE. BUT IT IS PRETENDED THAT SOME
CAUSES ARE NECESSARY, SOME NOT NECESSARY.

HUME

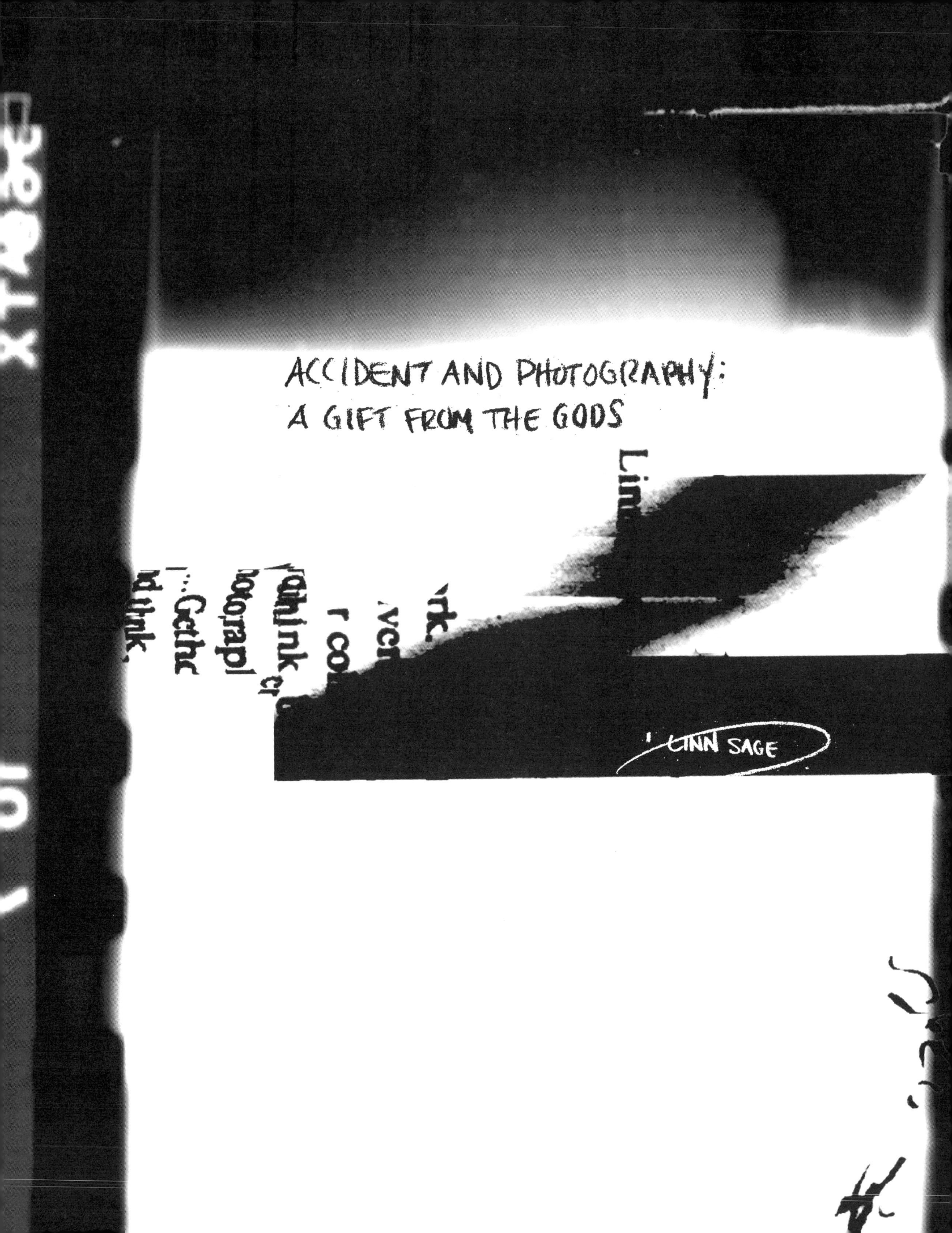

ACCIDENT AND PHOTOGRAPHY:
A GIFT FROM THE GODS

LINN SAGE

Lin

rk.

ver

r co

think

otorapl

Geth

d think,

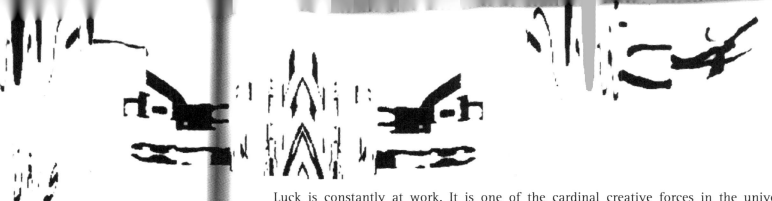

Luck is constantly at work. It is one of the cardinal creative forces in the universe, one which a photographer has unique equipment for collaborating with. ...Goethe wrote that it is good to think, better to look and think, best to look without thinking.

James Agee, *A Way of Seeing*

Once in a while I'll say, 'what idiot did that? I couldn't have done it.' But it's on my roll of film. I accept it as a gift of the Gods if I like it and throw it away if I don't.

Minor White, *Photography: Essays and Images*

These are inspiring words in our era of programmed cameras, auto-focus, matrix metering, sonar strobe, zoom everything, and fool-proof machines that are built to make accidents impossible and leave little to chance. Photography has always been plagued by the "How-to" ethic. However, I noticed in the early Kodak manuals that the "DON'T!" sample pictures were the most exciting—the luminous double exposures, the velvet blacks of a silhouette shot directly into the sun, the figure amputated, the horizon tilted.

Minor White, one of the masters of the previsualized photograph, said:

I know fairly well how to eliminate accidents and, paradoxically, in so doing I have learned that the happy accident can be cultivated! ...I put myself into the position of the reckless driver of whom it is said, 'there goes a maniac in search of an accident.'

Interviews with Master Photographers

Daring to flirt with accident, one sees as the camera does. Taking risks—courting the unexpected, shooting to see what it looks like—releases a new dynamic. Unhindered by gravity or logic, the camera can be a third eye, pure vision, the world freshly seen. Contact sheets can surprise you with astonishing images that were unplanned. Sometimes there are exciting relationships between frames, or the end-of-the-roll throw-away shot turns out to be the most dramatic because of a dynamic angle.

Photography is a wonderfully spontaneous medium, full of surprises and accidents. Rather than being foiled by them, one should be liberated.

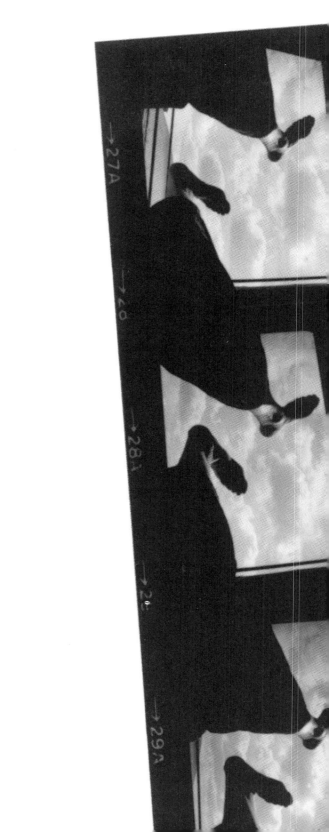

0101010101010101010001010101010101001010101010101010011001
1010101010101010101010101010101000001010001010001010101010
1010100000101010001010101111011001010100111010100101
1010101001000010111010010010101011100100010101010101

1NFORMAT1ON OUT OF 11P1ACE

John Kadvany

CHANCE TODAY IS RELATED TO DANGE

100101010101010100101010010101111101000101010010101010100000010101010111010010101010101010101010101010101010101010101010101010101
010101010101000101010101010010101010000010101000101010111101100101010010111010100101001000101111010101010100111100101010101011110

000100101010101010010101010100101111101000101010010101010100000010101
0001010101011101000110000100011101010010101001011100010101010101010100

ROUGH INFORMATION ABOUT RISK: RISK OF GLOBAL WARMING, OVERCONSUMPTION, AIDS, OZONE, ELECTROMAGNETIC FIELDS, BIODIVERSITY COLLAPSE, AND THE LOT.

Risk is "adverse consequences under uncertainty," meaning bad things may occur that you don't completely understand or completely control because

of our uncertainty about them and their causes. Today, instead of Greek *tyche* or Renaissance *fortuna*, we often appeal to mathematical probability and statistics as a powerful appa-

ratus for managing and taming chance, even as their empire of control is partial and fragmented. Nobody should deny the great value of mathematical probability to represent uncer-

tainty—to track HIV infection rates, or to communicate the odds of impending California earthquakes, or to help judge a vaccine's effectiveness through mass trials—even though not

our dangers are quantified so handily. When scientists argue over, say, the possible dangers of global warming, it's the arcana of meteorology and climate circulation, or metro-

politan heat islands that are uncertain; to study these problems is indeed to use probability and statistics, but the science itself, which includes probability, and how the world turns

out to be, is still subject to chance, unquantified and not subject to probability. Not that we should dismiss the numbers, for they have much to tell. But at various points we stop turn-

ing uncertainty into numbers, because we are up against chance and a danger's resistance to control.

The role of modern probability as the stand-in for chance, as far as dangers are concerned, parallels a change in habits of thinking about risks. In olden days, before the 1960s or so, many risks we face today were thought of as "pollutions," or generalized dirt, but without our current heightened consciousness about their associated uncertainty. As a cultural and political tool, pollution is only slightly less inclusive than risk: even as risk foregrounds uncertainty, pollution foregrounds dirt. For a scientist or engineer, this role for uncertainty is handy, since what counts as dirt is a value judgment, supposedly outside of scientific choice, while probabilities reduce uncertainty to a technical, apparently value-free act of counting. In practice, you can never completely separate value judgments about what dirt is—about what should count as hazardous waste, or dirty air, or polluted water (polluted for whom? for us? for the fish?)—from judgments about how much dirt there is, how uncertain we are about how much dirt there is, and our chances of harm. "Dirt is matter of out place," is how William James perfectly described pollution in *The Varieties of Religious Experience*, meaning that dirt becomes *whatever* is unstructured, uncertain, out of control, subject to chance. Plagues, poisonings, floods, crop failures, collapsing granaries, unsocializable miscreants, and the diseased are all subject to our interpretations of germs out of place, vermin out of place, water out of place, or people out of place. These are pollutions all, and out of place is out of local control, so subject to chance and uncertainty. Risk and pollution may not share the same exact meaning, but they coordinate equally well danger and our uncertain knowledge of it—and the special relationship between dirt and chance.

The translation of pollution into risk and chance into probabilities tends to make us miss how pollution practices may express subterranean crises of a whole culture.

Old-time pollution beliefs and risk rituals, such as purification ceremonies or witch hunts, encourage accusations of "irrationality" or scientific ignorance. So it's good to recall that in ancient Athens, right within the origins of Western rationalism, it was the celebrated scapegoat or *pharmakos* who was the focus of pollution practices, and a social means for acknowledging disaster by distributing blame. The pharmakos was often some poor wretch chosen to be celebrated for a day, then cast forever out of the city, the city's pollutions with him, the scapegoat turned into less than a slave. *Pharmakon* has the same double meaning in Greek, of either poison or cure, as does "drug" in English: a drug, properly administered, can help you overcome sickness, but if taken in the wrong way or at the wrong time, can lead to death. The person administering the drug is then also a bad wizard or beneficent doctor, a *pharmakeus*, and as a social character has a role whose logic is like that of a drug.

Our crop failure A lost battle This dread p

The dangers were to follow the scapegoat outside the city, and the whole process was literally a catharsis, or "off-scouring" of pollution from the city, which naturally enabled the residents to come to terms with the danger, confront chance, and overcome a shared trauma, whatever its causes. The most famous ancient scapegoat was the ugly Socrates, convicted in court of corrupting the young by helping them think about moral problems independently of political power. Socrates, in beautiful paradox, had the physical features of a scapegoat candidate, but his whole character was about argument and abstraction, about *not being physical*, and it was for this reason, in part, that he was to be expelled. As philosopher he was also a *pharmakeus*, practitioner of philosophical therapy and dispenser of dangerous ideas. But Socrates refused the scapegoat role: he would not be made inhuman by being turned out of the city, preferring death by a toxic hemlock tea. At least in Plato's tragic formulation, Socrates thereby masterfully created and subverted his role as scapegoat par excellence, a victim of politicians, and used that role to enact the contradictions of Athenian democracy in decline. Rationalism and philosophy are built into pollution and its paradoxes from the start, and the scapegoats of history, from the Jews of the Black Plague to the witches of many eras and places, are not just victims; they tell about the logic of social strife, power, and the assertion of control in the face of chance.

Today the best recognized such figures are the AIDS-risk scapegoats of the 1980s. But moral transgression is just one of several vehicles by which risk carries out pollution practices by other means. What matters is to elaborate current dangers and encounters with chance, and risk is every bit as good a machine for social debate as pollution. In addition to the morality plays of AIDS, risk is invoked when some social work needs doing about the limits of science, or about the conflict between economics and the environment, or about the experts' "actual dangers" versus lay "perceptions."

Instead of scapegoats *per se*, risk entails a kind of scapegoat logic, meaning the potential subversion of danger through some nefarious dialectic. The "first law of toxicology" says that *anything* is dangerous in the right amount or under the right circumstances, which in scientific terms may be put as "the dose makes the poison." Nothing is dangerous in itself, only in relation to what it is not. You may drown in a room full of milk; a plutonium baseball is harmless in outer space. Those on the conservative right are sometimes fond of such comparisons, in the form perhaps of numerical "risk ladders" showing the apparent triviality of many risks perceived as serious: the low probability of developing cancer from eating an Alar-tainted apple, or the high probability that death by gunfire is due to suicide, and so on. But the finer point is that toxicology is one of the great under-rated sciences, being based philosophically on its profound "first law," which repeats in heuristic terms the ancient ambiguity of the *pharmakon* as simultaneous poison and cure. "All is poison, nothing is poison," wrote Paracelsus, the great Swiss alchemist and medical doctor, about one hundred years before the invention of probability in the seventeenth century. Paracelsus didn't need those numbers to know that toxins contain their own magic and that "toxic" is a kind of magic itself.

Today it is uncertainty, and probability or statistics, that help coordinate dirt with modern ideas of knowledge. Though he didn't invent the idea, risk is Plato's mathematical revenge on his teacher Socrates' ironic and morally freighted death. The wicked turn of our risk ideas is that the cross-dressing of chance as uncertainty enables uncertainty itself sometimes to parade as danger. Risk tends to summarize social conflict not through the wretched outcast, but through a picture of danger projected through the lens of information: an avalanche of epidemiological studies, risk assessments, computer simulations, and proliferating models of your favorite risk. It's not always science, since often there's no settled uncertainty, no clear confirmations nor refutations, just a continuation of uncertainty by other means. Even so-called "risk perception" is now a scientific topic, with our own responses to the variety of risk messages we receive daily being as much a problem for social engineering as the design of safety systems.

Sometimes we in the risk management business do learn better how to communicate about dangers.

But you never completely tame chance, and at some point you end up recreating uncertainty through restatement, rephrasing, or representation. Risk becomes an inversion of old-time pollution as the management of chance. Instead of "matter out of place," dirt to be controlled, there is "information out of place," and perceptions and interpretations to be managed alongside dangers. If risk means "adverse outcomes under uncertainty," then our twist on pollution is to let the first law of toxicology, which says anything is dangerous under the right conditions, turn our uncertain knowledge into part of danger itself. Danger and chance are turned about through the languages of risk.

→ One way to find the new contradictions within the scapegoat role is to look at probability as contemporary chance. All specialized probabilities, it turns out—whether you want a "bell curve" to propagandize IQ's and eugenics, or calculate casino odds, or estimate the distribution of bomb hits on London during the blitz—can be created by transforming one master set of probabilities, what's called the "white noise" of mathematical uncertainty. White noise is a concept of mathematical information theory, which explains how to ensure accurate transmission of messages (as across phone lines, for example) against a background of unavoidable interference or random errors. White noise is also the engineer's idealization of processes like the uniform rush of sound that envelopes you during a jet flight, or the visual haze encountered between television channels, or the cacophony of a party conversation in which you momentarily hear everyone at once but nobody at all. For an engineer these constellations of sounds or light are easily described using uncertainty and probabilities: within a certain range of sensory signals, any "input" from white noise is equally as likely to occur as any other. The product is "white," random and uniform, like the equal distribution of all colors in the visible spectrum making up white light.

The odd white noise phenomena surrounding us are unexpectedly fantastic. Our experience of white noise is often a pure and complete loss of meaning. The cocktail party becomes like a chatter of cicadas we can't understand, and the gray-flickered television burns into a smear of non-information. The engineer sees this too. "It's all in the maths," she'll telegraph, "maximum entropy and minimum information content," meaning that in a ghostly televised glow, all signals, all messages and codes, are equally likely. For the engineer, information is at a minimum because, mathematically, information is measured by how unlikely a specific pattern—of sound, or light, or whatever material alphabet—is compared to the background. Make all the elements in the background—the cicadas, the sound bites, the party-goers, the pixels on your computer terminal—equally likely to be "on" or "off," and you get the white noise of chance.

The creation and destruction of information through reduction of entropy and noise in this engineering sense is a key idea of modern mathematics. Anything at all can be made "white," and therefore, subject to chance: that is, anything can become sound's imitation, a dead information space in any medium at all. White noise is potentially a site of danger because it puts information in the context of meaningless physical signals, of what it is not. Not that it's inevitable that white noise becomes danger or pollution, or even information out of place. You may, after all, simply leave the noisy party, safely; change the channel or fall asleep; or attend to something other than buzzing cicadas. Yet you might keep encountering the white noise wherever you turn; you might even be intoxicated by it, especially if one of the signal constructions of your culture is a surround-sound continuously produced for your regular consumption. As through advertising, for example.

TOYOTA COROLLA TOYOTA CRESSIDA TOYOTA CICADA

al Sponsor of

Official Sponsor of

The pervasiveness of advertising in American culture, though not discussed in school histories, is nonetheless one of the more salient facts of our shared sensorium. By adolescence we've seen tens of thousands of commercials, and even in old age we might be capable of enumerating brands with the mnemonic prowess worthy of a Homeric poet: *Sears Roebuck and Company, Arm and Hammer, Model T Ford, Band-Aids, Listerine, Coca-Cola*. Brand names are the principal component of advertising, garlands of signification in our history of consumption. They have become, as Don DeLillo suggests in his novel *White Noise*, the social background to sense, the American environment for a sophisticated consumer epistemology. The white noise of advertising is more than merely ubiquitous. The continuously evolving alphabets of brands and logos, cartoon characters, sports heroes, actors and actresses become voices of inner transformation, the background to an emergent self. That's not to romanticize our relationship with ads, even though there's a fair bit of romance in much of the best advertising. But ads do change us as they create or change our preferences about product choices: whether to have a smoke, invest in a mutual fund, change vodka brands, select among fashions or foods, or buy the car that's "fun to drive."

Coke is It

Olympics 1996

An important step in the advertising professional's education is coming to appreciate the uncertainty associated with a typical advertising campaign, the impossibility of determining cause and effect between most ads and action. Advertising works, but don't waste time trying to prove it, at least in great detail. Nobody, including information engineers and marketing analysts, can measure the "information" in the constant background of messages we encounter in the hum of name brands, product symbols, logos, and product sponsors, even as that information is there. You can't, for example, simulate an ad campaign because its very power depends on its continuous presence, and cumulative impact, not the individuated response of Controlled Subjects. Advertising requires reality to simulate its effects.

Anyone who lives in an advertising culture like our own can directly experience the "noticed-but-almost-ignored," the "perceived-but-not-quite-recalled" character of much advertising. Just shop the aisles, or read the magazines, or watch TV, or drive by billboards, or attend professional sporting events. DeLillo's apt characterization of ads and brands as white noise, as background moving in and out of foreground, suggests that the almost informationless, surrounding cicadian buzz of symbols become secular *mantras*, means for experiencing complicated transitions between consumer products, brand symbols, and states of mind. The history of many brands and ad campaigns, from *Listerine* to *Trojan*, is the history of images of our own projections into ideal scenes of domestic bliss, business success, leisure, romance, sport, or adventure, and all are based on imagined opportunities to recreate one's own person. But this happens as the white noise of brands moves in and out of consciousness, becoming meaningful, inciting or failing to incite desire, and then drops back into the thrashing, cacophonous sea of signs, where uncertainty reigns. We seem to continuously experience brands as physical signs, as information vectors deployed in marketers' stimulus-response experiments, while also consuming an ad's delightful projected meaning in preparation to consumption itself.

Most any advertising book will tell you that ads generally work by being purposefully repeated through a multitude of media, with complementary and reinforcing messages to their "targeted" audiences. We live in the white noise of brands because for ads to be most effective, they need to be round and about, always and everywhere, throughout your life. Not to be conspiratorial, but in communication terms our advertising culture is a propaganda culture, and to compete effectively for our limited attentions and memories, propaganda plays its continuous symphony of messages and media as background, so that the product aria may be sung when chance allows, so that your desire may be transformed, and so that you may buy and consume. Such, at least, is the engineer's account of the white noise of consumer culture.

The engineer can delight in observing that as messages become repetitive and similar, they take on the characteristics of chance events—they become information-less. To be internalized, to attain maximum "audience reach" and "intensity," the brand needs to be repeated ad nauseam, but with too much repetition the slender association between brand and product slips into a din of voices. For advertising to work, it runs itself up against the limits of chance, as messages turn into white noise: which means that sometimes they are nothing because ignored, sometimes they induce—stimulus-response style—a quick grab from the market aisle, and sometimes they work like a drug, exciting a greater probability of product choice. The whole process is one of meaning coming in and out of existence. Product messages are the cicada's hum from the standpoint of a cicada joining the swarm, or the party-goer getting drunk in the noise, or the denizen of late-night TV who notices she dozed off after awakening to the post-channel sign-off: an experience of not quite meaningless information. While we often attend, even with great care, to ads as useful communication, we also move in and out of ads and brands as mantras, taking us from a blur of background hum, to meaning, and then back again.

Engineering information marks a profound point of consciousness: it is where meaning holds on or just lets go. The mantras of advertising and brands are the triumph of an information engineer's philosophy of meaning.

Cambridge University Press **Oxford University Press** **Harvard University Press**

In Tibetan Buddhism, a key premis chants for meditation role of chance.

While your future death is certain, it is the uncertainty of when you will die, and the associated fear of this risk, that is continually negotiated during life. The transition from life to death in this view is the fundamental transition of human existence, *the* change to understand and partially control. The concept of risk is therefore implicitly at the center of Buddhist philosophy, and its importance is to inform daily habits in experiencing change and uncertainty about death. Mantras are intended to help you in the practice of other transitional states, especially in preparation for the change at death, and so to develop the skills needed in moving through to the after-life. You may learn care in experiencing all such transitional phenomena—or *bardos* as they are called—available to us: the passage from sleep to dream and back again; the shock of awareness when touching a hot plate or hearing a loud noise; the eruption of feeling in a sneeze; or the transformation of a cicada's single chirp into a peaceful, enveloping buzz.

For our engineering friend and information theorist, and not really too crassly, there are the transitions between dead signs, or symbols, and meaning, the passages from signal to data to information to meaning and back. One of the valiant hopes of some 1950s engineers was that information theory, and the use of probability to explain how dead signs, in any medium, are transformed into statistical information, would become the foundation for a new social science of language and meaning. That turned out to be another fad idea that failed, the failed romanticism of "cybernetics." The engineers neglected, as usual, the social dimensions of language use, and the congeries of meaning laid atop one another through metaphor and layered communication about communication, even as they perfected long-distance dialing. But what's missed in discarding the engineer's reductive calculus is the discovery of these peculiar notions of white noise and mathematical information, through which mathematical uncertainty was used to make statistical information-but-not-quite-meaning, and dead physical symbols, equivalent as mathematical abstractions. The engineers of information theory stumbled into one of the primal scenes of what is characteristically human: the obscure relation between meaning and its physical expression in voice, or print, or electrons burning into light. White noise, for an engineer turned philosopher, is the place in human experience where dead signs become alive in meaning, in us, and then die again. A bit abstract, perhaps, but white noise is a Tibetan *bardo*, par excellence.

h using mantras as repetitive nd prayer is found in the

Don DeLillo once thought to name his novel T*he American Book of the Dead*, in half-parody of the Egyptian and Tibetan books of the dead, those most venerable risk management guides for facilitating the changes occurring at death. *White Noise* is about American consumer culture and its relation to danger through the languages of risk, uncertainty, and advertising. *White Noise* is not a guide as much as a social autopsy; it is about risk in a society for which uncertainty and perceptions about technological and environmental dangers have made information and meaning indistinguishable from the danger itself. What's strange about this world is that it is full of images of brands and advertising, and interactions and reinforcements between the languages of risk and consumerism.

The narrator of *White Noise* is Jack Gladney, a kind of death scholar and expert in "Hitler Studies" at a midwestern college, whose family is exposed to the "airborne toxic event," a toxic cloud released from a nearby railroad car accident. In the novel we live with and learn about Jack and his American family through their encounter with the toxic cloud and other uncertain dangers. Nobody dies. There are adverse consequences, though, from the toxic cloud, bouts of *déjà vu* throughout the community. The toxin's impact is that people are *seeming* to remember, *appearing* to recall the past, so that the danger to be feared is itself, with only half-comic intent, a fake experience. Experience in *White Noise* is created through all kinds of stand-ins for what was negotiated more simply, and not untruthfully, in olden times as "reality," whether dangerous or romantic. Instead of a visit to the country, for example, there is a visit to its managed image, "the most photographed barn in America"; or travelers on a plane that nearly kills them all rush to hear the narration of their near miss with death on television in order to calibrate their own dread. The *déjà vu* created by the airborne toxic event is that of the most photographed barn.

Risk, in this hilarious parody of the modern management of danger, has gone postmodern. Risk is danger of simulation, like a fake memory, because advertising and the culture of brands, which largely become the environment of *White Noise*, have rendered "reality" a bit obsolete, and so danger is only confusedly related to old-fashioned hazards or pollutions. Jack Gladney is similarly connected to danger through this confusion of circumstance. He is a fake academic who, though an "expert" in the central symbol of death for the twentieth century, i.e., Hitler, conceals that he doesn't know German, the permanently contaminated language of the holocaust. Jack is also the perfect "victim" of the central risk event in *White Noise*, the hard-to-name "feathery plume," the "black billowing cloud," and finally the "airborne toxic event."

The airborne toxic event in *White Noise* is just the sum of the data and information representing it, not much more. The event, this risk, is the totality of its simulations, and that's how Jack and his family experience it as danger: the computer models, the media reports, the Gladney family's partially mistaken and reinforcing perceptions, the worrisome *déjà vu* episodes. Risk managers, as they are called today in government and industry, are well-versed in the idea of "risk perceptions," and especially the problems in communicating about uncertainty, but *White Noise* takes this already subversive idea to its logical, and largely realistic, end. For Jack Gladney, it's uncertainty and chance, generated through a welter of simulations and risk representations, that dominate his life and his interactions with technological risks and death. When Jack talks to health risk assessors about his exposure to the toxic cloud, he is confronted with the uncertainty of his own death through the language of scientific uncertainty: "The general consensus is that we don't know enough at this time to be sure of anything," they say, interpreting the probability distributions for the community appearing on their computer consoles. "Am I going to die?" asks Jack. "Not as such," "not in so many words...." Jack learns, finally, that statistically he was dead, "technically dead...though we'll know more in fifteen years. In the meantime we definitely have a situation." Jack's life had been fused to his future death through chance in the form of a probabilistic risk assessment. From the perspective of a sardonic, socially-critical, and risk-conscious Tibetan Buddhist, and if we can hold a churlish laugh, Jack is really centered. For through the probability of his death he has finally focused on the chance inherent in his future end, and has begun the transition toward it.

Jack's postmodern condition, his simulated environment, and his management of chance and danger through risk, are parallel effects of a culture that has simulation and uncertainty built into it. Jack's daughter Steffie, for example, is a member of an emergency team called SIMUVAC that practices "simulated evacuations," and who were surprised in the midst of one of their exercises by the airborne toxic event; the toxic cloud, therefore, gave SIMUVAC "a chance to use the real event in order to rehearse the simulation." (On the day of the Northern California Loma Prieta earthquake of 1989, just such a simulation was being conducted in the state capital, Sacramento.) Jack is at the center of this odd, simulated world, acknowledging the strange dissociation of symbol and referent all about him. "I am the false character that follows the name around," says Jack of "Jack," his own name being psychically disjointed from his non-personality. Even Jack's family, in this domestic novel of postmodern pollutions, is the antithesis of an ordered kinship structure. They represent a random family in a comic state of maximum social entropy, with Jack's four children being the result of as many marriages, but for Jack only three wives and one remarriage, and no two of the children sharing a common set of parents or a full sibling.

Among the several paradoxes underlying the Gladney family's woes is that their fear of death, and their experience of chance and uncertainty, is ambiguously physical and not-physical. At Jack's secret German language lessons, which he desperately needs to maintain his credibility in Hitler studies, his instructor reaches into Jack's mouth, grab's Jack's tongue and moves it about, trying to get Jack to make the effortless transitions from body to meaning, but Jack just doesn't get it, he can't embody the death language and simply make meaning out of physical movement. And "what if death," asks Jack's son Heinrich, himself a junior risk expert and adroit at skeptical tricks revealing the uncertainties implicit in ordinary conversation, "is nothing but sound...electrical noise...uniform, white?" That's in part an allusion to the constancy of TV images always haunting the

Gladney house. But Heinrich means the electro-physical stuff too, the media carrying the information, and which Heinrich knows may be the true hazard. "The real issue," he says, is "the kind of radiation that surrounds us every day...TV...power lines...It's the electric and magnetic fields." The danger of the "data" and the medium itself are one: more information, more signals, more danger. Published in 1985, *White Noise* was almost prescient about this "real" risk. The potential health hazards of magnetic fields from the electric power transmission and distribution lines that surround us was only starting to be researched in the early 1980s, and whether a danger from power lines exists is a controversy still simmering today among cancer researchers and epidemiologists. So Heinrich is referring to the power lines

cart only with generics, or *unbranded* products. It's this backdrop and the mantra of brand names that is weirdly coordinated with the airborne toxic event, with other risks including Heinrich's electromagnetic fields, and the underlying uncertainty in the Gladneys' lives. Shopping in *White Noise* is like the transition between life and death, the supermarket an ironic Tibetan lamasery: the "large doors slide open" to a place where "most of us like the packages themselves," the brands which we often sport as decorative insignia on tee shirts, on the rims of sunglasses, on shoes or luggage. "Here we don't die, we shop," says Murray. "But the difference is less marked than you think."

as a physical danger, but also to a danger whose scientific uncertainty has been almost impossible to resolve, making it a paradigm case of scientific uncertainty about danger, a risk whose uncertainty is only tenuously quantified through mathematical probability. But in the domestic world of *White Noise*, Heinrich's "waves and radiation" are not just physical, nor just a famously uncertain risk. They are the conveyance for brands as mantras of consumer culture, ironic "sacred formulas" for danger, which simply *are* waves and radiation in images and sound. To choose just one of several ululating refrains punctuating *White Noise*, and representative of the Gladneys' surround:

Clorets Velamint Freedent

The environment for the Gladney family, through which Heinrich's electronic mantras come to life, is the American environment of advertising, of branding, of the department store and supermarket, sites of the quintessential and most intense consumer experiences, *ever*. *White Noise* begins with students returning for the fall at Jack's college, escorted by parents helping carry in stereos, hair dryers, hot plates, and all manner of products we learn to consume. Many conversations and interactions in *White Noise* occur in the supermarket, our characters surrounded by aisles of products and their magical aura, even as it's noticed once parenthetically that Jack's colleague in popular culture, Murray Jay Siskind, fills his

All uses of names, not just brands, share the miraculous arbitrariness of language to create a conventional, tribally assumed relation between a dead sign and the thing named, like the product, that is supported by all kinds of social reinforcements, ways of organizing our lives around the bare name so that the word can come to life. Nowhere, in our culture at least, are the ceremonies and social ties making naming possible as convoluted, intense, ritualized, and spectacular as they are for branding. The profound humor about consumer culture in *White Noise* is that our lived relations with the names known as "brands," and the commodities they signify, have become one of our most primary shared experiences of death and rebirth, and hence a background to risk and chance, the consumer's *bardo*. The tale of risk in *White Noise*, the tale told of the "airborne toxic event," the obliquely named and continuously uncertain danger, is an allegory for the danger of consumer culture. It's the simulated experience created by advertising and the pervasiveness of disjointed simulation in consumer language that's become information out of place. The lived danger about branding that is a startling "anthropological" insight in *White Noise* is that the weirdness of naming objects in general, not just in advertising, and its importance for us as human beings as language-users, is perpetually played out, destroyed, and created through the notions we project in identifying with the objects we buy. *White Noise* is dark comedy, but not for that reason any less a realistic description of experience.

0010010101010101010100101010101010100101011111101010001010101010010101010101010100101010101010101101101010010101010101010101010101010101010101
0101010101101010101010101010101010101010101010101010100000101010101010100010101000001010001011110110010101011

Tony the Tiger
Winnie the Pooh,
and Tigger Too.

Branding might be thought of, then, as the revenge of D.W. Winnicott, the English child psychiatrist who noted the importance of his famous "transitional objects" (your child's favorite blanket or piece of a pillow or stuffed animal: Christopher Robin's teddy bear, Pooh, or Linus' blanket in the cartoon "Peanuts") but in a pathological mode. Branding helps maintain a sort of infantilized society; since consumer "needs" never are satisfied, we always yearn for more. The "yearning" comes by taking the fortuitous relation between names and things, and making the contact between brand and thing thoroughly uncertain, or at least as uncertain as our conceptions of ourselves, communicated via utopian messages of who we might be: of young girls as Barbies and boys as Lego-engineers or GI Joes, of generation X-ers as Gapped sex objects, of yuppies as comfortably mortgaged, safe and secure minivanists, of tribal elders as satisfied members of their HMO. And nothing today is more paradigmatic of chance, *fortuna*, than the accidental facts of our precarious psychological existence. These accidents are reflected all around us in communities of branded objects that look like fragments of ourselves. Nothing is more representative of chance than this constant reminder of the contingency of language, and nothing more powerful than its obsessive reminder of advertisements questioning who we are. Nothing, that is, unless it's the further uncertainty expressed in our understanding of environmental or technological risk. *You've come a long way, baby.*

Dirt is matter out of place, and it would appear that branding is information out of place. Merchandising is a danger because it makes the forms of life surrounding advertising dissociative of language and things, supportive of simulation and perhaps therefore of the "perceived" risk of chance versus the "actual" risk of pollution. Chance and uncertainty are dangers because the lived process between words and things has become a compulsive, continuous re-enactment of destruction and recreation, either of simulated fantasies through advertising, or simulations of risks. Branding, and the consumption of meaning through labels and logos and ads, is our latest modern *pharmakon*, a cultural jewel reflecting the importance of the meanings that we buy, as much, or more so, than the products. The particular social contradiction at work is that, while there are limits to the earth and the natural resources used up in consumption, the consumption of meaning is literally insatiable: meaning is recycled into white noise, while products are recycled mostly into energy consumption and old-time creation of old-time dirt. There are no inherent limits to the consumption of symbols and imagery, and there is no satisfaction for the consumer. Branding is an infinitely renewable, imaginary force for the consumption of finite and real natural resources. That bizarre confluence of material world and language is one of the odder events of the late twentieth century.

The skeptic not buying into the dangers of information out of place will want to know what the real hazard is, beyond the psychosocial fantasies lived out through branded shirts, cars, and backpacks, beyond the fictionalized "affinity" between the social meaning of advertising, perceived risks, and a society well-practiced in simulated experience. But it takes no great leap to step between consumption, advertising, and risk. The overconsumption of natural resources is one of the greatest environmental risks facing the world today. The exhaustion of fossil fuels and the associated impact on global climate, the contamination of finite water supplies worldwide, the spectacular extinction of species and biodiversity: these are all real dangers that have come about because of the scale of consumption in developed countries and its spread across the globe.

During the late 1980s, the "green consumer" movement helped stimulate the commercial development of environmentally friendly consumer products: non-toxic cleaners, recyclable containers, non-bleached paper products, minimum-waste packaging, low-energy appliances, and so on, all part of an effort to mitigate their related dangers. But insofar as we need advertising as our home-grown propaganda to keep consumerism going, it is information out of place, not just the products, that is part of the environmental danger, traditionally conceived. While low-impact products are naturally a laudable goal, the idea of moderating consumption in our present culture is at least naive and perhaps even absurd. "Green consumption" is an oxymoron, but that's really what "green products" are supposed to create. The need underlying advertising is the consumption of meaning, the temporary annulment of chance in the bond formed between language and things, and that fantasy, never fulfilled, is inexhaustible. How should a consumer bond with a product that says, *"Become me and consume me, but not to excess"*? Take, for example, one attempt to make good

through green marketing, the Esprit clothing company's launch in 1992 of their "Ecollection" line—as in "ecology" plus "collection"—of fashionable garb responsibly produced using post-consumer waste, naturally colored fabric, native-labor buttons, reconstituted glass beads, and the like. It's worthwhile, of course, to eliminate toxins and dangers from production processes of all kinds, but near impossible to sell a product whose meaning is not to consume. If the American environment is branded, and branding is the danger, you can't eliminate this environmental risk through a new "product line." You might as well sell cigarettes as a delivery system for nicotine. Forget the product, just market the risk.

In olden days it was enough for a Socrates to dispense good and bad drugs to Athenian youth, becoming himself both good therapist and Athenian malevolent wizard, and thereby showing the human truth behind the first law of toxicology: that anything can be poison or cure under the right conditions. At least then you could probably recognize the drug, though Socrates did his part to show up the madness behind scapegoating. Today it appears that risk, pollution, danger, and information are themselves becoming the objects of cultural inversion and perversion. The inversion is that information about risk, and the white noise of merchandising, are starting to convey the contradictions of the world's foremost consumer culture and the spectacular relations among people, products, and meaning, parleyed via our current love affair with chance dressed as uncertainty. "We passed a family shopping in sign language," writes DeLillo in *White Noise*—no doubt a completely normal family on an ordinary shopping trip. The beautiful young model of the Ecollection ads is a heroine and scapegoat of consumer culture, Socrates in drag, drinking hemlock to prove she's no mere consumer of meaning, just an environmental engineer minimizing post-consumer waste, tidying up her community's information out of place.

OBLIVION

oblvion ...
beyond the black wind
Light a candle
to preserve ladies' fingertips
in a pink, orange and black icecube
shoes that bite my feet
a swedish blue color
that melts in my mouth
whisper about politics
BOB DOLE pineapples
we think ...
scarred fruit
sweet but unguided
devil loving apples
blue oranges that melt in my mouth
blue unguided thoughts
wander aimless through
somewhere
wheat hair grey aimless
wanderer
where will she end up
when she closes her lashes.
and lets her dark pupils guide her
blind uncertainty
POLITICAL SHOES

Caroline Hagood

We cannot bear to regard ourselves simply as playthings of blind chance; we cannot admit to feeling ourselves abandoned.   Ugo Betti

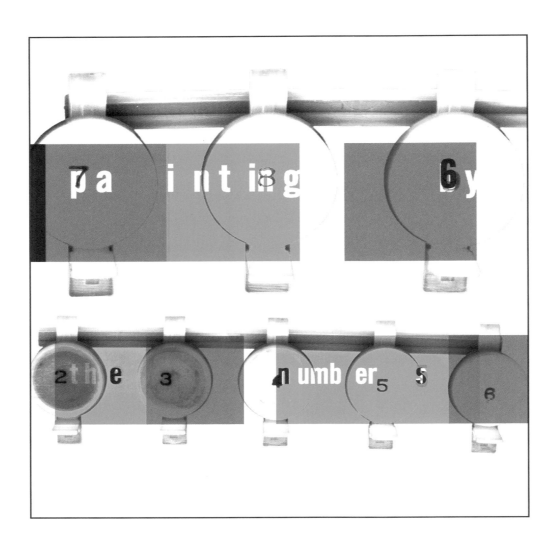

Most of my life I have been intrigued by geometric art of one sort or another. In the second grade in Kinston, N.C., I made geometric shapes to help Miss Kinsey decorate our classroom. In high school I made, for no reason other than the pleasure of it, a portfolio of drawings of the various temples on the Acropolis. At Chapel Hill (UNC), I designed sets for a production of Karel Capek's future-drama "R.U.R." Also at Chapel Hill, while not listening to "Prof. Koch" hold forth on Shakespeare, I doodled a checkerboard on the end paper of the book open in front of me. But it had a difference. Instead of the expected alternating red/black/red sequence, the squares alternated tiny landscape/blank/tiny landscape. In Japan, after World War II, the watercolors I rendered of Noh costumes frequently incorporated geometric designs, including checkerboards. While attending the Art Students' League in New York in the fifties, I came to enjoy the occasional use of the checkerboard by Herbin, Max Bill, Paul Klee, Mondrian, and Kandinsky.

Henry Pearson

Marilyn Pearl Gallery

The first artist I knew personally who painted checkerboards for their own sake was Ellsworth Kelly. I met him in 1956 when he was about to have a show at the Betty Parsons Gallery. He was in the gallery office touching up one of his paintings, and we struck up a conversation during which he explained that the choice and arrangement of colors in the painting he was working on were by chance!

A year later when I was visiting with an old friend, Charmion von Wiegand, who was also a friend of Mondrian and the Dalai Lama, she showed me a checkered painting that she had done based on the *I Ching*. She had used three colors and the white of the paper in a chance arrangement. I was deeply moved, and I thought to myself, "One of these days I'm going to have to try that."

In the 1980s, the Irish poet Seamus Heaney introduced me to the ancient Irish text, *Buile Suibhne (Mad Sweeney)*, and I began a long series of totemic paintings, tall and narrow and geometric, based on its characters and situations. While working on one that was to be called "In the Valley of Bolcain," I learned of Charmion's death, and in her memory I incorporated a checkerboard area. With this experience in the actual doing, I could hold back no longer. I had to paint checkerboards.

Ready to begin, I took a canvas and pencilled in the sixty-four squares of the typical checkerboard. Next, I selected several colors that I wanted on the first canvas and squeezed the contents of each tube into small applesauce jars. With a bit of tape I numbered each jar and identified the color and the manufacturer. I then cut small squares of paper and gave them corresponding numbers. It turned out that there were seventeen colors—the number of syllables in a Haiku, it was pointed out to me later. Having spent four years in Japan I felt that perhaps Fate was giving me a little nudge, so I decided to make seventeen colors a "given" for future paintings as well.

I put the seventeen little paper squares into a large glass jar, shook it sincerely, then emptied it onto the tabletop. Without looking, I drew a number at random, and this became the color of the square in the upper left-hand corner. I repeated this procedure for each successive square, moving from left to right, row by row. At times a particular number or numbers would persist. On one occasion a light green and a dark green became so insistent that on the bottom row of the painting they alternated light green, dark green, light green, dark green, light green, dark green before they finally gave up and allowed the last two squares to become other colors.

Sometimes the fact that a color turned up only once created a certain awkwardness. On one painting that number was sixteen—white. It might have been tolerable if it had chosen to be somewhere within the canvas, but it happened to be on the left edge. I couldn't get it out of my vision; my eye was constantly caught by it. Nevertheless, through gritted teeth, I grumbled, "Okay, you chose to be in that spot, so there you stay no matter what!" But then a friend came to visit, saw the white square and exclaimed, "Hey, how did you come to think of that placement? It's really strong. Such a fresh idea!"

Of course it wasn't my idea at all. It was pure chance.

& en changer les fondements, c'est à faire à ceux qui veulét a-
mender les deffauts particuliers, par vne confusion vniuer-
selle, & guarir les maladies par la mort. Le monde est ine-
pte à se guarir: Il est si impatient de ce qui le presse, qu'il ne
vise qu'a s'en deffaire, sans regarder à quel pris. Nous voyons.
par mille exemples, qu'il se guarit ordinairement à ses des-
pens. la descharge du mal present, n'est pas guarison, s'il n'y
à en general amendement de condition. Pour nous voir
bien piteusement agitez, car que n'auons nous faict?

  Eheu cicatricum & sceleris pudet,
  Fratrumque: quid nos dura refugimus.
  Aetas? qui
  Liquimus
  Metu Deo
  Pepercit ar

ie ne vay pas so

  Seruare pr

ous ne somm
periode. La co
blablement sur
tunes, nous no
& regardons ve
qui est au desso
ue mille exemp
qui dresseroit
aucun, qui ne
qui'l a, que de
hommes, de ce
Nostre police

MONTAIGNE'S GODDESS FORTUNA

MARCEL TETEL

When Michel de Montaigne left for Italy in June of 1580,
he carried with him the first edition of his own *Essays* (composed
only of the first two books), which had just been published.
Upon arrival in Rome in November most of his books, including the *Essays*,
were confiscated by the authorities and were not returned to him until the Monday after Palm Sunday, 1581. Montaig
noted in his diary:

On this day in the evening my *Essays* were returned to me, corrected according to the opinion of the learned monks. The Master of the Sacred Palace [the official censor] had been able to judge them only by the report of some French friar, since he did not understand our language at all; and he was so content with the excuses I offered on each objection that this Frenchman had left him that he referred it to my conscience to redress what I should see was in bad taste. I begged him on the contrary to follow the opinion of the man who had made the judgment, admitting in certain things—such as having used the word "fortune," having named heretic poets, having excused Julian [the apostate Roman emperor]....

Montaigne records this lengthy censorious list in his *Travel Journal to Italy*, and the Vatican's reaction to it, because he had mentioned the word "fortune" no fewer than 399 times in his *Essays*.

Of course, the notion of fortune is an integral part of the Medieval and Renaissance humanistic tradition. In the fourteenth century, Boccaccio, in the prologue to his *Decameron*, wonders whether the plague that has befallen Florence and Europe may be, in fact, some manifestation of bad fortune. Later in the same century, Petrarch writes a treatise on *De remediis utriusque fortunae (On the remedy of both good and bad fortune)*.

The situation in Montaigne's time, however, is quite different. The Counter-Reformation dominates the religious and political scene. Referring to fortune in one's philosophical discourse has its place, but if excess sets in, it could easily appear that Fortune, with a capital "F," is replacing God; and the stage is set for censorship. Montaigne, the masterful rhetorician, admits to his abusive reference to "fortune," and promises to correct it, but he never does. On the contrary, "fortune" will find its way into both the third book of his *Essays*, published in 1588, and into the additions he made to all the essays from then until his death in 1592. What is most significant is that, despite his failure to keep his promise, the *Essays* did not appear on the Vatican Index until 1676, when Montaigne's relativism and skepticism were attacked in France by the Jansenists, a sect that gained favor through its belief in predestination. Mankind has always felt subject to fortune, and in the Christian era struggled to reconcile fortune with God. In the face of the existential triangle of fortune, God, and man, the relationship among them can shift from submission, to conflict, to causality, to acceptance. However, in his essay "On prayer," Montaigne distinguishes the Word of God from human language, which is essentially discursive:

...the language of men has its own less elevated forms and must not make use of the dignity, majesty and authority of the language of God. I myself let it say—*verbis indisciplinatis* [using undisciplined words]—fortune, destiny, accident, good luck, bad luck, the gods and similar phrases, following its own fashion. I am offering my own human thoughts as human thoughts to be considered on their own, not as things established by God's ordinance, incapable of being doubted or challenged; they are matters of opinion, not matters of faith.

In later editions of the *Essays*, the admonitions of the Vatican censor were not forgotten. What has occurred, however, is a distinction between the earthly and the heavenly realms, between reason and faith. This separation does not necessarily propose a hierarchization of apparent opposites but rather acknowledges the constraints on human understanding. The principal purpose of philosophy, as stated in "On educating children" is "to provide a serenity in the face of the tempests of fortune." Ultimately Montaigne seeks an accommodation with fortune as one of the elements inevitably present in making life livable, and thus having a purpose as well as limitations. Since fickleness and the uncontrollable arbitrariness of fortune mirror the contingencies of reason (what reason means to one may not be so to another), uncertainty cannot be resolved by them. This equation provides the hard core of the longest essay of all, "An apology for Raymond Sebond." Its principal thrust is to show the limits of reason in the light of faith: "From that [rival schools of philosophy] we can learn that Fortune herself is not more varied, fickle, blind and ill-advised than human reason." Yet an accommodation with fortune is premised on one's ability not to challenge events beyond a certain point, but to accept both the inevitable and above all the possible. Hence, if needed, a measure of reason can reappear not necessarily to produce a contradiction but rather to manifest the exigencies of the moment, of the context, as here in "On vanity": "I am deeply indebted to Fortune in that, up to present, she has done me no outrage, at least, none above what I can bear. (Might it not be her style to leave in peace those who do not pester her?).... I am content to be at grips with Fortune through attributes which are strictly necessary to my being without extending her jurisdiction over me in other ways." The passive control exhibited here also implies an ongoing, if not constant, tug-of-war.

de à Dieu qu'il luy maintienne fa fanté entiere & vigoreufe, Ceft à dire qu'il le remette en ieuneffe,
Stulte quid hæc fruftra votis puerilibus optas:
N'eft-ce pas folie? fa condition ne le porte pas. Mon bon hõme, c'eft faict, on ne vous fçauroit plus redreffer, on vous plaftrera, & eftançonnera vn peu, et alongeron voftre mifere.
Non fecus inftantem cupiens fulcire ruinam,
Diuerfis contra nititur obicibus,
Donec certa dies omni compage foluta,

maux ont leur vie, & leurs bornes, ... donner paſ-
ſage ... arreſtent moins chez moy qui les laiſſe
faire, & en ay perdu de ceux qu'on eſtime plus opiniaſtres &
tenans, de leur propre decadence; ſans ayde & ſans art, & cō-
tre ſes reigles. Laiſſons faire vn peu à nature, elle entēd mieux
ſes affaires que nous. Mais vn tel en mourut; ſi faires vous, ſi-
non de ce mal la, d'vn autre, & combien n'ont pas laiſſé d'en
mourir, ayant trois medecins à leur coſté: l'exemple eſt vn
patron libre vniuerſel, & à tout ſens. Si c'eſt vne medecine vo-
luptueuſe, acceptez la; c'eſt touſiours autant de bien preſent.
I'ay laiſſé enuieillir & mourir en moy, de mort naturelle, des
reumes, defluxions gouteuſes, relaxation, battemēt de cœur,
micraines, & autres accidés, que i'ay perdu, quand ie m'eſtois
à demy formé à les nourrir. On les écoiure mieux par cour-
toiſie, que par brauerie. Il faut ſouffrir doucement les loix

the other hand, to acquiesce does not imply total acceptance but rather a
ed situation. A certain recalcitrance mitigated by a constant but subdued
ancholy then often rears its head despite some pseudo-materialistic sleight-
and: "Fortune has helped me in [the simultaneous need for travel and
ing at home]; my chief aim in life being to live it lazily and leisurely rather
busily, she has taken from me the need to proliferate in wealth to provide
proliferation of heirs." A very personal bittersweet note, rather than a
of resignation, surfaces here. Although Montaigne had six children, all
one, a daughter Leonor, died in early childhood. The absence of a wished-
nale heir will mean the extinction of the short-lived Eyquem de
ataigne lineage. Of course, the presence of the *Essays* has assured a
thy posterity.

Finally, the inexplicable and the power of the imagination become synonymous with fortune, which is, therefore, represented as a projection of
man's fears and desires—the very tenets of the human condition—and in a
sense as the acceptance of the unacceptable, as the impossibility to know
unequivocally. This paradoxical conviction is articulated in "On the lame,"
albeit not without a smile, in regard to an erotic belief: "On the point or off
the point, no matter; it is said as a common proverb in Italy that he who
has not lain with a lame woman does not know Venus in her sweet perfec-
tion. Chance, or some particular incident, long ago put that saying on the
lips of the common people." Thus, if fortune comprises, in essence, arbitrariness, instability, the negation of free will, it also embodies, above all,
the constructs of epistemology and ontology. Absolute knowledge seems
beyond reach, and existence on earth is fraught with uncertainty and constant variability. Without a doubt, Michel de Montaigne had Fortuna on
his side when the "learned monks" of the Vatican allowed him to slip away
with his *Essays* in hand.

Kathleen Bartoletti
Madonna of Chance
30"x 30" acrylic & mixed media

LIVRE TROISIESME.   483

maux ont leur vie, & leurs bornes, donner paſ-
ſage & trouve qu'ils arreſtent moins chez moy qui les laiſſe
faire, & en ay perdu de ceux qu'on eſtime plus opiniaſtres &
tenans, de leur propre decadence; ſans ayde & ſans art, & cõ-
tre ſes

Ipſum cum rebus ſubruat auxilium.

...IT IS IMPOSSIBLE THAT THE COLLOCATION OF MATERIAL ENTITIES
SHOULD PRODUCE LIFE, OR MINDLESS ENTITIES MIND.
NO ONE...WOULD PRETEND THAT A MERE CHANCE MIXING COULD GIVE SUCH

RESULTS; SOME REGULATING PRINCIPLE WOULD BE NECESSARY,
SOME CAUSE DIRECTING THE ADMIXTURE. THAT GUIDING PRINCIPLE WOULD BE—SOUL.

PLOTINUS

Tremor

Far below, the earth has stopped shivering.
The corpulent roots begin to forget
themselves in the quiet soil, the tree tops
unbelievably still, though the local
animals seem to think nothing of all
this new peace. They dart and call anxiously.
Our neighbor Hank, not a likely talker,
says over the fence he feels damn lucky
today. No, not exactly that, he cautions,
embarrassed. (He speaks so softly I have
to lean his way.) You know, *spiritual*.

From our hilltop I can see the new spread
flame of daylight kindle our lives, at least
for now. The human day moves with a fresh
shine, all the thin and glistening runners
gliding over all the other still hills
for the love of it, the sharp cars flashing,
the gas station attendants smiling and
pumping. Inside the house my two-year-old
charges with mock alarm at a big fly,
then soon at the spider on the front porch.
She knows only to laugh today, nothing more.

Beneath me, nothing is happening but
chance. The blue-streaked ores in the fissured depth
may speak to me any minute, but for
now I try to ignore the birds screaking
in the liquid amber. I'm envious
of their certain bedlam. Hank retreats
into his jonquil garden as I step
further out into the backyard, wanting
a message from all this bright air. Even
my old dog is sick with alarm. I'm calm,
weary, sure this nothing's got to give.

Kevin Clark

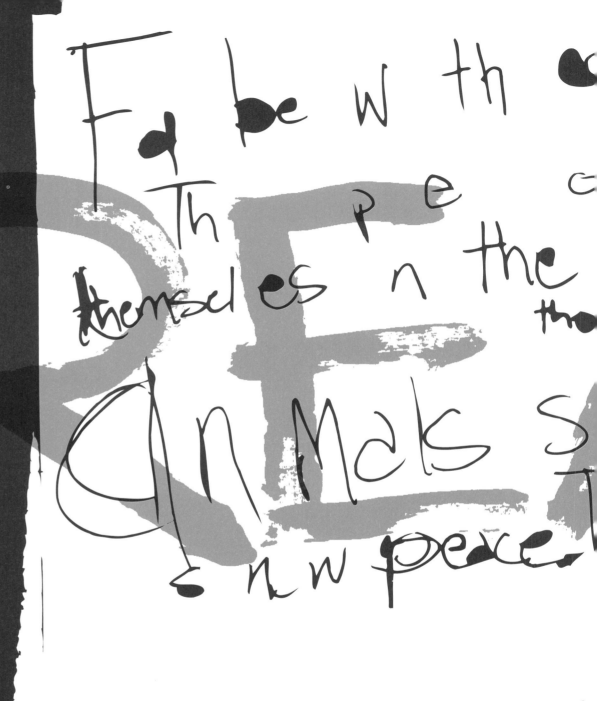

has st pped

the three

the

dart a d ca

nx US

the fence he feels

1

Mr. X drops by unexpectedly when I have an exciting guest. Mr. X is a kind of chance machine as long as he gives results within a certain range. We call Mr. X's visits chance visits as long as their causal arrangement appears to be without reference to events which are of interest to us. The concept of chance aligns with that of **independence and shares its relativity.**

George Spencer-Brown. Probability and Scientific Inferences. Longmans, Green, 1957.

If three out of six times the car doesn't start with Mr. X in it, we think it may not be chance. What, then, do we mean when we say that we think the car's behavior is chance? We mean that we think its relationship with some other event will not continue. Similarly if we say that its behavior is not chance, we mean that we expect the association to be continued. The observation is also retrospective, and all past failures of the car to start are classified as not chance. The unreal becomes real. Vice-versa is also possible. Or, if suddenly the car starts with Mr. X in it, **we say that Mr. X has changed.**

George Spencer-Brown. Probability and Scientific Inferences. Longmans, Green, 1957.

2

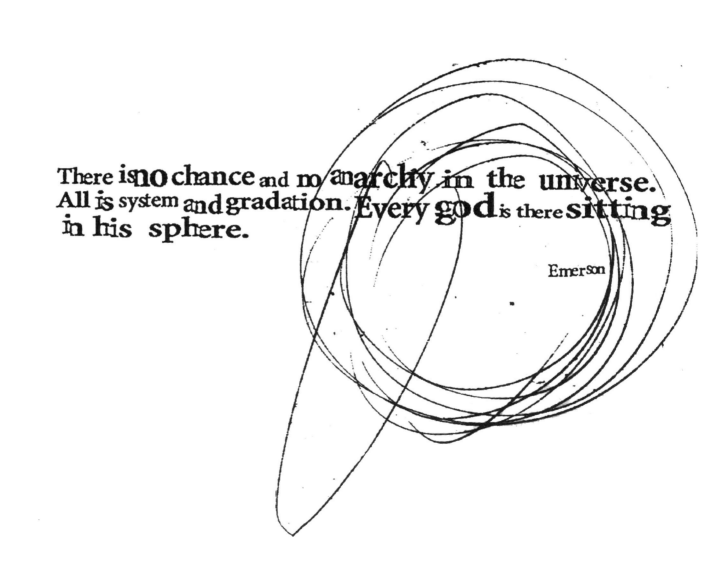

There is no chance and no anarchy in the universe. All is system and gradation. Every god is there sitting in his sphere.

Emerson

CHANCE

Robert Fowkes

Emerson asserted in his essay "Experience" that life is a series of surprises, adding that "it would not be worth taking or keeping if it were not." I am not sure about the validity of the latter part of the claim, but if surprises are to be equated with chances, there's a chance that he is right about the rest. He goes on to say that the ancients, struck by the irreducibility of the elements of human life to calculation, exalted "chance" into a divinity. By the ancients, he seems to have meant the Greeks and Romans—the latter rather more than the former—although he was well-versed in Indic matters too.

He certainly knew the story of King Nala, who was cheated out of his kingdom and practically everything else by a false dice player who had rigged the game. The dice were heavily loaded, for the evil Dvapara had entered the dice on command of the malicious Kali.

Fortuna was the Roman goddess of chance (*fors, forte:* "chance, luck"; *forsan, forsitan:* "perhaps, perchance"; and *fortasse:* "perhaps"). The Emperor Trajan founded a temple to Fortuna, who seemed to favor him in his campaigns. Fortuna's Greek counterpart was Tykhe (as in *tikhein:* "to obtain, attain, receive, be favored with").

Welsh *siawns* ("chance") was imported either from Middle English or French. *Siawns* rhymes with *bounce, flounce, ounce, pounce,* and *trounce.* The term *dim siawns* is not a reference to a dim or slight chance, for it means no chance at all. Welsh *plentyn siawns* is a euphemism for "illegitimate child," "child of chance." Whether "fat" chances or slender ones depends on designations like *plentyn trwy'r berth,* "child through the hedge," or *trwy'r llwyn,* "through the bush or grove."

The late Lewis Thomas, scientist, physician, and word-watcher by his own admission, said that chance "came to us" (etymologically) from the stem *kad,* in Indo-European, meaning "to fall" (see also *befall,* and the German *zufall:* "chance, coincidence"). What he calls the element of pure chance in human affairs he envisages as extending to the universe at large through physics and cosmology. Determinism, he claims (in *Et cetera, et cetera*), said goodbye to us at the beginning of the century, and even biology must now deal with the effects of "undeterminancy." Randomness and probability seem to govern things. As Emerson said, "We thrive by causalities."

We are, it seems to Emerson and Thomas alike, caducous, the stem of which is the same element *kad,* "fall." Emerson was, in success or failure, sure that it was a matter of the quantity of the vital force supplied by the Eternal. But even that seems to him to be administered randomly.

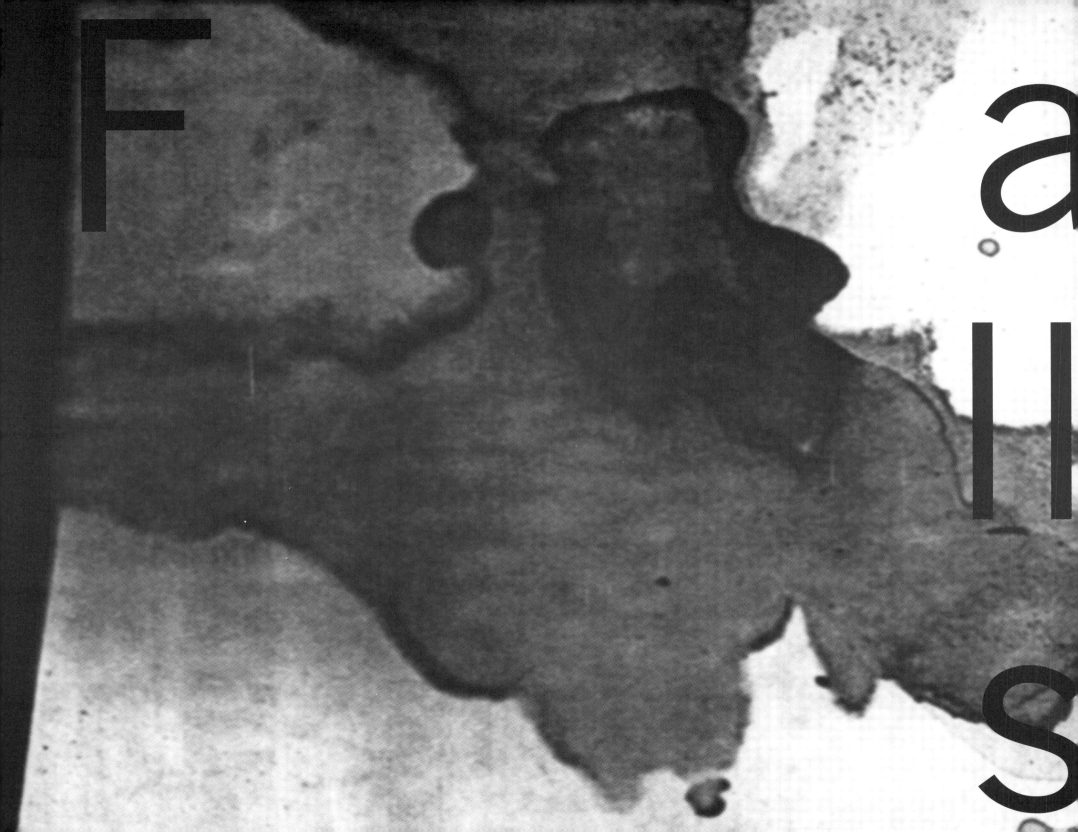

FALLS

Back falls, prat falls, falls that take us by surprise, show me one that didn't. Even the ones

you knew were coming, the ones you could see,

as in the circus when the guys jump from the high wire ladder into the webbed net below

stun us. There she goes.

And you fall with her. The inside of the body all locked up. You don't breathe. I've often

questioned if someone took my pulse

at that moment if it would be there. It must be close to death. As when the baby is tossed
in the air, stops breathing,

the hair held high above the head, held at attention, and as soon as he hits the heavy hands

a grunt of breath and a cackle of laughter burst out.

The net gives way and the body bounces back up just a bit higher than the edge of eye

level, rolls off

the side and bows as the crowd cheers for more, as the baby tugs the long fingers and begs

"more."

More falls, lip falls, take-a-fall, water falls, Great Falls, Potomac Falls, hell Niagara Falls,

nothing is ever enough.

Dave Johnson

Papa Was A Gamblin' Man

John Boe

A Gambler's Occupation

My father, for whom I am named, became a salesman during the Depression when he discovered that his brother-in-law was actually making money selling magazines door to door. "If that guy could make twenty dollars, I knew I could make forty," he'd say, telling the story. He was also attracted to the freedom the job offered. If he made a few sales, he could always knock off work and go to the track.

When I was born in 1944 in Detroit, the youngest of five, my parents still didn't have much money. When my mother was in the hospital with me, she worried because my father didn't have enough money to pay the bill. My father, in order to avoid the hospital authorities, had to sneak up the back stairs to visit. My mother was afraid they wouldn't let her keep her baby. Luckily, my dad's company, *Collier's Encyclopedia*, was holding a regional contest: whoever sold the most encyclopedias that week got a hundred dollar bonus. And so the story goes that it was only because my father sold the most encyclopedias in the region (winning the hundred dollars) that he was able to pay the hospital bill and bring me home.

For my father, as for any good salesman, the only really hard part in selling someone a set of books was getting in the door. You figured that if you got to give your whole pitch, you'd make the sale at least half the time. The salesman needed a good "door opener," a line that would get him invited into the house to finish the pitch. My father's biggest early success came when, having worked his way up to sales manager, he invented one of the all-time great door openers: "I'm taking an educational survey." The results of the survey would always amazingly show that "your family"—by virtue of children, anticipated children, whatever—"qualified for a special deal," for example, a free set of encyclopedias with only the obligation to buy the annual yearbooks (which, the customer seldom realized, cost exactly the same as a set of encyclopedias with the standard free yearbooks). The success his crew had with this door opener led to a promotion (and to one of our many moves around the country).

Having started as a door-to-door salesman and becoming, in the 1960s, president, then chairman of the board of P.F. Collier and Son, he took on a legendary quality for the men in the field. Once when I was a graduate student at UC Berkeley, a slick, well-dressed *Collier's Encyclopedia* salesman came to my door and began his pitch.

"I'm sorry," I explained, "I already have a set. You see, my father is president of the company."
The guy smirked as if he didn't believe me.
"Yes, really, my father is John Boe . . . ."

The guy stopped smirking and his eyes opened wide: "Not Boe who worked his way up?"

The motivation for working his way up was, of course, money. He made, spent, and gambled lots of it. We had lots of money when I was growing up, which was nice, and we spent all of it. My father insisted on picking up every check. He also paid for the college education of any cousin who asked for it. He bought a new Cadillac every year. For a time, I was embarrassed to come to school in a new Cadillac: I'd ask my mother to let me out a block from school so the other kids wouldn't see me.

I never had an allowance. I just asked for money whenever I needed it. My father figured that if his children grew used to the daily pleasure of spending money, they would of course want to make a lot of money themselves when they grew up. He spent money with incredible freedom, and he encouraged his wife and kids to follow his example. He would say to my mother, if out of our profligacy we ran short, "Don't worry, I can always make more money." And he could. He always knew he could, if needed, just ring a doorbell and sell someone a set of encyclopedias.

A lot of his money went for gambling. A salesman working on commission necessarily is a kind of gambler, wanting to make money but never knowing if he is going to. But the good gambler also has to have a contempt for money. If you really love money, you don't risk losing it. But if you don't really love money, losing it may just be the next best thing to winning it—at least you're in the action, not just sitting there holding it.

125

Anyway, when you've got a salesman's or a gambler's courage, if you lose your money, big deal—you can always go make some more.

My father treated money with a certain contempt not only in his spending and gambling, but also physically. He would jam money messily into various pockets, always having a lot of it, but never needing to know just how much. When he'd leave a tip at restaurants, he'd just reach into his pocket and throw a huge handful of bills and coins onto the table, leaving an excessive but undetermined sum behind.

A GAMBLER'S PRINCIPLE

Image compliments of C.S.A. Archive

Once, in the later 1940s or early 1950s, my father went to Santa Anita with three fellow *Collier's* salesmen, Cal (an amateur magician), Commie (a former Chicago Bear), and Woody (his brother-in-law). They had knocked off early, having sold a few sets of books, and they got to the track for the third race. They decided to pool their money and let my father, the best handicapper, choose the bets. They bet twenty dollars on Aladdin's Lamp at 5 to 1. It won, wire-to-wire, they were up a hundred dollars, and they had a drink to celebrate.

For the fourth race, my father announced they were going to let the hundred ride on Lazy Susan, at 8 to 1. "Shouldn't we save some of our winnings and just bet twenty again," Woody suggested. My father gave him a withering glance. "Go big or stay home," he announced as if that decided the matter. When Lazy Susan won, they were up nine hundred dollars. They had another drink to celebrate.

My father didn't like to bet favorites, but he really liked B.J.'s Blaze in the fifth (at 2 to 1). "Nine hundred dollars on B.J.'s Blaze," he announced. Woody just shrugged, but Cal and Commie chorused: "Go big or stay home!" B.J.'s Blaze won, and they had $2,700.

They had more drinks and skipped the sixth race (my father thought any of five horses could win it). In the seventh, though, he really liked his pick, Running Star. "John," Woody said, "why don't we take some of the money and split it and . . . ."

"Woody, my friend," my father said, "You've got to go big or stay home."

"Go big or stay home," Cal and Commie chorused, raising their drinks in a to[ast]

When Running Star did win (at 6 to 1), they had almost $19,000.

What was there to do but have one more round of drinks while my father stud[ied] the racing form for the feature race, the eighth? Finally he announced his de[ci]sion: $19,000 on Distant Star to win.

"Distant Star is at 8 to 1 now," he announced. "That means we'll each take ho[me] $38,000 if he wins."

"John," Woody said slowly, with some pain.

Once more father repeated the day's mantra: "Go big or stay home."

"Well, John," said Woody, "in that case, I'm staying home. I'm taking my sha[re,] it's almost $5,000, and I'm going to buy a new Cadillac El Dorado converti[ble,] one like you have, and then I'm going home."

Woody held to his course, went home and surprised his wife—she had thought [he] was selling encyclopedias that afternoon—with a new car. My father, Cal, a[nd] Commie went big. They put a little more than $14,000 on Distant Star (the [size] of the bet bringing the odds down to 6 to 1), and Distant Star ran a distant fi[fth.]

My father told this story many times, but he never suggested even a touch [of] regret for his decision. He was happy Woody got a Cadillac, but, hey, Distant S[tar] could have won. And he had, that day, formulated (and stood up for) a basic p[rin]ciple of his life: go big or stay home.

One Saturday, in the 1940s, before he began making real money, my father had a great day at the track. Driving home, he told his friend he wasn't going to tell his wife he had won a thousand dollars. He was going to keep the win a secret. Then he could have the money all to himself! His buddies thought the plan made sense and promised not to tell.

He invited them all in for a drink, and my mother welcomed them as she always did. No sooner had she given them all their drinks when my father burst out: "Margaret! I won a thousand dollars at the track!" His friends were aghast. As much as he wanted to keep the money (to play with), he wanted to share his happiness, and he wanted to show off, to brag to his wife. He had kept his secret for perhaps two minutes.

It was in L.A., when I was four or five, that we began occasionally to go as a family for a day at the races. My older brother and sister were usually off on their own (they were ten and twelve years older than I), but my sisters Margaret and Karen and I became very familiar with the track. We loved gathering the multicolored tickets off the ground (before computers began generating tickets that all looked the same, each race's ticket was a different color). And my parents would give us two dollars to bet on each race. At my mother's encouragement, we would bet to show. We'd take turns making the pick. At first, we picked the horses by their names or sometimes by their looks (my mother said grey horses never won), but I soon figured out the tote board and the idea of odds, realizing that by betting the favorite to show I stood a good chance of winning money. So while my sisters continued to bet by name, I began playing the favorite.

One afternoon we did pretty well and my father had done very badly. Out of money, he asked if he could borrow some of ours. We of course would have been willing, but my mother quickly made him realize that he simply couldn't be serious about taking (even to borrow) his own children's legitimate winnings.

When I was little, I was mystified by how my father "read" the racing form, filled as it was with numbers and symbols. I was more comfortable with my mother's folkloristic approach. She would, for example, always bet any horse whose name referred to fire. She also had three systems: the Holy Ghost, the Alphabet, and the Chinese Remainder.

Her favorite was the Holy Ghost—perhaps because she had been a Catholic until she divorced her first husband and married my father. According to the Holy Ghost, if a number won twice on any day, it was sure to win a third time. For example, if number two won the second and the seventh race, you could bet (and she always would) that number two would win the eighth or the ninth. The first two wins were the Father and the Son; that third win would be the Ghost. And the Ghost did come in an amazing amount of the time.

I liked to help her with the Alphabet system. For any given race, you start with the first letter of the name for the first horse in the program and say the alphabet, moving your finger one letter at a time as you say each letter of the alphabet. When you get to a correspondence between the letter you are saying and the first letter of the horse's name—for example, say you say "S" when you come to a horse named Silver—you bet that horse (you sometimes have to go through the horses several times until you get your pick).

Unfortunately, the details of her Chinese Remainder system died with her. All I remember is the name and fact that it involved some strange and complicated and supposedly Chinese mathematics.

In L.A., too, there were frequent weekend-long poker games at our house. They'd begin on Friday, when my father as sales manager would pay his crew. Then he'd invite the crew to his house for a poker game. He figured if they were going to lose their money, they may as well lose to each other (or, even better, to him). Our dining room table would fill up with smoking and drinking poker players (mostly men, but there would usually be a few women, including my mother). I loved to sit next to my father or mother and watch them play, figuring out their strategy, feeling a part of the action. I'd go to bed Friday night with the poker game going on, and when I'd wake up Saturday morning, the game would still be going. My mother would leave the table to make me and my sisters breakfast or lunch, and we would go out to play, but when we came back in, the game was still there. I loved it. If I didn't have anything else to do, I could always watch an hour or two of the poker game, listen to the jokes, learn the games, watch those reds, blues, and whites piling up in the middle of the table, moving from player to player. I'd stack them up and count them for my father, who usually just kept his chips in a messy pile.

Over the years there were card games of all kinds, always for money: canasta (especially popular for couples), bridge, cribbage, and almost always high-stakes gin rummy. My father used to play gin with one guy, Al, who beat him regularly. My father was a good card player, so this really rankled. He finally figured out that Al, who had a great memory for cards, never shuffled very thoroughly, putting himself in a position to make some pretty good guesses as to where certain cards were in the deck. So my dad invited Al over to play some gin. As I had been instructed to do, I asked if I could watch. "Sure," Al and Dad said. So my dad got out two decks of cards. He shuffled one, dealt and played the hand. After the hand, I scooped up the cards, and shuffled them while they played a hand with the other deck. I shuffled all day long and my dad cleaned Al's clock.

It's possible my father was not a very good father: he was away much of the time, and even when he was home, he didn't really know how to relate to children. But I did love, and relate to, his gambling. After all, the word gamble probably comes from the old English *gamian*, meaning "play": that my father was a gambler meant that he played, so there were card games to watch, sporting events to go to, and the father-son pleasure of TV ball games (where we rooted according to Dad's bet).

Through a lifetime of marriage, my mother became a bit of a gambler herself (she learned to read the racing form and play cards well). In the early days, though, when they didn't have much money, she didn't like the gambling, wanting a more conventional and responsible husband. She used to tell about the time she had to leave me and my sisters (toddlers at the time) in the care of my older sister Joan so she could drive from Detroit to Indianapolis to bail my father out of jail (I never did learn exactly why he had been incarcerated). When she got to the jail, she discovered he had no money with him, only a pocketful of poker chips, which he had almost convinced the guard were actually negotiable currency and could be accepted in lieu of bail money.

One morning, also in the early days, my mother told my father that she had dreamed about a racehorse named Sir Charming. My father opened the sports page and announced that, amazingly enough, there was a horse named Sir Charming running in a maiden race at the Detroit track that very day. My mother saw what was coming and made my father promise not to give up a day's work (ringing doorbells to sell *Collier's Encyclopedias*) to go betting a dream horse at the racetrack. My father assured her that he would put in a full day's work. Then, of course, he worked half a day, went to the track, bet on Sir Charming—and won! My mother was not pleased, but the much needed money appeased her anger.

Some months later, she had another dream. In the morning, she told my father she'd had another racehorse dream, but she wouldn't reveal it unless he promised (absolutely guaranteed) that he wasn't going to go to the track and bet on it. My father reminded her that he was driving out of town that very morning for a Midwest regional sales meeting. Even if he wanted to, he couldn't go to the track that day.

And so my mother confided that the horse's name was Windstorm. My father looked in the paper and to my mother's relief reported no Windstorm running that day.

And so my father drove out of town, let's say it was to Akron, Ohio. In Akron, as so often happened as part of his salesmen's meetings, he ended up at a bar. And, coincidentally, this bar had a handbook in back (a small-time bookmaker's place). So my father looked at the races being run around the country and did find a Windstorm running. He put a bundle on it, and Windstorm won.

My mother should have been pleased when he got home early the next morning with a bundle of money, but she swore she'd never tell him another horse dream. And she claimed she never had another one.

While mother consciously wanted to discourage my father's gambling, her dreams showed that she unconsciously supported it. She did want him to be a hard worker, not a gamester, but her unconscious gave her these dreams that sent him to the track, dreams that picked winners.

A Gambler's legacy

When my father died in 1977, he left my mother a nice pension and a few stocks, but no fortune. Men who had worked for him had become millionaires, but he had gone through his money, had gambled most of it away. He was really good at the horses but protested that over the years the vigorish (the percentage the track or bookie skims off the top before distributing money back as winnings) had increased so much that even horses had become impossible to beat. And he regularly lost his money in TV sports, betting all games that were on TV and some that weren't. Once he drove my college roommate Victor and me from our home in Ridgewood, New Jersey, to Amherst College for the start of our sophomore year. On the way, we talked football, my father asking Victor who he thought was going to win the Ohio State-Michigan game (Michigan was a three-point underdog). Victor opined that he thought Michigan would flat out win the game. My father raised his eyebrows, pulled off the turnpike, stopped at a pay phone, called his bookie, and bet $200 dollars on Michigan (who lost by ten.)

It was his money. He made it, and he enjoyed the hell out of throwing it away. He'd fly to the Super Bowl or the Kentucky Derby (the family never took vacations). He even bought some racehorses, some of whom I saw relentlessly lose at Golden Gate Fields when I was a graduate student at UC Berkeley. One time, he claimed a horse for $10,000 (for a claiming race, you pay the money before the race and then you own the horse as soon as the race is over. The old owner gets any purse for winning). His agent, who handled the transaction, mistakenly forgot to buy insurance for the horse, so when the horse stumbled and fell at the finish line, having broken its leg and having to be shot immediately, my father not only had to pay $10,000 for a dead horse, but he had to pay the cost of the horse's killing and disposal. At least he did get another story to tell.

Once he was on a train in England with the *Collier's* vice-president, Joe Chapell. They got into a card game with two strangers, and soon my father realized these strangers were con-men working together to cheat him and Chapell. My father's response to this was to raise the stakes and buy the men a drink. He thought it was such fun to be cheated by English con-men (Chapell never noticed) that he kept the game going for the whole train ride, trying to figure out every nuance of the men's system. He felt that the loss was worth the entertainment the crooks gave him.

Of course, the biggest gambling pleasure comes when you are on a winning streak. In 1966, I met my parents at my grandmother's ninetieth birthday party in St. Louis (my wife and I were driving from New Jersey to Berkeley). After the celebration, we went to the track with my father and some other folks. My father was hot, hitting the daily double, exactas, long shots, raising his bets with each win. He sent me to make his bets for him (what fun to be at the hundred dollar window!) and to collect his winnings. Near the end of the evening, I wised up enough to start betting the same horses he was betting, and so I won a couple hundred dollars myself. He ended up some thousands ahead, but I'm not sure exactly how much. What I remember is the feeling of magic he gave off. For a while, you just knew he could tell the future, that he was going to predict the winner of the next race.

There is something occult about gambling. What you are doing is clearly divination. You study some numbers, look at the horses, and bet some money that you can tell the future. And when you do it successfully more times than you should, you get this rush, this almost otherworldly experience that is more than just the high of making money.

One Christmas, the whole family played a board game called something like Intuition or ESP (my father was always a good Christmas father, playing games with the kids all afternoon while the turkey cooked). After playing for an hour or so, it was obvious to all of us that my father had the best intuition, that he was better than we were at looking into the future.

My father taught me, by his example, one secret of using intuition in gambling: try to be rational. Try, for example, to figure out the statistics in the racing form. Use your thinking as much as you can, because if you're an intuitive person, your intuition will come in anyway, will lead you to your pick (which you can always find rational reasons for betting on). This rationale for handicapping reminds me of one I once heard about writing in rhyme: for some poets, rhyme is an aid because it distracts the conscious mind (which has to think of rhymes) and therefore lets the unconscious come in undisturbed to do the real work of the poetry. Similarly, the rational gambler occupies his mind enough with rationality so that his intuition can function undisturbed.

My father was intuitive, but he was also lucky. It had to have been luck when in 1965 he won a brand new Cadillac Eldorado convertible in a church raffle. Since he already had one, he told my mother he was going to give it to me for a wedding present. My mother assured him I wouldn't want such a showy car, but I was no longer embarrassed by money, so I said thank you and drove out to graduate school in a new Cadillac (which my wife drove to her job as a sixth grade teacher in Newark, California).

While I gamble only a little, I feel that in gambling I am aware of my father's legacy. So I study the form before going to the track, trying to figure it all out. I have a little legacy from my mother here, too, for once I did have a dream of a racetrack winner. It was just after graduate school, and I was marginally or not at all employed, so I spent a lot of time at the track. The races must have been on my mind a lot, because one night I had a dream of the daily double winner. The first was won by a horse named Zabu, but I couldn't quite remember the second winner's name. I only remembered that it had something to do with sleeping or bathing.

I checked out who was running every day and sure enough, within a couple of weeks, there was a Zabu (a horse new to California) listed for the first race. I went to the bank and took out some money (telling my dream to the tellers, who gave me some of their money to bet for them). I put twenty dollars on Zabu to win at 20 to 1. Then I looked at the second race. For some reason, I associated Sweet Jo Mama with sleeping and bathing (my sister Joan used to take care of me a lot when I was a baby, when, for example, my parents were at the races). So I bet fifty dollars worth of daily doubles: Zabu and Sweet Jo Mama. Zabu won the first race, giving me four hundred dollars, but the second race was won by At Your Leisure. Of course! Sleeping and bathing is being at your leisure! Why hadn't I seen that? I would have won $5,000. Still, my dream did bring me four hundred.

Like my mother, I never had another racetrack winner dream, but when I know I'm going to the races, I always make sure I have my little dream pad next to my bed. The experience of having a dream tell the future, predict a racetrack winner, didn't make me an inveterate gambler; it instead made me an inveterate follower of my dreams. If my dreams can predict a horse race, then they ought to be able to tell me something about my own life.

From my gambler father most of all I received lore. I take my wife and daughter to the track and give them what is now my lore. My wife regularly bets the Ghost (and wins a lot of the time). We can't afford to give my ten-year-old Lily two dollars for each race, so we book her bets ourselves, at 20 cents a bet. I'm happy to say she follows Boe family principles (go big or stay home) and bets to win, not show.

like my father, I try to stay away from favorites (if you hit two 8 to 1 shots in a day at the races, you'll win for the day). And like my father, I have a certain contempt for money, which makes gambling easy for me. It really is only money. When I gamble, my father is with me, I am my father, I am John Boe.

So I am pretty good at it. I do win a lot of the time. I've done well at table stakes poker (those years of watching adults play helped), but I like the track best of all. I don't bet TV spots, mostly because I don't have a bookie. Actually, my father used to tease me about the fact that I, an academic, a Berkeley hippie, a whatever it was I was, no doubt couldn't find a bookie if I wanted one. He offered to bet me I couldn't get a bet down in Berkeley, and I wanted to take the bet, but I knew I'd lose. My world is not the world of bookies. This is probably for the best.

A couple summers ago, driving home from a Wyoming backpacking trip with three of my friends, we stopped at Reno. I decided to play roulette, having fallen in love with the game after reading Dostoyevski's *The Gambler*. My friends didn't want to play, so they hovered around the table watching. We must have looked pretty funky, having just come out of the mountains, and security seemed to take a special interest in us.

I decided to play number 17 because my father's lucky number was 17. Once at a race track in Japan, he bet nothing but 1 and 7, any combinations that suggested 7, since he couldn't read their racing form, and he won all day. I figured I might have inherited his lucky number, so at the roulette table I put a dollar on 17, and it came up. I was thirty-five dollars up. I put another dollar on 17, and it came up again! Now I was seventy dollars up, and the croupier proceeded to spin the wheel as I bet 17 one more time. This time, though, he "accidentally" threw the ball onto the ground. Security guards scurried over to pick up the ball and check out the scene. My momentary magic spell was broken by a required change of balls, so I soon quit. I was up a few dollars, but I knew I had blown it. I still think back on the chance that was given me (like the chance given me by the daily double dream). After I had won the first time, I should have let the whole thirty-five dollars ride on number 17 one more time. After all, you've got to go big or stay home.

Essay from John Boe, "Papa Was a Gamblin' Man" originally appeared in *Life Itself: Messiness is Next to Goddessness and Other Essays*, (©1994 by Chiron Publications. Reprinted by permission of the publisher).

Paris Distractions
1992 Gouache & water color
Collection of Dr. and Mrs. David Skinner

Snake Eyes
Original Lithograph

Rolland Golden

a. Those occupations are most truly arts in which there is the least element of chance.

Aristotle

b. Where observation is concerned, chance favours only the prepared mind

Pasteur

Chance is a word devoid of sense; nothing can exist without a cause.

Voltaire

LEAVING THE CENTURY

ON A DOUBLE TREK

ANNA BALAKIAN

loin qu'un endroit

fusionne avec au delà

hors l'intérêt
quant à lui signalé

selon telle obliquité par telle déclivité

vers
ce doit être
le Septentrion aussi

froide d'oubli et de désu

pas
qu'eli
sur quelque surface
le heurt

d'un com— LE HASARD

veillant   doutant   roulant
br

lume
à rythmique suspens du sinistre

s'ensevelir

aux écumes originelles

d'où sursauta son délire jusqu'à une cime

flétrie

par la neutralité identique du gouffre

LE NOMBRE

EXISTÂT-IL
autrement qu'hallucination éparse d'agonie

COMMENÇÂT-IL ET CESSÂT-IL
sourdant que nié et clos quand apparu
enfin
par quelque profusion répandue en rareté

SE CHIFFRÂT-IL

évidence de la somme pour peu qu'une

ILLUMINÂT-IL

(chance)

When Stephane Mallarmé, the French poet

best known as the author of

"The Afternoon of a Faun," died

unexpectedly at the age of fifty-six in 1898,

he left a desk cluttered with

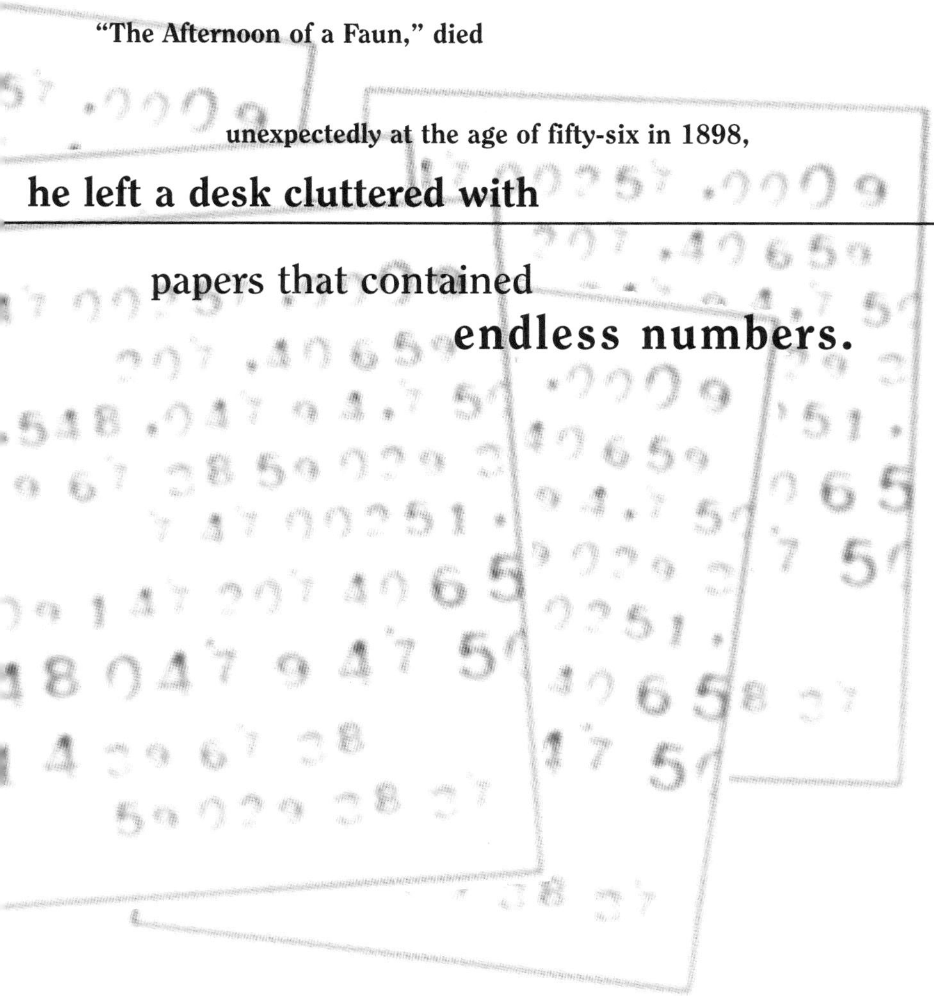

papers that contained

endless numbers.

From a man who had spent his entire

adult life writing and teaching, one would

have expected **words** instead.

He had taken early retirement

FROM A PARIS LYCÉE TO DEVOTE THE NEXT TWENTY YEARS

to a special project. Mallarmé experts had assumed that the **Great Work** he had in

MIND WAS A LITERARY OPUS.

But considering how ultimate in appearance, tone, and thought

was his enigmatic poem of 1897,

"Un Coup de dés jamais n'abolira le hasard,"

perhaps it was not so

surprising that words

no longer sufficed.

Instead, in the fin-de-siècle atmosphere, Mallarmé was **turning a corner.** He had moved from literature in the direction of the new theories of calculation and probability which several French mathematicians were exploring. Before them, an Englishman, Robert Brown, had studied the random movements of particles in water, the erratic circuits of flies, and the irregular patterns of the dice player who is called an **"aleator"** because his good or bad luck is assumed to be the result of accidental factors. Calculations in the field of uncertainties were creating a rift between philosophers who espoused positivism and determinism and thinkers who were moving toward the aleatory character of a more dynamic materialism. This dynamism unsettled the positivists' explanation of human character and activity through factors of race, place, and moment. Although determinism allowed for a certain degree of free will, the general sense of indeterminacy implied in the new mathematics—and reflected in the writings of the Symbolists— **delivered a serious blow to rationalism.** Mallarmé, the leading theoretician of Symbolism, was a cool agnostic in an environment that included fervent religious believers as well as militant atheists. Half a century before Jean-Paul Sartre, Mallarmé was looking into the cosmos and finding a universe totally indifferent to human travails and turmoil, so he substituted for it his own virtual reality.

MALLARMÉ

reacted to the imperial powers of "objective chance" (random/impersonal) in two existential poems: a strictly versified traditional sonnet and an amorphous, non-linear piece of writing, graphically overt, and verbally dispersed that he called "Un Coup de dés jamais n'abolira le hasard." So different in form but so related in thought, these two poems have catalyzed interminable critical dialogue about the subject that they have in common: **the abyss that separates chance from the wants and workings of the human will.**

The sonnet in "yx" (as it is called because of its strong rhyme in "yx") suggests what the human habitat looks like when the owner, reflected in all his furnishings, leaves it to go drink in the waters of the river Styx, from which, according to Greek mythology, no one returns. The rays of the North Star fall on his study in total indifference.

The "Coup de dés" was first printed in folio; its meaning was suggested as much through the disposition of the words on the page and their varied proximities to each other as through linguistic significations. The type-set is constantly modified, and the words that compose the title are magnified as they run on various levels of the page through the poem that asks to be read like a musical partita.

The human creature is floating in a shipwreck in space instead of water, no gravity pulling it to any pole except in the direction from top to bottom of the page and bridging the center of the folio. As you absorb rather than read the words that rain down the page, they arouse thoughts such as these: NEVER will "objective chance" pay any heed to the human casting of the dice although, as the last line (and only complete sentence) says in a whisper: each throw emits a human thought. "Jamais" evokes a longing for the "otherwise," the poignancy of the irrevocable, reminiscent of the word "nevermore" as used in "The Raven" of Edgar Allan Poe, to whom Mallarmé was greatly attracted and whom he had translated. Double meanings or collisions of meanings occur in the poem: "feather" from a flying bird or "pen" from a writer's hand—"plume" means both things in French—lonesome and lost in the spheres, a Hamlet figure characterized not as a "sweet prince" but as a bitter one envisages the horrible dangers as he faces the neutrality of the abyss. NOTHING will take place given man's isolation in the numbers game. All action is void and empty, giving the lie to all we thought we knew, and all our realities are dissolved. Shall we laugh in derision at our own fate in the vertiginous nothingness? Shall we seek a rock to lean on or to measure space, to delimit the infinite? The poet, now old in appearance, tries to make the supreme contact with probability but the effort at connection fails; his ship's sail is a veil ("voile" has a double meaning) of illusions that he has shed in his sinister suspension in the void. Except, PERHAPS: the word hangs precariously in the non-air, then vanishes as does the ship, leaving the poet "Sans coque" (without his shell). The rock was a false shelter. The rational character of the human mind had sustained man with the idea that somehow he could control his destiny or trust some divine power to control it, or even, like Prospero, play games with the universe. But there is no support for "perhaps." Even that steadiest of stars, Polaris, has turned cold and is about to be sanctified in death.

Such is a paraphrase one might make of the poem, which is as untranslatable as it is abstruse in its own language. Ironically, in order to suggest a visible incoherence and random character, Mallarmé applies all the power of rational mind to find the right word, to put it in the right place, to keep his writing as far removed from being a product of chance as human control can achieve.

History is replete with philosophies of fatalism; but fatalism is not nihilism. It assumes that some force cares enough about us to manipulate us as puppets. But at the turn of the last century, Mallarmé was telling us that we were puppets no longer; instead, we were produced and destroyed automatically for no reason at all. Life was a tentative engagement ("fiançailles" is the word with which he characterizes his encounter with "objective chance"), not a marriage. No one made a lasting commitment to us, and chance ("le hasard") could extinguish in a split second all the efforts and nurturing of human endeavors. (Some of Mallarmé's biographers believe he himself died a random, irrational death, by choking on a chicken bone.)

Two centuries earlier the unconventional philosopher, Blaise Pascal, had stared mortality in the face and said: "I may be a mere reed but I know the unpredictability of my life and the reed does not know it." Is there a stoical bliss in knowing that every existence ends in bad news? There are the uncertainties of accident: a run-away car jumps the curb and there is a death; an airplane crashes upon a particular house. Thorton Wilder wrote a whole novel on the vagaries of chance, *The Bridge of San Luis Rey,* wherein a group of unconnected people happened to cross the bridge at the specific moment when it collapsed. Bitter chance! His inspiration was Voltaire's *Zadig,* a satire on cause and consequence that he had read in college. But the abolition of chance is the worst news of all. The older you grow, the more limited your chances of life become. If you don't die today, you will die tomorrow. You are not unlike the prisoner condemned to death, who knows that the moment of his dying is no longer subject to the caprices of chance.

But there is a sunnier side to chance. When four eyes meet in an unexpected place, from which each possessor of two eyes might well have been absent, and a spark occurs which leads to a happy life of two soul-mates, we call it "love at first sight." Is it not rather "love favored by chance"?

In fact, there is a twentieth-century movement in the arts that has capitalized on chance. The surrealists manifested an upbeat attitude and banked on the propitious character of chance. If it has such powers over us, why not go out and court chance? Seize it as a source of opportunity in our relations with people, and in the arts: in the fortuitous coupling of words that occurs in automatic writing, and in the haphazard disposition of objects that can be juxtaposed to make a collage or a painting on canvas. Practice aleatory walking and you may encounter a sight that leads to creative meditation, or you may meet the woman of your life. On that basis Louis Aragon wrote his most provocative book, *Le paysan de Paris (The Peasant of Paris),* and André Breton carried the cult of chance from his writings into his lifestyle in the way that he met his second and third wives, both of whom he loved passionately. I would go so far as to say that the term "automatism" as first used by the psychiatrist Pierre Janet and appropriated by the surrealists, is a misnomer. Serendipity is not automatic, but a disorder in the course of the automatic order of things.

Much of surrealist poetry makes of chance a necessity: unexpected events, unexpected encounters of words that catalyze entire poems, the *non sequitur* character of dreams, the relation of unexplainable irregularities in nature with those of metaphoric perceptions in language, the relationships that human desires can establish with the stars. Breton, like Mallarmé, appeals to the stars, but in doing so he links human dexterity with chance ("adresse et hasard"); he finds in the gouaches of Miro, and their title, the springboard for his own last series of poems, *Constellations.* In Breton's hands Mallarmé's battered vagabond of the spheres becomes an expert weaver who connects human endeavors to "objective chance."

Latin-American poets, influenced by European surrealists, have also cultivated the theme of "convulsive beauty" coined by Breton, and they have found a deep source of inspiration in the explosive character of the earth—such as earthquakes, geysers, whirlpools, volcanoes, etc.—which they have connected with the turbulences of the poetic mind.

One might ask: "How about Dada?" What about the games the Dadaists played, games based on chance encounter? Did they not arrange the cut-up pieces of a newspaper page in random fashion and identify as a poem the arbitrary sequence of chance pickings? But in accepting humans as creatures of chance they neither despaired, like Mallarmé, nor did they seek advantages from the mobility of chance, like Breton. They shrugged off nihilism in favor of the indulgences of language. Tristan Tzara called himself the anti-philosopher and Marcel Duchamp took up chess to minimize the power of chance through the challenge of human expertise; but it was to be the surrealists' experiments with the workings of chance that brought surrealism in line with scientific inquiry.

Whereas the surrealists related their aesthetic notions to twentieth-century findings in science—such as Werner Heisenberg's studies of the unpredictability of molecular movements, and in the field of chance and chaos—very few scientists avowed awareness of any connection with literature. A startling exception was Pierre Vendreys, whose work in the 1930s made allusion to "Brownian motion" as well as the research on aleatory phenomena pursued by the French scientist, Jean Perrin. Vendreys was so struck by the parallel between his studies and the surrealist approach to objective chance that he wrote an article for the surrealist journal *Medium,* in which he suggested that "the use that a human being makes of his motor autonomy in total independence permits him to enter into relations of probabilities in his environment. **Observing Breton's attempt to seek a state of grace in relation to objective chance, Vendreys noted its relevance to the mathematician's preoccupation with the mechanism of the laws of probability:** "To give a place to chance in the domains of science is to insert at the same time an element of mystery.... The existence, real and proved, of purely aleatory encounters in life, adds to this life an element of mystery and anxiety."

The sense of superiority over what physically controls us has in recent decades been implicit in the scientific inquiries into the mysteries of chance. Jacques Monod was to arrive at the philosophical explanation of randomness and chance through his studies in biology. In an attempt to popularize his theories for a general public, he related them to the intricacies of chance in the universe at large in his book *Chance and Necessity* (1970). James Gleick's *Chaos* (1987), coming almost two decades later, is upbeat and challenging in its identification of a series of scientists in various disciplines who have tried to break through disorder and chance in different aspects of the material world. Scientific explorations into space conclude, not with a Mallarméan sense of human helplessness, but with a sense of human power. Rather than despairing, the faces of astronauts glow with triumph every time that they return from their journeys after stealing each time a little more from the mysteries of concurrences outside of the causal perceptions previously assumed. We have not yet heard a single nihilistic remark by any astronaut or by any peruser of the telescopic probes of the unmanned voyagers.

What is uncontrollable has long been associated with chaos and chance. But the most recent developments in science tend to suggest that there may well be order in chance, and that the so-called indeterminable and chancy may be due to human ignorance. Everything may be explainable, if not yet explained. Psychology is already showing how such famous theories in art and poetry as "the fortuitous juxtaposition of distant realities" can be demonstrated not to be "distant" and "fortuitous" but part of an internal psychic cohesion that brings them together.

It would follow that some of those unpredictable atom movements discovered in quantum theory and applicable to the very functioning of the human body may be part of an order of things not yet comprehensible to us. Reality would then be as narrow or as vast as our developing power to envisage it. How far should the speculative forces of the human mind proceed to overcome the condition that Mallarmé calls "the useless head" of the MASTER? Gleick concludes his report on the series of scientists he calls "chaoticians" with the upbeat generalization that:

"God plays dice with the universe.

But they are loaded dice. And the main objective of physics now is to find out by what rules were they loaded and how we can use them for our own ends." This sounds like the triumph of man over the cosmos. But wait! In gradually narrowing the dominion of chance are we prepared to surrender the sunny side and the ever-refuelable excitement inherent in life's unpredictability?

One thing is certain. We are leaving the twentieth century on a double trek: in the postmodernism of some of our artists in all fields, Mallarmé's bewildered vagrant continues the battle with chance by turning the **bitter** into the more aggressive weapon of **the ironic.** But the starry-eyed voyager in space establishes with every "coup de dés" his own trajectory in the cosmos to put on it the human seal.

ARTICLE DESIGN BY PAMELA CANNON

EVERYWHERE THAT **MARIE WE**

POE ON THE TRAI

MARIE ROGÊT Daw

It has become a commonplace to link the birth of the detective story to the rise of positivistic science in the nineteenth century. Was the detective story simply "reflecting" developments in the scientific domain at the moment of its invention, or was it more actively engaged in formulating an outlook on the world favorable to the acceptance of a certain kind of scientific approach to reality? This broader question frames the remarks on Poe's "The Mystery of Marie Rogêt" that follow.

"Marie Rogêt" is the least known of the three stories published by Poe in which Dupin is the hero. The reasons are obvious. It is in many ways unfinished, and it lacks, therefore, the polished closure of the other two Dupin stories: "The Murders in the Rue Morgue" and "The Purloined Letter." The tale begins with the same narrator as the one in "The Murders in the Rue Morgue." Some two years after that tragedy, he takes up the story of his relationship with the Chevalier C. Auguste Dupin. Once again a mysterious crime has been committed—the murder of a young woman named Marie Rogêt. On the basis of his earlier performance in the Rue Morgue case, Dupin is solicited by the prefect of Paris, where the crime has occurred, to help solve this new and baffling mystery. Dupin agrees to assist, but his investigation assumes a novel form, quite different from the manner of proceeding in the earlier case. This time he hardly ever leaves his quarters while inquiring into the crime. In his quest for a solution, Dupin relies almost exclusively on police reports and especially on journalistic accounts of the crime and the circumstances surrounding it. After he formulates a series of conjectures prompted by what he reads and hears, the story abruptly breaks off with a cryptic remark indicating only that Dupin's inferences do lead to a solution, but the solution is not described. The closure upon which the detective story generally relies so heavily is imperfect and unsatisfying in this instance. The text ends on a strangely theoretical note, with reflections on the question of coincidences and the theory of probability. These final remarks have a crucial significance, but they most assuredly do not fulfill the traditional function of closure that a resolution to the mystery would have permitted.

The story is far richer than a mere summary reveals. In the first place, the newspaper accounts quoted in the text and upon which Dupin pends correspond to newspaper accounts of an actual murder that took place in New York, or so the narrator/editor claims. Thus, the crime that Dupin is trying solve is presented coincidentally as nearly identical to the New York murder of Mary Cecilia Rogers. Perhaps it is that very crime, since Mary Rogers would seem be none other than Marie Rogêt if one is to take the two names seriously. The French version of the name is a willfully amateurish transposition of the English— *vice versa.* A sustained interplay of footnotes in the story establishes the parallel between the two murders by providing street names, proper names, or newspaper titles from the New York case every time a French name is invoked. The story's narrator/editor professes to believe that the elucidation of the mystery in his narrative will have an impact on the actual investigation of the New York murder. The vexing relation between fiction and reality is, thus, explicitly evoked, and akes the story interesting to analyze from the standpoint of mimesis and literary representation.

"The Mystery of Marie Rogêt" explores, for example, the relation among the various newspaper accounts of the crime. By showing how they contradict one another, it undermines the belief that a newspaper article can actually capture the essence of any event. In a paradoxical way, the story puts its own ambition into serious question as well, since one of its stated purposes is to solve a "real" crime, the murder of Mary Cecilia Rogers, by reviewing the text-based accounts of it—even though these accounts have been transformed for the purposes of the story into accounts of a Parisian crime. The frame-within-a-frame effect created by the footnotes linking Marie Rogêt to Mary Cecilia Rogers most assuredly brings problems of representation and closure to the fore and invites a deconstructivist approach—especially since the footnotes were not present in the first version of the story but were added later. The first of those footnotes calls attention to the dilemma of the "writer" of the tale. (Is this also the narrator?) It speaks of the writer's ambition to reconstruct an account of Mary Cecilia Rogers' murder in the absence of any means to verify his conjectures by visiting the real place of the crime. Isn't this the very dilemma produced by Dupin's whimsical choice to stay at home to solve the mystery of Marie Rogêt's murder? Are the two stories really only one? The effect of the footnotes is to turn the text into a hall of mirrors. This technique ultimately turns literary representation into a caricature of itself and transforms the text into a handbook on postmodern literary practice before the fact.

I choose to make my own entry into the text along a different path, however. I use the term "path" advisedly here because a crucial problem to be resolved, if the mystery is to be elucidated, deals with a path, a circuit, or a route, and with the difficulties of deciding what points that route might have intersected. Marie Rogêt is murdered somewhere along a route that she was ostensibly to take from her mother's house to her aunt's house. As the narrator explains: "In going out, she gave notice to a Monsieur Jacques St. Eustache, and to him only, of her intention to spend the day with an aunt who resided in the Rue des Drômes. The Rue des Drômes is a short and narrow but populous thoroughfare, not far from the banks of the river, and, at a distance of some two miles, in the most direct course possible, from the pension of Madame Rogêt." The use of the adjectives "narrow," "short," and "direct" is crucial. They explicitly insist on the strict limitations imposed on the path that Marie was to follow. The "populous" character of this same path alludes to something like the probabilistic ease with which one might be able to verify exactly when and where she passed through certain points. What happened to Marie Rogêt is reputed to be the result of her straying from the simplest possible route, one that should have confined her within narrow limits without wavering or detour.

Where did Marie stray from her path? How can one calculate the location of that bifurcation? These are the questions that Dupin must answer. Almost from the beginning he envisages, in blatantly probabilistic terms, the manner in which she deviated from her course. He does this particularly when he deals with the comments made by one of the journalists who claims that it would have been impossible for Marie to follow the route she had projected without having been seen by at least one acquaintance. This would be the normal expectation, especially in the case of the journalist writing the article, as he tries to imagine what his own experience would be were he to take a walk in the streets comparable to Marie's:

This could only be the case were her walks of the same unvarying methodical character, and within the same species of limited region as are his own. He passes to and fro, at regular intervals, within a confined periphery, abounding in individuals who are led to observation of his person through interest in the kindred nature of his occupation with their own. But the walks of Marie may, in general, be supposed discursive. In this particular instance, it will be understood as most probable, that she proceeded upon a route of more than average diversity from her accustomed ones. The parallel which we imagine to have existed in the mind of Le Commerciel [that is, the newspaper in question] would only be sustained in the event of the two individuals traversing the whole city. In this case, granting the personal acquaintances to be equal, the chances would be also equal that an equal number of personal rencounters would be made. For my own part, I should hold it not only as possible, but as very far more than probable, that Marie might have proceeded, at any given period, by any one of the many routes between her own residence and that of her aunt, without meeting a single individual whom she knew, or by whom she was known. In viewing this question in its full and proper light, we must hold steadily in mind the great disproportion between the personal acquaintances of even the most noted individual in Paris, and the entire population of Paris itself.

143

The use of the term "probable" is not by itself decisive to the structure of Dupin's argument. The notions of average and of large numbers come into play in a fundamental way, as does a style of reasoning that is only one step away from expression in the form of mathematical equations. What does it mean, for instance, to suggest that Marie's route on the fatal day was "of more than average diversity from her accustomed ones"? Or to calculate that "the chances would be also equal that an equal number of personal rencounters would be made"? And what is the importance of the "disproportion between the personal acquaintances of even the most noted individual in Paris, and the entire population of Paris itself"? I would also draw the reader's attention to the term "discursive." The term has extremely complex resonances in this instance. It means both rambling but also, and perhaps simultaneously, proceeding to a conclusion through reasoning, as opposed to intuition. Discursivity in Poe's story is intimately tied both to an aleatory trajectory and to reason. Reason here seems clearly to be on the side of probability statements of a certain kind.

To explore more precisely the nature of the relation between probability and discursivity—envisaged as a rambling with a certain randomness to it—I must take a momentary detour away from Poe's story to examine a notion that belongs to the domain of probability: namely, the random walk. The random walk is a basic concept covered early in modern literature on probability and thus belongs to a clearly defined theoretical tradition. A nontechnical definition of the term goes something like this: the random walk is the simplest example of a stochastic, or conjectural, process. Consider a particle that can occupy positions at distances 0, ±1, ±2, and so on, from some starting point. Suppose that at each instant of a sequence of times the particle is moved one step to the right or left, with probabilities p and q=1-p, respectively. The sequence of positions thus plotted is called a random walk. That most classic of all probability examples, the flipping of a coin (with heads or tails considered as two equiprobable outcomes), can be formalized as a random walk.

The experiential feel that the notion of the random walk conveys to the non-scientist is not uncommon for probability problems more generally—they often have an aura of attachment to the world of experience. Indeed, at least one of the theoretical approaches to the foundation of probability theory, the frequency theory approach, tries to incorporate this experiential insight. Such an approach maintains that probability equations are conceptualizations meant to explain regularities appearing in data sufficiently repetitive to be organized into frequency tables. The mortality tables of insurance companies are a common example of this method quoted in every history of probability. The modern theory of probability and statistics finds its starting point in tables of this sort, frequency theorists would maintain, rather than in the exploration of idealized equiprobable situations such as the classic example of tossing a coin. Such tables record "actual" events. In the particular case of the random walk, the connection with the world of experience is suggestively brought home by a further example, frequently described in treatments of the random walk: namely, the drunkard's walk. A point beginning at the origin of a Euclidean plane moves a distance of one unit for each unit of time, the direction of motion, however, being random at each step. The problem is to find, after some fixed time, the probability distribution of the distance of the point from the origin.

It is particularly important and pertinent to underscore the way in which reflections about a trajectory or route, Marie Rogêt's route in this case, inevitably assume a probabilistic form in Poe's tale. It would seem that there is no other manner of dealing with the notion of trajectories or routes in detective fiction than by appealing to something very much like the random walk. The random walk was not formalized as a concept in probability theory until well after the moment when Poe was writing "Marie Rogêt," but this is precisely my point. Literature does not simply *quote* what exists in published scientific argument—it can also show the way at certain key moments. The problem of the random walk is consistently at the center of nineteenth-century detective stories well before it becomes a formalized notion. For example, Emile Gaboriau's pioneering *L'Affaire Lerouge*, published in 1866 and generally considered to be the first detective novel in the French tradition, contains an enigma of this sort—how to calculate who could have taken the path leading to the widow Lerouge's house on the outskirts of a village not far from Paris and murdered her within a given time frame. A mapping of the movements of the characters potentially involved in the crime is a *sine qua non* of its resolution, and this can only be done by reasoning about probable events and motives. Numerous other examples could be invoked. The dilemma posed by the mystery of Marie Rogêt's route, then, is more than a simple incident in one particular Poe story—it is an archetypal puzzle in nineteenth-century detective fiction generally. One can conjecture that the reason such a structure plays a key role in these stories has everything to do with the rise of probability and statistics in the nineteenth century and the crucial importance they assume as the century progressed. We are not speaking about just any science when we note the presence of scientific elements in the detective story. We are alluding to a very precise kind of science, one that is closely tied to the development of probability theory.

The notion of the random walk has a fascinating cultural richness at another level. The etymology of the term *random* is closely linked to the notion of the random walk. It comes from the old French *randon*, which means rapidity or impetuosity, force or violence. *Randon* became *random* in English, but not in French. A term directly comparable to the English *random* does not exist in French, but traces of its presence have not disappeared entirely. The term *randonnée* does indeed exist. It was originally a hunting term, meaning the haphazard route followed by the hunted prey from the point where it was flushed out. By the nineteenth century, it finally came to mean a long, uninterrupted trip or excursion, and is often used today to describe an extended hike in the mountains, for example. One sets out on such a journey to enjoy random bifurcations along the way, and not simply to get from one point to another in the shortest possible time—to the extent that one does not become totally lost. It is when Marie Rogêt's walk becomes a *randonnée* that disaster strikes. If she had simply adhered to the straight and narrow path laid out for her, she would not have fallen out of sight.

The particular problem created by Marie Rogêt's trajectory results also from the fact that it traverses a variety of spaces. A dense thicket is the locus of a discovery of personal objects that belonged to Marie. In the midst of urban space—"This thicket, although dense, was in the close vicinity of a public road"—is a different kind of space, a more rural one that tears the fabric of the presumed urban topological uniformity of Marie's route. This rift is perhaps far more important than even Dupin is willing to admit. The same thing could be said of the Seine River, where

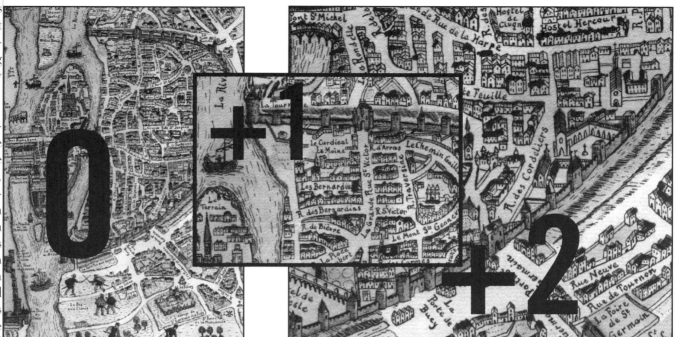

Marie's body is discovered. It turns out that Marie crossed the river. "An omnibus-driver, Valence, now also testified that he saw Marie Rogêt cross the Seine on a ferry." This crossing is another moment when a rift in the urban space must be bridged. The danger that Marie faced in her walk manifestly appeared at transitional stages in the topology of the terrain she covered, at points of rupture. The probabilistic notion of the random walk must be enlisted precisely because the uniformity of straight lines is inoperative in explaining Marie's murder, and this fact is reinforced by the breaks in her trajectory that are brought out one-by-one as the investigation progresses. The last piece of evidence that Dupin must interpret is none other than a rudderless boat discovered after the crime and subsequently linked to it—by Dupin, at least. The boat reiterates in symbolic terms the problem of path and trajectory at the heart of the tale, and the aporia into which Marie eventually fell. The etymology of the word *aporia*, from the Greek *aporos*, meaning the absence of a path, is an eloquent commentary on Marie's quandary. An *aporia* in philosophy is precisely a dilemma out of which there is no path. The Greeks considered the navigator of a ship to be the perfect example of the person who deals constantly with aporias, because the sea is that domain where there are an infinite number of paths and yet where no single correct path is discernible. Small wonder that the last element to appear in the mystery of Marie Rogêt's disappearance is an allusion to navigation and to a lost navigator.

Thematically, Poe's story deals with random walks and thus implicitly with probability theory. Simultaneously, however, explicit musings on probability theory frame the narrative. Clear reference is made to the theory itself, what Poe calls the calculus of probabilities after Laplace and others, both in the first paragraph of the story and in the last.

> There are few persons, even among the calmest thinkers, who have not occasionally been startled into a vague yet thrilling half-credence in the supernatural, by *coincidences* of so seemingly marvellous a character that, as *mere* coincidences, the intellect has been unable to receive them. Such sentiments... are seldom thoroughly stifled unless by reference to the doctrine of chance, or, as it is technically termed, the Calculus of Probabilities.

> ...we must not fail to hold in view that the very Calculus of Probabilities to which I have referred, forbids all idea of extension of the parallel.

Poe is speaking in the last paragraph of the parallel between the story of Marie Rogêt and the murder of Mary Cecilia Rogers. He goes on to set out his understanding of a wagering problem in a dice game, and the story ends on this note. Not only is the notion of probability present in the structure of the events recounted in the story and the explanations they elicit, but Poe quotes, at least indirectly, from literature on probability with which he was clearly familiar.

What are we to make of this reference to probability literature? One could debunk the scientifico-mathematical bent in Poe's story by arguing quite correctly that the description of the odds in the dice game referred to in the final paragraph gets the probability principle involved completely backwards. It has regularly been a strategy of literary criticism to denounce the scientific dimensions of literary texts, claiming that they never get the science right or that they are mere pale copies of real and creative scientific work taking place elsewhere. The references to probability theory are mere literary tropes, as this argument would put it, and can have little effect on the way scientific theories are being formulated elsewhere in the culture of a period. The literary critical strategy implied by this gesture—reducing the presence of scientific knowledge in a literary text to a kind of quotation and then making that quotation into something vaguely metaphorical—is hard to resist in our culture that divides science and literature so radically. But I think it is the wrong strategy. "Can one imagine [rather] that literature is a reservoir of science and not its exclusion?" as the French philosopher and historian of science, Michel Serres, has argued so eloquently. What is convincing about Poe's "take" on probability is not the direct reference to treatises on probability, but rather the whole atmosphere created by Dupin's method of reasoning.

> In that which I now propose, we will discard the interior points of this tragedy, and concentrate our attention upon its outskirts. Not the least usual error in investigations such as this is the limiting of inquiry to the immediate, with total disregard of the collateral or circumstantial events.... Yet experience has shown, and a true philosophy will always show, that a vast, perhaps the larger, portion of truth arises from the seemingly irrelevant.... It is no longer philosophical to base, upon what has been, a vision of what is to be. Accident is admitted as a portion of the substructure. We make chance a matter of absolute calculation. We subject the unlooked for and unimagined to the mathematical formulae of the schools.

The point must not simply be that Poe is a bad philosopher or scientist when he makes erroneous statements about probability theory. The point should be rather that, in an extraordinarily insightful manner, he was exposing his 1842 readers to a kind of reasoning that was to come into its own during the remainder of the century.

The themes Poe sets forth in Dupin's comments are far from bad philosophy or bad science. They capture quite succinctly the principal tendencies of thinking as it was developing in the nineteenth century. No longer, suggests Dupin, can we rely only on obvious and traceable Cartesian chains of seemingly immediate central elements to analyze the structure of a given event or series of events. We must search instead among the circumstances. Circumstances are contingent, apparently irrelevant parts of the event. They are found in the vicinity of the event—around it, as the etymology of the term would suggest—but not at its core. Dupin claims that we cannot neglect them. We must instead be attentive to them and eventually explore them in order to organize them in creative ways. Unexpected correlations will then appear, relations that are potentially as revealing as the more visible causal chains that seemed to contain the essence of the event. This attention and inventiveness in treating what is contingent and circumstantial reveals an unexpected order in things we might have considered to be trivial and chaotic. But there is more here. Dupin also suggests that it is precisely amidst the circumstances that new events are born. When he says that we cannot predict in a simple way what will come about by reasoning from what has occurred, he is alluding to the importance of chance— accident, as he puts it—which is the source of change and complexity, or to state it slightly differently, of invention in the natural world. With the fervor of an early convert, Dupin looks to the power of probability thinking in part for its ability to incorporate chance in its calculations. In our own time, chaos theory has returned to this insight.

What can we really learn from Poe about how truths of a scientific nature concerning the world are expressed in the literary text? In his paper entitled "Truth in Fiction," David K. Lewis claims that although fiction cannot take the place of nonfictional evidence, it can offer contingent truths about the world based on abundant evidence that has already accumulated. Occasionally there is a great deal of evidence favoring a certain position, but we have not seen it assembled in any convincing way nor have we seen a clear position articulated about it. This is what fiction does well. Even if Poe gets the probability example dealing with wagering and odds wrong, Dupin's way of seeing the world nevertheless amounts to a proposition about a new manner of understanding how correlations among circumstances can be formulated. The fact that Dupin, and through him Poe, so easily adopts such a stance demonstrates clearly that Poe's invention and use of the detective story must be considered an important moment in any history of the development of probability in the nineteenth century.

CHANCE DANCES IN THE MIND OF A BUDDHIST

The chaotic history of my relationship with the concept of "chance" starts in the form of a wrestling match with the flow of changes and climaxes, in the evolution of an interest in what comes next. "Chance" sets off reverberations. Blowing an opportunity or seizing an opportunity is one reference point. Suddenly, for a moment, there was a possibility. Was I awake, or was I asleep? If I was asleep, where was I? When I look, I find that I was in a predictive dream. When I live in the dream world of my predictions I miss opportunities. My predictions keep me walking in my sleep. I try, as instructed by an eleventh-century samurai, to "seize opportunity by the forelock."

BERNARD WEITZMAN

My views have been formed both by my training and experience as a psychologist and by the "rational" world view of science that often seems to dominate modern thought. My ongoing education in Buddhist teachings has shown me that these competing viewpoints, or lenses, are themselves incomplete though valuable.

THE CONFINING ROLE OF LOGIC

Horse races, roulette wheels, and stock markets. I walk by store windows advertising lottery tickets. This week the New York State Lottery jackpot is ten million dollars. I don't buy a ticket. "The odds are ridiculous," I think. Then, "Maybe this is the one." I hesitate, but walk on. Does that make me sane?

I pick up the *I Ching, The Book of Changes,* and cast an oracle. Why? The odds are easily as ridiculous as those involved in buying a lottery ticket. Nonetheless, in my experience, the questions I ask and my relationship with the book are part of "a situation." I find the answers presented in the book meaningful. I have no idea how such a thing could be. I accept it, although I don't believe it. On the other hand, I don't buy lottery tickets.

The conceptual problem in trying to join these frames of reference is that reality can't be reduced to a formula that is logically satisfactory. I think of the Italian proverb: "When it comes to food, good is good enough." Logic, applied to learning how things work, is often "good enough." But, in its long history of attempts to provide an account of the deep structure of reality, logic hasn't produced a nourishing meal. The question of the place of concepts such as chance in the matrix of "things as they are" continues to plague philosophers, and what they say about it leaves me hungry.

Logic is inherently unsuited for and incapable of providing the nourishment we seek, but it is an indispensable help-meet. Guided and instructed by Buddhist teachers and by my experiences in the practice of meditation, I have come to believe that my former teachers, among them Freud and Jung, were insufficiently discriminating in their reliance on logic. Even where they seemed to put experience first, they stopped too soon. Mistrusting the capacity of direct inspection to reveal the nature of their subject matters, they resorted prematurely to abstract conceptual formulations. Today I regard their views as "relative truth"—truth which holds for a given moment and from a particular perspective. At the same time, my appreciation of their genius has deepened immeasurably.

The same kind of change has turned my awe at the accomplishments of the physical sciences to admiration and respect. Scientific theories no longer emanate the sacred light of truth. Scientific doctrines and even "facts" are relative. At the very foundation of my perspective as a psychologist and a person, I now understand Freud's views of human nature as unambivalently nihilistic and Jung's conception of "self" as ambivalently eternalistic. Buddhism presents a middle way by which I attempt to weave these strands together.

In experiential terms, applying logical classifications to behavior dehumanizes people. For example, "You are a liar" imputes an essential characteristic to a person, who may thereafter be seen as a carrier of the characteristic "liar" even while speaking the truth. If a person imputes such an essence to himself, then logic reaches a limiting case. If he says "I am a liar," he is lying only if he is telling the truth.

Logical thinking requires that we assign things to categories based on their characteristics. There are, for example, liquids and solids. Logically, a liquid is not a solid, and a solid is not a liquid; logically, but there are hidden problems. Imagine a piece of ice lying on the palm of your hand. I present you with the question: "Is ice water? Yes or no." You might want to hedge and say, "They're both H_2O." That reaction identifies the problem but avoids it. "H_2O" invokes another system of categorization.

Logic requires a simple "yes/no" answer. From the side of logic you might answer, "Yes, ice is water." That makes sense. Or you might choose, "No, ice is not water." Clearly that also makes sense. Given this problem you might want to violate the rules and say, "Yes and no." Or you might want to say "It both is and isn't water," or, "It neither is nor isn't water." Those four possibilities exhaust the logical alternatives. We're left with the melting ice cube and are forced to acknowledge that we want to qualify "water": "It's frozen water." The experience is transformative; things change and turn into one another. The boundary between them is not sharp and clear. Logic deals with the rules of thinking, not with life. When that is clear, then logic is a great and valuable friend.

Time provides the limiting case for logic. Experience changes constantly, as does the material world. Logic invokes concepts like chance in order to mediate between fixed, unchanging reference points that it establishes by abstraction. However, in reality, nothing is fixed. Reality slips away from every formula.

Most of us, when we learn how something works, develop confidence that it will continue to work that way. If it doesn't, then we expect an intelligible reason; there is always room for the unexpected. We have confidence in things that rarely go wrong but accept that, eventually, something may go wrong. Then there are things that, if they happen, will invariably be followed by a particular something else: if you are born, you will die. Practically speaking, there is no chance that you will be surprised.

When not corrupted by neuroses, our native intelligence sees in this way; we have an intuitive grasp of probabilities. If we are as open to learning as children; we notice this. When we react with delight to a magician's trick, we are enjoying the unexpected. What we "expect" is so much a part of the atmosphere we live in that we may rarely notice it as an attribute of our probabilistic thinking.

On the other hand, when we impute essences we are sleepwalking. The expectations that essentialist thinking generates allow us to absorb our minds in worry and fantasy. We can move around on automatic pilot, until reality shocks us awake. Experimental studies demonstrate that this tendency is universal. We organize situations into categories in such a way that we don't need to pay detailed attention to them. "Oh yes! It's a type 'A' situation. I can go on about my business."

To the extent that we impute essences, we live in worlds of labels; logical categorizations seem "true." The problem here is that "true" has more than one meaning. It may mean logically coherent and valid in accordance with a given set of stipulations; in that framework there is no problem. Typically, however, "true" is also a claim of validity in empirical reality. But what is logically coherent and true is often empirically false. If we pay close attention, we are often surprised by what happens, even delighted. Things are never the same from one moment to another, but we ignore that fact. In some instances, we believe it doesn't matter. Up to a point we do well to be creatures of habit. In other cases, however, it is enormously important that we are awake and paying attention; it could mean the difference between life and death.

We are most likely to be surprised when we are awake. We can notice that we were looking at things through the lens of a particular theory or preconception. The spontaneous reaction of our native intelligence is to revise the implicit or explicit theory which was just then disconfirmed. We say, "Oh, the magician must have...."

THE MEANING OF MIND IN A CAUSAL AND DETERMINISTIC WORLD

The idea of chance is a handmaiden of causality. Up to a point, causality is not an abstraction from experience, but a measure of our understanding of the world. It can be given theoretical form, but the experience doesn't need theories. Thing "A" bumps into thing "B," so thing "B" moves. Things influence other things by contact. When we look at the world, we see sequences of causes and effects unfolding in linear time. When we can't see the relevant bumps, we imagine them. Sometimes what we imagine is sophisticated: quantum mechanics, for example. Sometimes what we imagine is primitive: "Things are going badly for me; I must be doing something wrong." Suppose I'm side-swiped by another car. I can identify reasons that account for my being at that spot on the road. There are causes that could be specified for why the other driver was at that spot. My reasons and his reasons have no discernible connection with one another. Therefore, it's reasonable to say it was a chance event. However, we might also feel an impulse to say that it was fate. These alternatives point to the existence in our minds of competing theories about the nature of reality. "Chance" is our rational conclusion about the accident; it didn't have to happen. "Fate" is our emotional response; some hidden meaning exists because this happened to me. The rational choice describes us as isolated units in a cold and silent universe. The emotional response embeds us in a personally meaningful cosmos. We believe and fear both alternatives.

Freedom and determinism are poles of a continuum: the outer world as a realm of causality and the mind as a domain of freedom. We are a creative nexus from which meaning flows in the dance of will and chance. "I can think and do anything I want to think or do. My reasons for doing or thinking are 'reasons'; they don't compel anything. They are chosen, not caused; I could chose to do or think something else. I have executive privilege in a world of inanimate things." We believe in our experience of freedom. But anyone who has tried to stop smoking or to break some other addiction might want to demur. Better to say that we all believe we have free will some of the time. If we weren't so neurotic, maybe we'd have it a lot more of the time. But for the person trapped in an addictive pattern, or caught in the prison of depression, the idea that we have free will is questionable.

For others, the idea of free will is a burden. We struggle to escape our minds, jog in order to control our moods through aerobics. We have a martini, a toke of dope, or a snort, to take a vacation from the nuisance of who we are. We wrestle with our minds to change them; we would like to have the courage not to lie, the discipline to hold back and not inflict pain on someone we love. With distressing frequency we fail. We experience temporary success but then, again, we sneak a cigarette, bolt down a cookie, or lash out at a loved one. We might conclude that we are powerless to overcome and control our minds. A Buddhist understanding teaches us to stop struggling. Our struggles are hopeless because we are fighting the nature of things as they are—above all, the fact of transitoriness. Ceasing to struggle makes possible a reacquaintance with the ineffability of experience.

Although, as has been argued in the sociological literature, the average person has adopted Freud's language, at the same time he has paid little attention to what Freud was really talking about. In my reading, Freud posited absolute determinism—our every thought and act is motivated by and shaped through a complex network of causation. There's no room for chance.

If chance is a gap in a deterministic framework, it is also the possibility of freedom. In Freud's cosmology there is no freedom whatsoever. Freud regarded the causal ideas of the physics of his time as participating in sane intelligence. We supply whatever meaning we find. Meaning is the connective tissue we weave through the empty spaces between things. Freud's approach has permeated our culture. Freud claimed that there is no "world" at birth, only visual "stuff," bounded regions of space with nothing to do with one another: chaos. Thus he conceived psychological reality, the unconscious mind. In the reality of the psyche there's no point of view, no coherence, and no world: that's who we are, and what we remain. Our points of view and our "worlds" are transitory fabrications that we play only a minimal part, at best, in making up.

The Buddhist view presents an uncomfortable alternative: mind as a field of awareness where everything is already woven together. A medieval Christian metaphor says: God is a sphere of intelligence in which every point is both the center and the periphery. Contemplatives trying to express their experience often use such metaphors. Here, meaning is relational; nothing is local or means anything in and of itself. The field of being is an ecological whole; relationships already exist. Meaning is always contextual; meaningfulness is our experience of the relationships among things. In the Buddhist view, everything is what it is by virtue of its relationship with everything else that is, at a given moment.

This idea is uncomfortable because it contradicts the familiar atomistic view. We have problems taking our own experience seriously because "mind" is the most obvious fact of our existence. When you say "I," you are pointing to "your awareness." There have been extraordinary, even awesome, contortions made to argue away the significance of that experience. Despite the effort expended, no one has even come close to providing an adequate reductive account of awareness. It is now as it was then: awareness is the medium in which everything is given to us and to which everything returns for its stamp of legitimacy.

"Mind" is difficult to argue away because it doesn't exist to begin with. In Buddhist logic it exists precisely because it doesn't exist. Is this logical? To say something exists you must have posited nonexistence. Existence "sticks out" of nonexistence, or else it has no meaning. The difficulty is that experience has a vanishing point, that is its perceptual "origin," as in a perspective drawing. This center is a nonexistent point in mental/geographical space. "Mind" seems to look at itself through this point. It's difficult to ignore "mind" because mind seems to be what is doing the ignoring.

Jung took the step of defining "ego" as the center and the field of consciousness—who we feel ourselves to be. Descartes' "cogito ergo sum" is another familiar view. There is the extended world spread out around us, and there is the mental world that does not exist but is nonetheless real while still the source of the problem. A point of view is a rhetorical device for describing the logical necessity of the centeredness of the phenomenal world for which the pre-Copernican, Sol-centered vision of the universe is an apt metaphor: for each individual the center of the universe is the center of the field of consciousness. That consciousness does not have a self-evident center requires reflection. The world extends from the body symmetrically in all directions to infinity. Each sense specifies a point in space. The senses, in their interpenetration, create a world. We each identify ourselves with the universe given to us directly: the one in which we live. Any other universe is an abstract theory. According to the laws of perspective, what a person perceives points to that center. In cognition, everything I experience refers to me, is most meaningful to me, has consequences for me, and points to me as a center.

Using "me" in this way brings up another difficult instance of triangulation: time. The psychological origin point is a geographical point and also a temporal one, identical with the perceptual center of the senses at this moment. This moment is located in a flow path of transformations of experience. "Me" is the momentary, "right now," verge of a stream of experience. Its flow of experience has continually conditioned the psychological perspective of my world view, and has unfolded and evolved in a unique concatenation of moments. For example, if I pass a restaurant where I fell in love, that restaurant glows with special coloration. Everything I experience is colored in that way; something not thus colored isn't in my field of consciousness. I don't see anything that can't take up residence in that stream.

The spatial and temporal point of view I call "me" exists because it doesn't exist. It exists as the condition for the existence of the world it organizes. In itself it has no determinate qualities or characteristics. "Subject" is defined, etymologically, as "that which suffers the presence of the object." Everything you find in your experience is a picture of "that": of something, of the world. That picture of the world relates to a nonexistent dot in space-time. If a person insists that these mind pictures are truly objective, that they are outside, or correspond to truly existent outside objects, then, as for Descartes, mind and world will be felt to be utterly incommensurable. In that framework, glimpses of transitoriness will give rise to fear; the world will be alien and always a threat. One lives in the empty, silent spaces of Pascal. In those spaces "chances," even vanishingly slim ones, seem to be our best hope.

STABILITY IN A TRANSITORY WORLD

The basic teaching of Buddhism could be said to be the truth of transitoriness. Everything that comes into being is going out of existence at the same time. In contemporary physics the basic particles, the ultimate building blocks of the material universe, seem to become ever smaller and smaller. After discovering the divisibility of atoms, we found divisible subatomic particles that come into existence and disappear with extraordinary rapidity. Will we find something like the eternally existent building block the atom once promised to be? Some doubtful physicists argue that what we call "world" is a field of energy phenomena displayed, through the activity of our senses, as wave forms.

Buddhist psychology holds that fear of transitoriness motivates frantic efforts to hold change at bay. We struggle to secure footholds; we attempt to defend ourselves against the ravages of time. Even though we try to avoid glimpses of transitoriness, we experience the constant eroding of whatever ground we have worked to secure. We attempt to analyze and to understand the flow of events so that we can predict coming disasters and avert them, so that we can maximize what we want and minimize what we don't. From one perspective all of this seems quite intelligent. Our safety and well-being require unclouded attention to the flow of change. When, however, we are driven to establish security, no accomplishment is fundamentally satisfying and gratifying. The most secure ground is threatened with disintegration.

The urgent task we face in our struggle against transitoriness is to find some ground for believing in the continuity of "me." Is my continuity a matter of chance or not? If I turn right, will I meet a stray bullet; if I turn left, the elixir of immortality? When as a boy I used to think I'd really like to lie in bed and miss school, I got the flu frequently. Can I avoid disease by thinking properly? It seems, on the basis of the evidence, that everyone who has ever been born has died. Does that really need to happen to me? Against the fear of death even the slimmest of chances is a straw at which to grasp. Death is at the emotional heart of our fear, the living context of the dance of chance.

Why talk this way? Things are the way they are, and nothing is going to change them. At the same time, "the way things are" is also a function of the lens applied by consciousness to the eye that is its center. Carl Rogers said the beginning of psychological wisdom is to observe that how you think about things has a determining influence on how you experience your life. The psychoanalytic form of this understanding is expressed by those analysts who devote themselves to midwifing the rewriting of the autobiographical narratives of their patients. Acquiring the lens of a new and better story is hailed by them as a cure. Jung, similarly, thought that "revisioning" one's autobiography is the authentic journey of a human life, discovering that one's personal life is an archetypal expression of the human condition. Psychotherapy, in most of its forms, assumes that a person's well-being is tied to his or her lens, to his or her way of looking at reality.

For example, suppose we're out in a boat, and we see a wave coming, off in the distance. It moves along, it lifts us, and drops us; we can see its shape clearly as it passes to either side of us and moves off into the distance. It's difficult to doubt the existence of the wave. We not only see it; we know that if we were in the water, we'd feel its power, its energy. If we were body-surfing near the shore and caught the wave's curl, we'd feel the tremendous force and energy of it driving us in toward the beach. If, however, we miss the curl, the wave will merely lift and then drop us. How can that be? Why doesn't it carry us with it?

The horizontal motion that we call "a wave" is an illusion. The passage of wind over the surface of the water energizes water molecules that express this increased energy level by the increased amplitude of their vertical oscillation. In rising they spend the energy acquired from the wind and they fall. The rising and falling of successive molecules of vitalized and then spent water molecules are organized by our perceptual process into an illusion of horizontal motion. There is a horizontal motion: the invisible motion of the wind. The motion of the water is vertical. The pattern of the wind's passing, its footprint, is perceived as the wave in horizontal motion. Understanding in this way, we acquire a new lens. We can begin to understand why, when we are floating in the water, the wave may merely lift and drop us.

In the perceived horizontal world of waves there is determinism and chance. In vertical "reality" there is the rising and falling of energy. The union of the two describes the truth of unbiased experience. Seen with two eyes, the rising and falling of energies paint patterns. When we lose sight of these patterns, our world becomes a wasteland, and our motivational patterns lead to struggle and the constant recycling of misery.

This is a metaphor of the Buddhist view of the nature of the world. There are risings and fallings, a play or dance of energy. "I" is a wave form, a horizontal motion; when it reaches the shore it falls. Vertically, however, the dance is the rising and falling of energy. The horizontal motions that give the impression of causality are illusions. In this new lens the conventional view of emotional compulsion is false; instead, a person has the option of suppressing or expressing emotional reactions. It is commonly believed that being angry with someone necessarily includes a compulsion to strike that person. The lens presented here suggests instead that the waves of emotion that rise in you do not have the power to move you horizontally; instead, they lift and drop you. The abusive parent is not compelled to strike his child; he chooses to do so.

We say that stillness is the root of movement, or that dance expresses stillness. Dance makes the invisible visible. In the same way, sound articulates silence. A melody truly heard is heard as intervals, as a cascade of spaces, as temporal and tonal distances between the notes. When we hear in this way, notes are jewel-like. Seen or felt from a horizontal perspective, risings and fallings are the sense perceptions of the phenomenal world. In the Buddhist lens they are the wave motions our minds impose, our interpretations of the play of energy.

Buddhist thought speaks of two truths: relative and absolute. These are the two eyes with which experience needs to be viewed. Relative truth is the accurate perception and understanding of how things work, the truth of how to bake a good loaf of bread. Absolute truth makes it clear that these motions take place against a background of stillness; in truth, nothing is happening. The phenomena that comprise our experience articulate and bring the stillness into view.

MEMORY AND CONTINUITY

Chance and destiny are ideas that have been woven through the fabric of my life. My study of Buddhism has led me to the conclusion that anxiety about my own mortality drives my preoccupation with this idea. Earlier I said that

logic "invokes concepts like chance in order to mediate between fixed, unchanging reference points that it establishes by abstraction" to point out the limitation of logic in its attempts to map reality. A person who clings to logical categories as a cure for pain brought about by the exigencies of transitoriness suffers both the pain of change and the pain of rigidity. I have come to believe that the transitoriness of "me" is, explicitly or implicitly, the subject of all my inquiries.

When I was a little boy, I played a game familiar to many of you in one form or another: if, on my way to the dentist, I didn't step on a line on the sidewalk, the drill wouldn't hurt me. I'm not sure if I really believed it, but at some point I just stopped. While I was doing it, I was really serious about it. Looking back I can see that I was holding my fear at bay, pretending that my ritual could protect me. "Me"! Why do I say "me"? Well, my memory is continuous. I remember me remembering me as far back as I can remember. I can't remember not remembering me. And I have a stock of memories that are landmarks. They are supposed to make my continuity certain. Still there is doubt. I claim the events of my life, from moment to moment, from situation to situation, as "me," on the basis of the continuity of my memory. I press every logical resource to the task. Nothing is more urgent to me than my sense that I am the continuously arising agent who is responsible for the actions that locate "me," my consciousness, as a purposeful and pivotal causal influence in the unfolding of my life.

By contrast, Freud's fundamental argument for his notion of the "unconscious psyche" is the discontinuity of memory. "Psyche" of course meant "soul" and was, in his time, widely used as synonymous with "consciousness." Freud's "unconscious psyche," however, had none of the characteristics attributable to a point of view. Therefore, the structure of the unconscious domain was beyond representation; psyche had no point of view. Freud was fully aware that calling something unconscious a "psyche" would, to his sophisticated readers, make no sense at all. His argument was that on careful observation consciousness is discontinuous. For considerable periods of time, we move through our daily routines absorbed in fantasies, ruminations, and other forms of discursiveness, more or less detached from the activities with which we are engaged. The activities for which we are most fully present are the ones we find represented in our memory. During the periods of time when our memories are fuzzy or missing, our attention is absorbed in a scene other than the one entering our senses.

Still, coherent action takes place. Therefore, Freud properly asks who is it that is acting in the absence of an executive point of view, what we like to call our "selves." He answers that there is an unconscious psyche capable of all those activities, including the highest reaches of intellection, without any trace of consciousness or agency, even though, logically, that doesn't make any sense. "Myself" has several identifiable possible meanings. I may use a designation that refers to a set of ultimately biochemical processes accompanied by some form of reflective representations. I could make the error of imagining that there is an entity that justifies the label "I." A third meaning would refer to a geographical point in space-time: the center of this universe of experience. If all the functional capacities that have seemed to require a relationship among "mind," "awareness," "point of view," and adaptive interaction with a world can be explained without the need for mind-like ideas, then we can move freely and confidently toward computer models of human intelligence. How could a system without a point of view perform as if it had one?

The Buddhist view is critically different from Freud's. Each moment includes the existence of an awareness reflecting a world. In each moment a point of view arises and then dissolves; from moment to moment, there are sparks of awareness that are discontinuous. As in Einstein's account of the physical universe, "being" can be viewed from an infinite variety of vantage points. The point of view in question will have an organizing and determining influence on the world arising from the field of being. One moment of awareness arises, then another. The second moment is conditioned by the first; there is indeed continuity. That continuity, however, is not based upon memory. From the perspective of relative truth, it is based upon discontinuity. In terms of absolute truth, it is based upon being.

The Buddhist view identifies the panic-driven urgency to cover over the discontinuity in our moments of consciousness as the cause of our misery. We twist logic into a "proof" of the continuity of "me." Glimpses of discontinuity undermine the narrative of "me" to which we are attached. We feel compelled to spin narratives that convince us that we are continuous entities and agencies. Our attention is obsessed with supporting the claim that discontinuous moments of consciousness are in fact the ongoingness of a single quantum of consciousness. Examined and raised to consciousness, the capacity to deploy attention is seen to be embattled. The enemy who must not be engaged is the gap-filled consciousness that reveals the truth of the transitoriness of "me."

Experience caught up in this dizzying, hopeless task of finding reliable confirmation of the existence of "me" will be characterized by a constant, frustrated struggle to secure ground and to establish a territory of certainty. Moments of awareness arise, reflecting a world seen from a particular point of view. Thoughts arise and fall, dissolve as they come into being. Discontinuity is continuous. Space, or gap, is the matrix, empty of preconception from which phenomena appear. "Chance," the absence of specifiable, deterministic relations, is the womb of potentiality.

When the search for predictive power returns to an interest in how things work, the concerns that drive the use of concepts like chance and causality recede into the background. My encounter with Buddhism has somewhat freed the cramp that accompanied the decision as to whether to turn right or left. Instead of being forever hopeful or fearful, I sometimes find myself interested in discovering what I will encounter when I turn right or left. I am confident that whatever I encounter will have something to say to me.

Buddhism differs from physics and from psychoanalysis in its non-dualistic view. No dualism and no dogma survive in the crucible of direct experience. As with the ice cube on the warm palm, no formula will neatly fit. While form is form and emptiness is emptiness, form is also emptiness and emptiness is form. That is the conclusion of an unbiased investigation when one's posture is upright and one's mind is at rest, when one has a vertical as well as a horizontal axis. Reality cannot be reduced to a logically satisfactory formula. **Even so, what will happen to us is not entirely a matter of chance.**

Oh, the infinity of possibility!… Fate just didn't intend Gay to go on the frog hunt and Fate took a hell of a lot of trouble and people and accidents to keep him from it.

IT'S ALL RIGHT NOT TO BELIEVE IN LUCK AND OMENS.
NOBODY BELIEVES IN THEM. BUT IT DOESN'T DO ANY GOOD TO TAKE CHANCES WITH THEM AND NO ONE TAKES CHANCES. CANNERY ROW, LIKE EVERY PLACE ELSE, IS NOT SUPERSTITIOUS BUT WILL NOT WALK UNDER A LADDER OR OPEN AN UMBRELLA IN THE HOUSE.

Steinbeck

ON THE ROAD

LOUIS HAGOOD

A young man leaves home to avoid his fate. It was foretold that he would grow up to kill his father. On the road to Thebes he chances upon a chariot that grazes his foot. The young man is sensitive about this foot, deformed by a childhood wound for which he is named. Enraged by the accident, he slays the charioteer and resumes his journey to Thebes. But, alas, it was this very charioteer who was the youth's real father, not the man back home whom he had hoped to save by his departure. Was Oedipus's encounter on the road a stroke of bad luck or was it fated? Perhaps his sensitive foot made him cranky—a mere character flaw. Of course, it was his real father who had wounded him in the first place. Not one to take a chance on fate, the father had dispatched the future patricide, feet pierced and bound, to die on a mountain top.

In Greek mythology, as in Freudian mythology, father and son were never left to chance or fate alone. Mount Olympus loomed over every mortal conflict, like Jimmy the Greek. Unlike Jimmy, the gods let their petty emotions interfere with their handicapping. They were easily angered. Oedipus's father, Laius, had seduced a boy "beloved of the gods," and was fated for a payback from his own son. It further angered the patriarchal oddsmakers on Olympus that Oedipus's mother was a priestess of the man-eating Sphinx, who talked in riddles. Both Freud and the Greek gods preferred patriarchal fate to feminine riddles.

By chance or fate, Oedipus answered the Sphinx's riddle and put an end to her devouring ways. Unfortunately, he got her priestess, his mother, as reward. Some riddle! Please note that it was the Sphinx and not Laius that he killed in order to wed his mother. The gods celebrated the demise of the pedophile and the man-eater as if they had won the daily double. Meanwhile, mortal Oedipus was left with his mother and his fate.

Freud did not base his theory of psychoanalysis solely upon Oedipus's fate. It was really Oedipus's quest for insight that appealed to Freud from the start. When,

following his own father's death, Freud found himself on the road in self-analysis, he relied on dreams for insight. Freud's road book, *The Interpretation of Dreams*, was dedicated to the insight, not the complex. The complex was emphasized later in order to found a school. Schools are not built on dreams.

Just as Freud consulted his dreams for guidance in his mid-life crisis, Oedipus consulted Tiresias when Thebes was suffering from the plague. Tiresias had insight because he had lived life as both a male and a female and had been blinded—by the gods, of course—for the privilege. Blind insight or blind fate? Oedipus chose his mother's brooch to blind himself when he had had enough of insight. Tiresias had warned, "How dreadful knowledge of the truth can be when there's no help in truth!" Oedipus, and later Freud, disregarded this warning. Both were fated to "bring what is dark to light."

Tiresias's insight in the *Odyssey* did manage to get Odysseus on the road back home—not to mother's bed, but to Penelope's. At mid-life Freud descended into the night world of dream for insight, while Odysseus descended into the underworld for Tiresias's counsel. Once again, Tiresias spoke of limits, limits to one's paternal and maternal aspirations. Odysseus was advised to spare the livestock of the sun god, Helios, and to bury the oar at the end of his voyage. He ignored the first part and was blown off course again. Fortunately for Odysseus, at long last he **was** able to renounce the oceanic/maternal sea voyage—he buried the oar—and return to Penelope.

Insight came too late for Achilles. When Odysseus met him with Tiresias in the underworld, Achilles lamented that he would rather be a slave on earth than lord of the underworld. Like Oedipus, he also had a foot problem, but his fate-l flaw was a gift from his immortal mother. Freud and his followers would call these shortcomings character flaws rather than fate-l flaws. Oedipus's father-inflicted flaw drove him beyond the limits of insight, while Achilles's maternal wound drove him to glory. Oedipus compulsively enacted Freud's family drama while Achilles suffered from Narcissus's ailment and died young, but gloriously. Freud says that these fates were not accidents, but character disorders—the unconscious repetition of patterns.

Aeneas had mother problems of his own. Just when he had gotten his father off his back and settled in with the attractive widow Dido, in stepped Aphrodite, his immortal mother, to remind him of his glorious fate—not an early death like that of Achilles—but the royal road to Rome. While Odysseus found the shade of his mortal mother in the underworld, Aeneas's and Achilles's mothers were immortal and refused to let go. Call it naval-cord psychology or call it fate.

While Freud and his followers offered character as an alternative to divine intercession, Jung reduced the gods to their archetypal essences in our collective unconscious. For example, Hermes was the guide to both the demonic opposite sex and to the underworld. He counseled Odysseus in his trickery of the terrible Circe and retrieved him from Calypso's cave when Odysseus had had his fill of the divine female. Freud would be concerned with the conflict within Odysseus's crafty character, while Jung evoked the trickster archetype. So we can say that it was not only the winds that returned Odysseus to Ithaca, but also his crafty character and a little archetypal assistance from Hermes and Athena.

Penelope's bed was not heroic Athena's goal for Odysseus, but only a reward for fulfilling her higher purpose. Athena was more concerned with patrimony than marital bliss, which she left to Hera, or even with bliss itself, which Aphrodite manipulated to start the fate-l war in the first place (The Judgment of Paris). The suitors were wasting Odysseus's estate, the inheritance of Telemachus, his son, while Odysseus's father worked feebly in his cottage garden. Not only Odysseus, but all three generations of men in his family needed empowering. It was Athena who dispatched Telemachus to learn of his father from Helen of Troy—some mentor. Of course, by then the beauty that had launched a thousand ships was standing by her man, Menelaus. Next, Athena orchestrated the massacre of the suitors and gave Odysseus his mortal reward—a warm homecoming. Next morning our hero was on the road to his father's cottage, not with patricide on his mind, but patrimony. When the old man heard about the carnage, he dropped his hoe and armed himself to join his son and grandson against the outraged families of the dead suitors. Three generations together on the road.

Even blind Oedipus was forced to hit the road again when banished from Thebes. In *Oedipus at Colonus,* Sophocles offered his hero a more regenerative road experience, similar to Odysseus's morning after. Odysseus reunites with his son, while Oedipus is exiled with his daughter, Antigone, to wander to Colonus, his place to die. James Hillman, in his *Oedipus Variations,* sees the journey from Thebes to Colonus as a move from parents to children, from duty to love, from obsession with origins to preparation for ends. Could it be that the gods are concerned ultimately with man's death, the one thing that eludes them? Odysseus was promised a peaceful death from the sea, and Oedipus at last finds peace at the end of the road in Colonus. Who knows? Ask Tiresias.

[As divine
beings do not give direct expression to their knowledge, a
means had to be found by which they could make themselves
intelligible. Suprahuman intelligence has from the beginning
made use of three mediums of expression — men, animals, and
plants, in each of which life pulsates in a different rhythm.
Chance came to be utilized as a fourth medium; the very
absence of an immediate meaning in chance permitted a
deeper meaning to come to expression in it. The oracle was
the outcome of this use of chance.]

I Ching
wilhelm ed.

THE I CHING AND I

Efrem Weitzman

My experience of the *I Ching* covers a period of almost fifty years, and during that time I have gone from youthful curiosity to profound respect for its depths of understanding of human affairs. I have also come to see that what it asks of me is that I reflect my respect for it by not coming to it with trivial questions. Rather, I am asked to pose a question only at those times that I feel "stuck," when life has presented me with a problem for which I cannot see any solutions. What the *I Ching* proposes is that you allow it to introduce you to a broader field of perception. This has certainly been my experience. It is as if my understanding is being lifted above the situation in which I find myself "stuck," so that I can see a broader field of possibilities.

CHANCE

imagine yourself high above the earth, traveling by airplane to some destination. You see what has always been there but what you did not see when down on earth. Not only do you have a wider perspective, but your state of mind can differ as well. Luckily, you are given a window seat on the airplane. The air is clear—no clouds—and you can see the earth far below, the very same earth that you will come back down to in order to pursue the goals you have set in the environment you have chosen to go to. Behind you is someplace you have left. You are in between, en route, perhaps un-stuck, and, one might say, experiencing a degree of what Eastern thought calls "detachment." While others may be conscious that they are at risk in this airborne situation, you are in a state of pleasant hiatus.

A number of years ago, during a flight from Kansas City to New York, I clearly experienced myself in that state of quiet detachment and experienced as well the process of losing it. The change began as the plane made its final descent into the airport. The earth below me, which for a while had possessed the quality of a beautiful still-life, began to change, to become animated. And I began to see details, such as the cars on the highways moving in opposite directions. Patterns emerged, implied complexities that triggered my awareness of what I was descending to, the world of relationships, concerns, and anxieties that constituted my daily life: a world gradually becoming more and more specific. By the time I stepped out of the plane and entered the hustle and bustle of the terminal, I had entered into an entirely different state of consciousness similar, I suspect, to the return-to-body state undergone by people who have had out-of-body experiences.

What is it that happens in a moment of breakthrough when the deductive mind is "stuck," when the whole being of the subject is poised, and suddenly there is a flash of intuition? We cry out, "How could I have missed it?" or "Why didn't I see that? It was right there under my nose all along." This is what it is often like when the *I Ching* is consulted by someone who is "stuck." It is not unusual to receive a reading that lifts you above what at first might be barely recognizable as **the** problem.

When I look at a newborn baby, I wonder how its life will unfold. Let's say that I know its parents to be good people, and that I know their financial situation to be solid. I think that I know enough to foresee what the future holds, but there are so many unseen elements—the genetic makeup of this new individual, for instance, and how that makeup will interact with what the world will bring to it. And what will the world bring to it?

Like the budget estimates of economists and the predictions of political analysts, all is subject to chance. The field of possibilities is vast; even if we choose to ignore the possibilities before us, they will somehow impinge themselves upon our reality whether we like it or not. We waltz with the element of chance from the outset and from the start we try to disengage ourselves from it. We are told to "leave nothing to chance." Civilizations are grounded in the effort to disengage us from it. The U.S. Weather Bureau and all of its subsidiaries strive mightily to defend us from it.

Carl Jung in his Foreword to the Wilhelm edition of the *I Ching* says that in the ancient Chinese view of reality,

The matter of interest seems to be the configuration formed by chance events in the moment of observation, and not at all the hypothetical reasons that seemingly account for the coincidence. While the Western mind carefully sifts, weighs, selects, classifies, isolates, the Chinese picture of the moment encompasses everything down to the minutest nonsensical detail, because all of the ingredients make up the observed moment.

I must confess that, all hypotheses aside, before my encounter with the *Book of Changes*, I found coincidence attractive. What was it, I wondered, that the artist was waiting for as he studied his canvas? He might tell you that he was waiting for "something" fresh and unexpected to suggest itself. Where was this "something" supposed to come from, this inspiration? The experience of "waiting to see" is not uncommon in the face of problematical situations. "What have I overlooked?" is a good question at such times. Or "Have I been looking in the wrong place?" The Chinese understanding seems to imply that if we take an aerial view, the answer is right there. For the artist who can "lift" himself, so to speak, the configuration he seeks, to use Jung's word, is simply waiting to be "seen," to be integrated into, or to totally transform, the image on the canvas.

Sometimes, on the other hand, things emerge into the field of awareness that are called coincidences for which we appear to have no need. They do, however, jog our awareness, and their advent can prove momentarily exhilarating. Since they seem to have no practical function in our lives, it would seem easy to forget them; however, though they do not fit neatly into a chain of meaningful events, they can remain intact as having a meaning in and of themselves.

TRIGRAMS

UPPER ▶

LOWER ▼

Ch'ien
☰

Chên
☳

K'an
☵

Kên
☶

K'un
☷

Sun

	Ch'ien ☰	Chên ☳	K'...
	1	34	
	25	51	
	6	40	
	33	62	
	12	16	
	44	32	
	13	55	
	10	54	

Key for Identify

☷	☴	☲	☱
11	9	14	43
24	42	21	17
7	59	64	47
15	53	56	31
2	20	35	45
46	57	50	28
36	37	30	58
19	61	38	58

Some forty years ago I was in France on a government grant to study stained glass. One day I turned a corner in a small village and encountered someone I had known casually in high school. There was a brief period of recognition on both our parts, and then we continued, each on his own way. What was he, of all people, doing there in that obscure little French village? Certainly neither of us recognized our encounter as especially significant, and yet I remember this coincidence—it resembles a finger pointing at something that wants to be seen and understood.

The old Chinese sages who acknowledged chance as a real element in their lives and tried to find ways to engage it have something to teach us. We are aware of the power of choice. We are aware, though we try to limit them, that there are myriad possibilities through which any situation can be altered or totally transformed. This state of affairs can feel at times like chaos, and at other times, like a blessing. We also are aware that there are times when we feel we have no alternatives. The field of possibilities appears to have dried up, and we survey a barren desert.

In the course of time, I have recognized the *I Ching's* function as a therapeutic tool and used it as such. I have a client, or I see a friend, in a state of ambivalence and anxiety. I propose that they ask the "Old Man," see what "he" has to say. Whether they are willing to deal with their problems in this way is open to question. When the answer is "yes," I feel that it is essential that I participate in the process. My chief function is to help the Questioner ask the essential question, the one at the heart of his situation. I believe that this question anchors the besieged ego as it receives the answers from the *I Ching*, as the terrain-of-answers unfolds its many possibilities. If the question is genuinely pressing, the Questioner is engaging in this process because he wants to survive. However, this desire, worthy as it is, can be the chief obstacle to attaining that end. The Questioner, as a rule, tends to grasp for anything in the text, any answer that relieves anxiety. And while this is understandable, the relief of anxiety doesn't mean that the richness of the answer has been accessed. It is not unusual for it to remain unavailable. As I see it, continually bringing the Questioner's attention back to the text and its relationship to the question gradually allows him to rise to a higher plane of awareness and subsequently to understanding. I encourage anyone who uses the *I Ching* in a time of crisis to do the reading with another person.

But, you say, look at the methodology offered. The book tells you to throw at random, six times, three coins or forty-seven dried sticks of the yarrow plant. Now that may seem like a peculiar "answer." It proposes that you engage the element of chance. Mysteriously, for those who are open to it, such an "answer" is relevant. Still, it is understandable that a Western mind might feel seriously challenged by the form in which the *I Ching* makes its wisdom available and that it offers itself as an Oracle whose oblique messages we must arduously interpret.

xagrams

While preparing this article, I asked the *I Ching* the question, "What is the nature of chance?" Its initial reply was surprising. The reading is #21 and is called "Biting Through." See if you agree.

Energetic biting through overcomes the obstacle
that prevents the joining of the lips; the storm
with its thunder and lightening overcomes the
disturbing tensions in nature. Recourse to law
and penalties overcomes the disturbances of
harmonious social life.

This is a brief portion of a long reading. It suggests to me that the nature of chance is to offer us the possibility of liberating ourselves from obstacles, from being "stuck." Look at those people who play games of chance in search of liberation from whatever in their life binds them, those who try to bite through the obstacle by taking risks—gambling, lying, cheating, etc.

The majority of "Biting Through" focuses on those elements that disturb harmonious social life.

When an obstacle to union arises, energetic biting
through brings success. This is true in all
situations. Whenever unity cannot be established,
the obstruction is due to a talebearer or traitor
who is interfering and blocking the way.

Before making further comment, I want to point out the obvious but significant fact that, as reader of this passage, I am the Questioner. This is important because I am bringing my own agendas to the question, the subject of being "stuck" and of being liberated by allowing chance elements to speak to me through the *I Ching*.

In general, being "stuck" implies a lack of unity, a being "split-off" from one's sense of wholeness. This condition, according to the *I Ching*, is due to some untruth that we have subscribed to, consciously or unconsciously. On the other hand, it could be equally true that our confusion arises from what is being said or has been said by others (parental messages, etc.). The *I Ching* seems to equate recovering from the painfulness of a situation with taking the risk of finding the culprit responsible, be it idea, feeling, concept, or person. Having the courage to expose the culprit and pass judgment would be "biting through," and would liberate the one who is "stuck" from whatever he is stuck in or by. The reading goes on to suggest that the judgment to be made should be based on clarity and excitement, and "that the man who makes the decisions is gentle by nature, while he commands respect by his conduct in his position." Certainly, coming into an active relationship with the element of chance brings excitement with it. We know we are confronting the unknown. To maintain clarity in the face of this excitement suggests that the Questioner put himself in a position of being able to grasp whatever might spring into view.

One might say that the *I Ching* is addressing human suffering and the release from that suffering. One might also say that the gift of the *I Ching* is simply hanging out with this wise old book. No matter how critical the situation feels to the Questioner, the clarity and wisdom it offers, if approached in a reasonably reflective manner, opens the field of possibilities to views that were always there but unseen. An *I Ching* reading can offer a sense of detachment and allow creative alternatives to emerge where there seemed to be none. After all, the *I Ching* itself is detached. It hears our question and then, if we allow ourselves to listen, it responds by offering us a perspective that includes us as subject and shows us the situation that surrounds us in the form of all the chance elements that are available in the present moment. In this way, our understanding can be opened to the possibility of significant choice and significant action.

HISTORY ABHORS DETERMINISM BUT CANNOT TOLERATE CHANCE

BERNARD DEVOTO

ON GODAND DICE: CHANCE DETERMINISM, AND THE BERLIN WALL

Nicholas Campion

Isaac Newton, the true founder of the modern mathematically perfect cosmos, is supposed to have proclaimed that "God doesn't play dice." In Newton's roulette-wheel universe, so popular in the heady days of the eighteenth and nineteenth centuries, when all was well in the best of all possible worlds, the correct balls always went down the right holes. Many people think they still do. Yet twentieth-century science has different opinions. We now have a dozen different post-Einstein, post-Quantum, post-modern variations on the old theme: God does play dice, God can't play dice, or even, the dice play themselves. Can a square die fit in a round hole? Probably.

Politicians are inveterate gamblers. They risk vast amounts of money, sometimes their own, usually other peoples', on speculative ventures of a truly mind-boggling scale: the invasion of Russia, for example. It is the job of the historian, the arbiter of what did and didn't happen in the past, to make sense of the politicians' gambles, to slot them into some sort of order where they have both clear reasons (beyond the fact that Hitler's mother had a headache one day) and definite results. Late-twentieth-century historians though, are in a muddle. And the muddle they got themselves into has consequences for the rest of us because they are part of the academic industry that trains the graduates who become the journalists who eventually become foreign correspondents and tell us what is happening in the rest of the world, exerting a profound influence on our views of ourselves and our fellow humans.

Humanity is in a quandary. There is now a fundamental dislocation between what the scientists say and what our senses tell us. The experts tell us that the physical world is an illusion. Our bodies tell us that it's precisely the opposite, as anyone who lies down in front of a truck will affirm. Most of us, including historians and political commentators, are therefore still addicted to a nice, sensible, cause-and-effect view of society and its workings. Look back to the past and we can identify the causes of the Russian Revolution. Tinker with interest rates or the money supply in the present and we will guarantee certain desirable effects in the future.

Go to any university and you'll find physicists playing with particles that can be in two places at the same time, or even, some say, take a little trip back in time. But down the corridor in the history department Newton is King. Historians have always had a problem with uncertainty. They don't like chance. Indeed, their entire discipline depends on the search for the causes to explain the effects that they are (if they're lucky) paid to study. Any student faced with a silly exam question like "The American Revolution of 1776— explain" will regurgitate a series of stock solutions: George III was mad, there was a new spirit of Enlightenment abroad in the colonies, greedy American merchants didn't want to pay taxes to London, British generals were stupid, Americans liked freedom, and Lancashire mill owners forced cotton prices up—or down. Taken together, all these small causes add up to the Big Cause.

Historical debate, such as it is, is based on the rearrangement of these causes. One historian might claim that the Enlightenment was really no more than a sham, another that George III wasn't really mad. Historians factionalize. Marxists look for economic causes. Old-fashioned types put it all down to "Great Men." Others psychoanalyze George Washington. Feminists say Mrs. Washington started it. Gurus in Afro-American Studies say it comes down to Washington's black man-servant. But they all agree they've found the cause that explains the effect.

Sometimes these somber debates are conducted in deep, leather, ivy-league armchairs. At other times, they arouse intensity bordering on hysteria. Not surprising, perhaps. After all, careers depend on the outcome. But the debaters have one thing in common; the conviction that they are all on the trail of a real sequence of cause-and-effect historical movements, just like real grown-up scientists.

The problem doesn't stop there. Historians are stuck in a completely schizophrenic world where not only is chance taboo, but so are big patterns—and, paradoxically, real Big Causes. To explain why this is so requires a short history lesson. Until the seventeenth century it was accepted that all historical events originated with God. By the eighteenth century, historians had decided that the existence of God wasn't a suitable explanation for the War of the Spanish Succession. Anyway, they reasoned, if God was so good, why were Christians so nasty? Fair enough. Let's look for human causes, they thought to themselves. Gibbon moved the debate one step further when he said that the Roman Empire collapsed, not because God punished the Romans for being corrupt and decadent, but simply because they were corrupt and decadent. So much so that they couldn't beat off a rabble of painted barbarians.

Removing God from history, though, didn't remove the search for patterns. It just changed their nature. The laws of history became secular instead of spiritual. If we look back over the last two hundred years we can identify three distinct forms of historical determinism. First there's "Whig history" (named after the eighteenth-century English politicians), which holds that European/Western culture is destined to triumph over all others. Then there's the Nazi/Fascist view, in which all history leads to the victory of one race over another. And there's the Communist/Socialist version, in which the workers and peasants are bound to destroy their bourgeois and feudal oppressors. No doubt about it. Well, not until recently at any rate.

All three versions are firmly discredited in the classrooms and corridors of academic history. Historians definitely don't like patterns. So, as fast as school kids are taught lists of causes, once they get to graduate school they learn that nothing really happened—and without effects there couldn't be any causes. "Okay," a liberal professor might say, "we know that the Declaration of Independence was signed, but was the Revolution of 1776 *really* a revolution? In fact, did anything really change? Well, on a very close examination, no."

Like quantum physicists peering through their electron microscopes, historians discover that history as we know it is an illusion. Of course, they don't tell anybody. If the news got out, cost-cutting politicians would soon close down their comfortable sinecures. Instead they continue their quest for causes: "There *must* be a real cause out there. Let's look just a little harder."

So, it's back to chance. Or more properly Chance with a big "C." This is the big one, the Uncertainty Principle as applied to history. Modern historians haven't even begun to grapple with the problems of unpredictability. If they did, they'd stop assuming that we can be certain about the past. But to the ancients Chance was something they had to live with.

By 2,000 BCE, the Sumerians had figured out that while some events (the rising of the sun) could be predicted, others (a cloud blowing over the sun's face) couldn't. They worked out that there must be two sorts of fate. One was called *nam*, or *šimtu* (pronounced shimtu). This was the sort of fate which cannot be avoided, the fate which turns a hen's egg into a hen and an emu's egg into an emu. Or an acorn into an oak, if you prefer. Alongside this was another fate, which they called *me*. This was individual destiny, perhaps best translated as personality, or that which makes us do the things we do and take the choices we take. *Me* allowed the Sumerians to be free, to get up with the rising sun or to duck inside when the rain came over. *Me* allowed them to make moral choices. They inhabited a world of perpetual paradoxes: there was no dodging fate, but they could choose how they tried to dodge it. *Shimtu* and *me* existed in a mutually exclusive, contradictory relationship in which the future both could and couldn't be predicted. The Sumerians, we might say, had their cake and ate it.

The Greeks got more elaborate. Among the many systems they worked out was the following, attributed to the fifth-century BCE professional thinker, Pythagoras. He constructed an elaborate theory to account for the divine order he observed in this most beautiful of universes. First, there was Destiny, the force (such as God) by which all things are brought to pass. Second was Necessity, the force which compels results to follow beginnings (or what school kids study in their history classes). Third

was Order, the interweaving of events and their temporal arrangement (or what medieval chroniclers recorded in their manuscripts). All very elaborate. Pythagoreans could bask in the stability of a perfect world in which the past led inexorably to the future.

But Pythagoras was a little smarter than many modern historians. He wanted nice little laws of history, but he realized that his efforts were basically absurd. So he built in a fourth form of Fate, which translates into English as Chance. At a stroke he demolished his previous Byzantine efforts. If something happened that could be explained, then it could be attributed to Destiny, Necessity, or Order. If it couldn't be explained, then it came down to Chance. Game, set, and match to Pythagoras. One way or another his theories were proved.

Modern historians have a grudging respect for chance in its most devastating form—death. The extinction of a Great Man is one of the few historical events which is not generally attributed to another historical cause. It might have general causes, of course, like lack of hygiene or an unfortunate encounter with someone else's sword, but not historical ones (if you like circular arguments, an historical cause is a cause which an historian believes to be significant). There is no conceivable historical cause which forced a Norman archer to shoot an arrow into Harold's eye at Hastings. The classic exam question asked about Henry IV, the king of France who died prematurely in 1610, is "It is as well for his reputation that he died when he did. Discuss." Chance, in this case, was presumed to be a savior, and the king was remembered only for his successes. As teenage students we used to pose the same question of Jimi Hendrix and Jim Morrison: "It was as well for their reputations that they died when they did." That the question must be answered in the affirmative is answered by the example of Elvis Presley: Chance was unkind and he lived too long. There's an obvious flaw in such questions; we can never bring the deceased person back to life to see if his reputation would have been enhanced given an extra thirty years. Had Elvis not died when he did, would he have checked into the Betty Ford clinic, lost fifty pounds, and cut some more great rock-and-roll songs? We'll never know.

But enough of such digressions. Historians don't like Chance, but neither are they fond of Pattern. They regard it as outmoded and authoritarian. It offends their liberal principles. The last historian to suggest that there might be patterns in cultural and political development was Arnold Toynbee, whose epic twelve volume *A Study of History* was published in 1948. In spite of his stature, he was held up to ridicule and his reputation never recovered. The attacks on him were little more than a hand-washing exercise by historians who wanted to pretend that they had had nothing to do with the excesses, mainly of Nazism, but also of Stalinism—and nothing to do with the embarrassing legacy of nineteenth-century Whig History, in which all historical theories agreed that the European world, with its wonderfully superior civilization, was destined to replace all other cultures. They understood that this theory was just a slight advance on earlier doctrines of the triumph of God, and that it was only a short step from there to the murderous doctrines of the triumph of race or class.

The historical world's hasty rejection of Toynbee, though, was a major mistake. Historians have painted themselves into such a corner that they can't acknowledge any patterns in history at all. Most economists assume the existence of business cycles, and most believe they recur at regular intervals, such as the fifty-four-year "Kondratieff Cycle." Paul Volcker, former President of the Federal Reserve Bank, even wrote a book in 1978 called *The Rediscovery of the Business Cycle*. The Foundation for the Study of Cycles invited Margaret Thatcher to be the guest of honor at its 1996 conference. Yet suggest to an academic historian that there might be political cycles, and that, just like business cycles, they might be regular, and you'll drive him to apoplexy. Historians have been forced to argue that, even though economic causes have political effects, economic patterns are not reflected in historical patterns. History, they agree, proceeds along cause and effect lines, but definitely not with any order, and certainly not with any purpose.

Whiggishness, though, remains the guiding principle of our culture. The belief in the triumph of the West stalks the corridors of political power, and the belief in the superiority of Western institutions is virtually unquestioned. Academic historians may have retreated from their Whig principles, but they had already done too thorough a job promoting them. As Jim Morrison sang (although he did it with multiple layers of irony), "the West is the best."

We see this implicit sense of superiority surfacing in the way that all other countries are compared to our own democratic values. We encourage other societies to adopt our view of "civil rights" and attack them when they don't. Watch CNN or the BBC and you'll constantly hear foreign correspondents criticize other nations for crimes and misdemeanors that Britain and America have committed with great regularity. Or you'll hear them talk about the risk of the "clock's" being "turned back" in Russia, as if not only is political life regulated by a predetermined mechanical process, but the West is now at about 4:00 p.m., while the poor old East is still having breakfast. Iran is back in the dark hours of the early morning.

But how democratic is the West? The argument that it represents the pinnacle of freedom tends to represent the establishment—those who benefit from society's current institutions. But from both right and left come allegations that these same institutions are deeply authoritarian. Ask the *ad hoc* militias if Washington holds the torch of freedom. This is not to say that they are right or wrong, merely to note that there is no single view of the character of our current political society. What we can see, though, is that just as history is written by the winners, who see their victory as the inevitable result of everything that came before, so those at the top of the political tree tend to assume that they, or their ideas, are destined to take over the world.

Chaos theory, our current fin de siècle fad, is challenging such comfortable views, posing new possibilities. We all know the basics of chaos by now: a butterfly randomly flaps its wings in Siberia and causes a tornado in Tennessee. But can the random event be predicted? A strict determinist might say that the butterfly was bound to flap its wings. Certainly, where once chaos meant precisely that, now some kill-joys are using it to make even more precise forecasts. The determinists are fighting back.

However, no billion gigabyte computer model can cope with the man who raises his arm during a demonstration and starts a revolution. Neither can any cause-and-effect theory account for the event which actually brought down the Berlin Wall. Let me take you back to November, 1989, the time when we in the West were still faced with the great Monolith in the East. Yet Communism was tottering. In Poland, Jaruzelski had welcomed Solidarity members into a coalition. In Hungary , the government had announced the end of the Peoples' Republic. But in East Germany, the linchpin of the eastern bloc, the raison d'être for the entire Soviet occupation of Eastern Europe, and the symbol of the Iron Curtain, the politburo had actually issued orders for the massacre of demonstrators in Berlin. In Dresden, on one November night, only a last-minute change in the route of the daily protest march prevented a blood bath and a terrible revolution. The "Tiananmen Square Solution" was being openly touted.

Then a curious event took place, one which was so startling, so unexpected, that it is said that it took on the mythical aura of the Angel of Mons or the leaning Virgin of Albert. Did it really happen, did the witnesses really see what they saw or hear what they heard? Even people who watched the event live on television have different versions. However, these seem to be the facts. Shortly before 7:00 p.m. on November 9, 1989, Guenther Schabowski, the East German Central Committee's secretary for the media, held a press conference to announce the latest decisions of the Council of Ministers. Much of it dealt with the Communist Party's new philosophy, its acceptance of pluralism and plans for the forthcoming party conference. All very droll. Typical Stalinist stuff.

A few months later BBC foreign affairs editor John Simpson interviewed Schabowski in an effort to find out what happened next. According to Schabowski himself, and Simpson's recollections, at a few minutes before 7:00 p.m. there was an awkward pause. The three hundred journalists who were sitting there became restless. Schabowski whispered something to the man next to him and shuffled his papers. The man next to him leaned over. A piece of paper then appeared in Schabowski's hand and he read from it slowly and hesitantly. "This will be interesting for you," he intoned. "Today the decision was taken to make it possible for all citizens to leave the country through the official border points."

Immediately and unexpectedly there was a buzz. A GDR journalist asked when the order would come into effect. Schabowski used the word *verzüglich*, meaning *immediately*. What *he* meant was that the government was immediately beginning to set up offices to handle visas and create the other necessary bureaucratic hurdles. Eventually, at 6:59 p.m., still holding the piece of paper and pestered by a group of journalists, Schabowski broke. In response to repeated questioning on when visas would be issued, he replied "straight away." The effect was electric. The news was flashed around the world within minutes. In East Berlin crowds surged toward the Wall. By 8:15 the checkpoint at Bornholmstrasse was open, and the Cold War was, to all intents and purposes, over.

The opening of the Berlin Wall was undoubtedly one of the great pieces of political theater in the modern world, comparable to the fall of the Bastille in 1789, or the seizure of the Winter Palace in 1917. Yet its dramatic power and consequences—the revolutions in Czechoslovakia and Romania and all the events in the communist world down to the Soviet coup of 1991, were entirely due to two utterly unpredictable events, both pure chance. One was Schabowski's muddle over words and the slight change of nuance from "immediately" to "straight away." The other was the case of the missing paper. When Schabowski entered the press conference the piece of paper containing the visa announcement was on the top of his sheaf of papers. If all had gone according to plan, it would have been the first item on the agenda, quite possibly scarcely noticed by the assembled journalists. Somehow, nobody knows quite how, it became mixed up with the rest. So instead of reading it first he had to go through other business in the hope of finding it later. He finally came across it at the bottom of the pile and, as an afterthought, read it out before going home, he hoped, for a quiet night. But history was about to change. Schabowski, the butterfly, had flapped his wings.

We arrive at the same second   just inside the door this cold winter night   as if we're synchronized from past millennia.

"Well timed," you say giving me your hand. the charm of your red knit gloves. -Jenifer Nostrand

"The artist stands naked and alo

Monica Kassan

Day Dream
Acrylic on canvas
2´ x 4´

the edge."

Tightrope Walker. Linn Sage

illustrated friends to be "scientific" —meaning unemotional and analytic—in approaching a vexatious problem.

We talk about the "scientific method" and instruct school-children in this supposedly monolithic and maximally effective path to natural knowledge, as if a single formula could unlock all the multifarious secrets of empirical reality.

Beyond a platitudinous appeal to open-mindedness, the "scientific method" involves a set of concepts and procedures tailored to the image of a man in a white coat twirling dials in a laboratory—experiment, quantification, repetition, prediction, and restriction of complexity to a few variables that can be controlled and manipulated. These procedures are powerful, but they do not encompass all of nature's variety. How should scientists operate when they must try to explain the results of history, those inordinately complex events that can occur but once in detailed glory? Many large domains of nature— cosmology, geology, and evolution among them— must be studied with the tools of history. The appropriate methods focus on narrative, not experiment as usually conceived.

JAY GOULD

The Burgess Shale and the Nature of History †

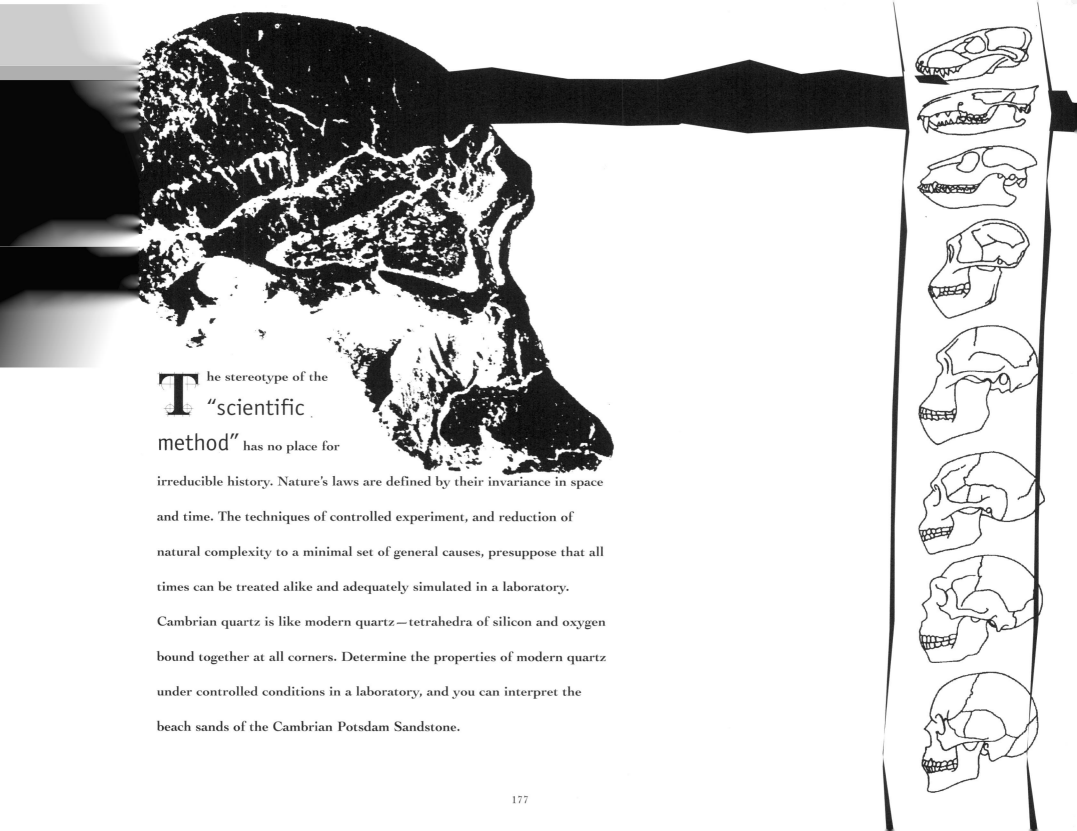

The stereotype of the "scientific method" has no place for irreducible history. Nature's laws are defined by their invariance in space and time. The techniques of controlled experiment, and reduction of natural complexity to a minimal set of general causes, presuppose that all times can be treated alike and adequately simulated in a laboratory. Cambrian quartz is like modern quartz—tetrahedra of silicon and oxygen bound together at all corners. Determine the properties of modern quartz under controlled conditions in a laboratory, and you can interpret the beach sands of the Cambrian Potsdam Sandstone.

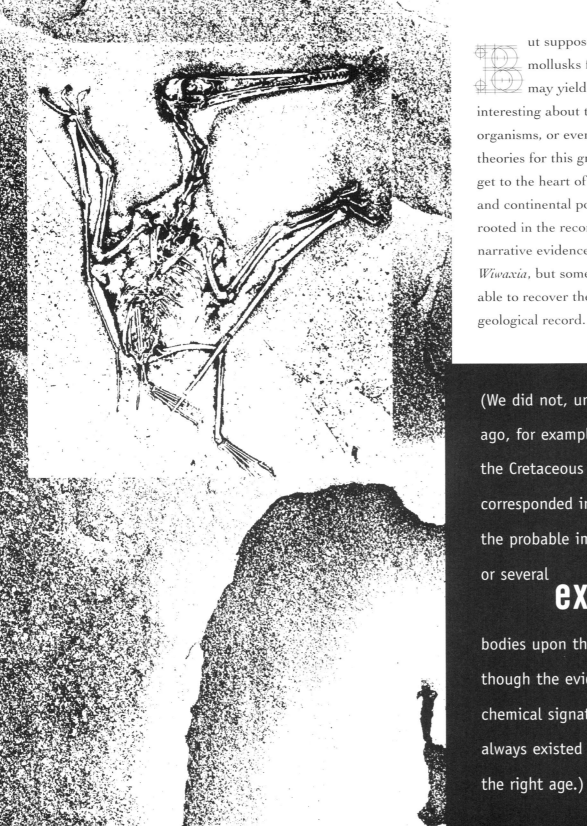

why dinosaurs died, or why

ut suppose you want to know **why dinosaurs died,** or why mollusks flourished while *Wiwaxia* perished? The laboratory is not irrelevant, and may yield important insights by analogy. (We might, for example, learn something interesting about the Cretaceous extinction by testing the physiological tolerances of modern organisms, or even of dinosaur "models," under environmental changes proposed in various theories for this great dying.) But the restricted techniques of the "scientific method" cannot get to the heart of this singular event involving creatures long dead on an earth with climates and continental positions markedly different from today's. The resolution of history must be rooted in the reconstruction of past events themselves—in their own terms—based on narrative evidence of their own unique phenomena. No law guaranteed the demise of *Wiwaxia*, but some complex set of events conspired to assure this result—and we may be able to recover the causes if, by good fortune, sufficient evidence lies recorded in our spotty geological record.

(We did not, until ten years ago, for example, know that the Cretaceous extinction corresponded in time with the probable impact of one or several **extraterrestrial** bodies upon the earth— though the evidence, in chemical signatures, had always existed in rocks of the right age.)

THE
IIRD

top to **Slime helps**
p to **top boffin**
wrap up
my serious
phenomena

Historical explanations are distinct from conventional experimental results in many ways. The issue of verification by repetition does not arise because we are trying to account for uniqueness of detail that cannot, both by laws of probability and time's arrow of irreversibility, occur together again. We do not attempt to interpret the complex events of narrative by reducing them to simple consequences of natural law; historical events do not, of course, violate any general principles of matter and motion, but their occurrence lies in a realm of contingent detail. (The law of gravity tells us how an apple falls, but not why that apple fell at that moment, and why Newton happened to be sitting there ripe for inspiration.) And the issue of prediction, a central ingredient in the stereotype, does not enter into a historical narrative. We can explain an event after it occurs, but contingency precludes its repetition, even from an identical starting point. (Custer was doomed after a thousand events conspired to isolate his troops, but start again in 1850 and he might never see Montana, much less Sitting Bull and Crazy Horse.)

These differences place historical, or narrative, explanations in an unfavorable light when judged by restrictive stereotypes of the

"scientific method." The sciences of historical complexity have therefore been demoted in status and generally occupy a position of low esteem among professionals. In fact, the status ordering of the sciences has become so familiar a theme that the ranking from adamantine physics at the pinnacle down to such squishy and subjective subjects as psychology and sociology at the bottom has become stereotypical in itself. These distinctions have entered our language and our metaphors—the "hard" versus the "soft" sciences, the "rigorously experimental" versus the "merely descriptive." Several years ago, Harvard University, in an uncharacteristic act of educational innovation, broke conceptual ground by organizing the sciences according to procedural style rather than conventional discipline within the core curriculum. We did not make the usual twofold division into physical versus biological, but recognized the two styles just discussed—the experimental-predictive and the historical. We designated each category by a letter rather than a name. Guess which division became Science A, and which Science B? My course on the history of earth and life is called Science B-16.

Perhaps the saddest aspect of this linear ranking lies in the acceptance of inferiority by bottom dwellers, and their persistent attempt to ape inappropriate methods that may work higher up on the ladder. When the order itself should be vigorously challenged, and plurality with equality asserted in pride, too may historical scientists act like the prison trustee who, ever mindful of his tenuous advantages, outdoes the warden himself in zeal for preserving the status quo of power and subordination.

Thus, historical scientists often import an oversimplified caricature of "hard" science, or simply bow to pronouncements of professions with higher status. Many geologists accepted Lord Kelvin's last and most restrictive dates for a young earth, though the data of fossils and strata spoke clearly for more time. (Kelvin's date bore the prestige of mathematical formulae and the weight of physics, though the discovery of radioactivity soon invalidated Kelvin's premise that heat now rising from the earth's interior records the cooling of our planet from an initially molten state not long past.) Even more geologists rejected continental drift, despite an impressive catalogue of data on previous connections among continents, because physicists had proclaimed the lateral motion of continents impossible. Charles Spearman misused the statistical technique of factor analysis to designate intelligence as a single, measurable, physical thing in the head, and then rejoiced for psychology because "this Cinderella among the sciences has made a bold bid for the level of triumphant physics itself" (quoted in Gould, 1981, p. 263).

UFO THEORY ON CIRCLES

Scientists check plane crash link

Myste circle baffle

N CIRCLES D RIVALS!

when you though it was safe back into the cornfield. ...

nds that may be t of this world!

By Jacqui Goddard

ut historical science is not worse, more restricted, or less capable of achieving firm conclusions because experiment, prediction, and subsumption under invariant laws of nature do not represent its usual working methods. The sciences of history use a different mode of explanation, rooted in the comparative and observational richness of our data. We cannot see a past event directly, but science is usually based on inference, not unvarnished observation (you don't see electrons, gravity, or black holes either).

The firm requirement for a science—whether stereotypical or historical—lies in secure testability, not direct observation. We must be able to determine whether our hypotheses are definitely wrong or probably correct (we leave assertions of certainty to preachers and politicians). History's richness drives us to different methods of testing, but testability is our criterion as well. We work with our strength of rich and diverse data recording the consequences of past events; we do not bewail our inability to see the past directly. We search for repeated pattern, shown by evidence so abundant and so diverse that no other coordinating interpretation could stand, even though any item, taken separately, would not provide conclusive proof.

The great nineteenth-century philosopher of science William Whewell devised the word consilience, meaning "jumping together," to designate the confidence gained when many independent sources "conspire" to indicate a particular historical pattern. He called the strategy of coordinating disparate results from multifarious sources consilience of induction.

I regard **Charles Darwin** as the greatest of all historical scientists. Not only did he develop convincing evidence for evolution as the coordinating principle of life's history, but he also chose as a conscious and central theme for all his writings—the treatises on worms, coral reefs, and orchids, as well as the great volumes on evolution—the development of a different but equally rigorous methodology for historical science (Gould, 1986). Darwin explored a variety of modes for historical explanation, each appropriate for differing densities of preserved information (Gould, 1986, 60-64), but his central argument rested on Whewell's consilience. We know that evolution must underlie the order of life because no other explanation can coordinate the disparate data of embryology, biogeography, the fossil record, vestigial organs, taxonomic relationships, and so on. Darwin explicitly rejected the naive but widely held notion that a cause must be seen directly in order to qualify as a scientific explanation. He wrote about the proper testing of natural selection, invoking the idea of consilience for historical explanation:

Now this **hypothesis** may be tested—and this seems to me the only fair and legitimate manner of considering the whole question—by trying whether it explains several large and independent classes of facts; such as the geological succession of organic beings, their distribution in past and present times, and their mutual affinities and homologies. If the principle of natural selection does explain these and other large bodies of facts, it ought to be received (1868, vol. 1, p.657).

But historical scientists must then proceed beyond the simple demonstration that the explanations can be tested by equally rigorous procedures different from the stereotype of the "scientific method"; they must also convince other scientists that explanations of the historical type are both interesting and vitally informative. When we have established "ju history" as the only complete and acceptable explanation for phenomena that everyone judge important—the evolution of the human intelligence, or of any self-conscious life on earth, fo example—then we shall have won.

Historical explanations take the form of narrative: E, the phenomenon to be explained, arose because D came before, preceded by C, B, and A. If any of these earlier stages had not occurred, or had transpired in a different way, then E would not exist (or would be present in a substantially altered form, E', requiring a different explanation). Thus, E makes sense and can be explained rigorously as the outcome of A through D. But no law of nature enjoined E; any variant E' arising from an altered set of antecedents would have been equally explicable, though massively different in form and effect.

I am not speaking of randomness (for E had to ar as a consequence of A through D), but of the cen principle of all history—*contingency*. A histor explanation does not rest on direct deductions fr laws of nature, but on an unpredictable sequence antecedent states, where any major change in step of the sequence would have altered the f result. This final result is therefore dependent, contingent, upon everything that came before— unerasable and determining signature of history.

Many scientists and interested laypeople, caught by the stereotype of the "scientific method," find such contingent explanations less interesting or less "scientific," even when their appropriateness and essential correctness must be acknowledged. The South lost the Civil War with a kind of relentless inevitability once hundreds of particular events happened as they did—Pickett's charge failed, Lincoln won the election of 1864, etc., etc., etc. But wind the tape of American history back to the Louisiana Purchase, the Dred Scott decision, or even only to Fort Sumter, let it run again with just a few small and judicious changes (plus their cascade of consequences), and a different outcome, including the opposite resolution, might have occurred with equal relentlessness past a certain point. (I used to believe that Northern superiority in population and industry had virtually guaranteed the result from the start. But I have been persuaded by recent scholarship that wars for recognition rather than conquest can be won by purposeful minorities. The South was not trying to overrun the North, but merely to secure its own declared borders and win acknowledgment as an independent state. Majorities, even in the midst of occupation, can be rendered sufficiently war-weary and prone to withdraw by insurgencies, particularly in guerrilla form, that will not relent.)

Suppose, then, that we have a set of historical explanations, as well documented as anything in conventional science. These results do not arise as deducible consequences from any law of nature; they are not even predictable from any general or abstract property of the larger system (as superiority in population or industry). How can we deny such explanations a role every bit as interesting and important as a more conventional scientific conclusion? I hold that we must grant equal status for three basic reasons.

1. A question of reliability.

The documentation of evidence, and probability of truth by disproof of alternatives, may be every bit as conclusive as for any explanation in traditional science.

2. A matter of importance.

The equal impact of historically contingent explanations can scarcely be denied. The Civil War is the focus and turning point of American history. Such central matters as race, regionalism, and economic power owe their present shape to this great event that need not have occurred. If the current taxonomic order and relative diversity of life are more a consequence of "just history" than a potential deduction from general principles of evolution, then contingency sets the basic pattern of nature.

3. A psychological point.

I have been too apologetic so far. I have even slipped into the rhetoric of inferiority—by starting from the premise that historical explanations may be less interesting and then pugnaciously fighting for equality. No such apologies need be made. Historical explanations are endlessly fascinating in themselves, in may ways more intriguing to the human psyche than the inexorable consequences of nature's laws. We are especially moved by events that did not have to be, but that occurred for identifiable reasons subject to endless mulling and stewing. By contrast, both ends of the usual dichotomy—the inevitable and the truly random—usually make less impact on our emotions because they cannot be controlled by history's agents and objects, and are therefore either channeled or buffeted, without much hope for pushing back. But, with contingency, we are drawn in; we become involved; we share the pain of triumph or tragedy. When we realize that the actual outcome did not have to be, that any alteration in any step along the way would have unleashed a cascade down a different channel, we grasp the causal power of individual events. We can argue, lament, or exult over each detail—because each holds the power of transformation. Contingency is the affirmation of control by immediate events over destiny, the kingdom lost for want of a horseshoe nail. The Civil War is an especially poignant tragedy because a replay of the tape might have saved a half million lives for a thousand different reasons—and we would not find a statue of a soldier, with names of the dead engraved on the pedestal below, on every village green and before every county courthouse in old America. Our own evolution is a joy and a wonder because such a curious chain of events would probably never happen again, but having occurred, makes eminent sense. Contingency is a license to participate in history, and our psyche responds.

The theme of **contingency,** so poorly understood and explored by science, has long been a mainstay of literature. We note here a situation that might help

to reach the false boundaries between art and nature, and even allow literature to enlighten science. Contingency is Tolstoy's cardinal theme in all his great novels. Contingency is the source of tension and intrigue in many fine works of suspense, most notably in a recent masterpiece by Ruth Rendell (writing as Barbara Vine), *A Fatal Inversion* (1987) — a chilling book describing a tragedy that engulfs the lives and futures of a small community through an escalating series of tiny events, each peculiar and improbable (but perfectly plausible) in itself, and each entraining a suite of even stranger consequences. *A Fatal Inversion* is so artfully and intricately plotted by this device that I must view Rendell's finest work as a conscious text on the nature of history.

Two popular novels of the past five years have selected Darwinian theory as their major theme. I am especially intrigued and pleased that both accept and explore contingency as the theory's major consequence for our lives. In this correct decision, Stephen King and Kurt Vonnegut surpass many scientists in their understanding of evolution's deeper meanings.

King's *The Tommyknockers* (1987) fractures a tradition in science fiction by treating extraterrestrial "higher intelligences" not as superior in general , wiser, or more powerful, but merely as quirky hangers-on in the great Darwinian game of adaptation by differential reproductive success in certain environments. (King refers to this persistence as "dumb evolution"; I just call it Darwinism.)* Such equivocal success by endless and immediate adjustment breeds contingency, which then becomes the controlling theme of *The Tommyknockers*—as the aliens fail in their plans for earth, thanks largely to evasive action by one usually ineffective, cynical, and dipsomaniacal English professor. King muses on the nature of controlling events in contingent sequences, and on their level of perceived importance at various scales:

I would not be the one to tell you there are no planets anywhere in the universe that are not large dead cinders floating in space because a war over who was or was not hogging too many dryers in the local Laundromat escalated into Doomsville. No one ever really knows where things will end—or if they will…. Of course we may blow up our world someday with no outside help at all, for reasons which look every bit as trivial from a standpoint of light-years; from where we rotate far out on one spoke of the Milky Way in the Lesser Magellanic Cloud, whether or not the Russians invade the Iranian oilfields or whether NATO decides to install American-made Cruise missiles in West Germany may seem every bit as important as whose turn it is to pick up the tab for five coffees and a like number of Danish.

*Our agreement on the theme, if not the terminology, provides hope that even the most implacable differences in style and morality may find a common meeting ground on this most important of intellectual turfs—for Steve is the most fanatical Red Sox booster in New England, while my heart remains with the Yankees.

Kurt Vonnegut's *Galápagos* (1985) is an even more conscious and direct commentary on the meaning of evolution from a writer's standpoint. I feel especially gratified that a cruise to the **Galápagos,** a major source of Vonnegut's decision to write the book, should have suggested contingency as the cardinal theme taught by Darwin's geographic shrine. In Vonnegut's novel, the pathways of history may be broadly constrained by such general principles as natural selection, but contingency has so much maneuvering room within these boundaries that any particular outcome owes more to a quirky series of antecedent events than to channels set by nature's laws. *Galápagos*, in fact, is a novel about the nature of history in Darwin's world. I would (and do) assign it to students in science courses as a guide to understanding the meaning of contingency.

In *Galápagos*, the holocaust of depopulation arrives by the relatively mild route of a bacterium that destroys human egg cells. This scourge first gains a toehold by striking women at the annual international book fair in Frankfurt, but quickly spreads throughout the world, sterilizing all but an isolated remnant of *Homo sapiens*. Human survival becomes concentrated in a tiny and motley group carried by boat beyond the reach of the bacterium to the isolated Galápagos—the last of the Kanka-bono Indians plus a tourist and adventurer or two. Their survival and curious propagation proceeds through a wacky series of contingencies, yet all future human history now resides with this tiny remnant:

> In a matter of less than a century the blood of every human being on earth would be predominantly Kanka-bono, with a little von Kleist and Hiroguchi thrown in. And this astonishing turn of events would be made to happen, in large part, by one of the only two absolute nobodies on the original passenger list for **"the Nature Cruise of the Century."** That was Mary Hepburn. The other nobody was her husband, who himself played a crucial role in shaping human destiny by booking, when facing his own extinction, that one cheap little cabin below the waterline.

Contingency has also been an important theme in films, both recent and classic. In **Back to the Future** (1985) Marty McFly (Michael J. Fox), a teenager transported back in time to the high school attended by his parents, must struggle to reconstitute the past as it actually happened, after his accidental intrusion threatens to alter the initial run of the tape (when his mother, in an interesting variation on Oedipus, develops a crush on him). The events that McFly must rectify seem to be tiny occurrences of absolutely no moment, but he knows that nothing could be more important, since failure will result in that ultimate of consequences, his own erasure, because his parents will never meet.

The greatest expression of contingency—my nomination as the holotype* of the genre—comes near the end of Frank Capra's masterpiece, **It's a Wonderful Life** (1946). George Bailey (Jimmy Stewart) has led a life of self-abnegation because his basic decency made him defer personal dreams to offer support for family and town. His precarious building and loan association has been driven to bankruptcy and charged with fraud through the scheming of the town skinflint and robber baron, Mr. Potter (Lionel Barrymore). George, in despair, decides to drown himself, but Clarence Odbody, his guardian angel, intervenes by throwing himself into the water first, knowing that George's decency will demand another's rescue in preference to immediate suicide. Clarence then tries to cheer George up by the direct route: "You just don't know all that you've done"; but George replies: "If it hadn't been for me, everybody'd be a lot better off.... I suppose it would have been better if I'd never been born at all."

Clarence, in a flash of inspiration, grants George his wish and shows him an alternative version of life in his town of Bedford Falls, replayed in his complete absence. This magnificent ten-minute scene is both a highlight of cinematic history and the finest illustration that I have ever encountered for the basic principle of contingency—a replay of the tape yielding an entirely different but equally sensible outcome; small and apparently insignificant changes, George's absence among others, lead to cascades of accumulating difference.

Everything in the replay without George makes perfect sense in terms of personalities and economic forces, but this alternative world is bleak and cynical, even cruel, while George, by his own apparently insignificant life, had imbued his surroundings with kindness and attendant success for his beneficiaries. Bedford Falls, his idyllic piece of small-town America, is now filled with bars, pool halls, and gambling joints; it has been renamed Pottersville, because the Bailey Building and Loan failed in George's absence and his unscrupulous rival took over the property and changed the town's name. A graveyard now occupies the community of small homes that George had financed at low interest and with endless forgiveness of debts. George's uncle, in despair at bankruptcy, is in an insane asylum; his mother, hard and cold, runs a poor boarding house; his wife is an aging spinster working in the town library; a hundred men lay dead on a sunken transport, because his brother drowned without George to rescue him, and never grew up to save the ship and win the Medal of Honor.

The wily angel, clinching his case, then pronounces the doctrine of contingency: "Strange, isn't it? **Each man's life touches so many other lives,** and when he isn't around he leaves an awful hole, doesn't he?....You see, George, you really had a wonderful life."

Contingency is both the watchword and lesson of the new interpretation of the Burgess Shale.† The fascination and transforming power of the Burgess message—a fantastic explosion of early disparity followed by decimation, perhaps largely by lottery—lies in its affirmation of history as the chief determinant of life's directions.

Walcott's earlier and diametrically opposite view located the pattern of life's history firmly in the other and more conventional style of scientific explanation—direct predictability and subsumption under invariant laws of nature. Moreover, Walcott's view of invariant law would now be dismissed as more an expression of cultural tradition and personal preference than an accurate expression of nature's patterns. For as we have seen, Walcott read life's history as the fulfillment of a divine purpose guaranteed to yield human consciousness after a long history of gradual and stately progress. The Burgess organisms had to be primitive versions of later improvements, and life had to move forward from this restricted and simple beginning.

---

*"Holotype" is taxonomic jargon for the specimen designated to bear the name of a species. Holotypes are chosen because concepts of the species may change later and biologists must have a criterion for assigning the original name. (If, for example, later taxonomists decide that two species were mistakenly mixed together in the first description, the original name will go to the group including the holotype specimen.)

† Located in British Columbia, this Cambrian deposit was discovered by C. D. Walcott in 1909. It yields an exceptionally diverse and well-preserved fauna. (Reprinter's note.)

The new view, on the other hand, is rooted in contingency. With so many Burgess possibilities of apparently equivalent anatomical promise—over twenty arthropod designs later decimated to four survivors, perhaps fifteen or more unique anatomies available for recruitment as major branches, or phyla, of life's tree—our modern pattern of anatomical disparity is thrown into the lap of contingency. The modern order was not guaranteed by basic laws (natural selection, mechanical superiority in anatomical design), or even by lower-level generalities of ecology or evolutionary theory. The modern order is largely a product of contingency. Like Bedford Falls with George Bailey, life had a sensible and resolvable history, generally pleasing to us since we did manage to arise, just a geological minute ago. But, like Pottersville without George Bailey, any replay, altered by an apparently insignificant jot or tittle at the outset, would have yielded an equally sensible and resolvable outcome of entirely different form, but most displeasing to our vanity in the absence of self-conscious life. (Though, needless to say, our nonexistent vanity would scarcely be an issue in any such alternative world.) By providing a maximum set of anatomically proficient possibilities right at the outset, the Burgess Shale becomes our centerpiece for the controlling power of contingency in setting the pattern of life's history and current composition.

Finally, if you will accept my argument that contingency is not only resolvable and important, but also fascinating in a special sort of way, then the Burgess not only reverses our general ideas about the source of pattern—it also fills us with a new kind of amazement (also a *frisson* for the improbability of the event) at the fact that humans ever evolved at all. We came **this close** (put your thumb about a millimeter away from your index finger), thousands and thousands of times, to erasure by the veering of history down another sensible channel. Replay the tape a million times from a Burgess beginning, and I doubt that anything like *Homo sapiens* would ever evolve again. It is, indeed, a wonderful life.

A final point about predictability versus contingency:

Am I really arguing that nothing about life's history could be predicted, or might follow directly from general laws of nature? Of course not; the question that we face is one of scale, or level of focus. Life exhibits a structure obedient to physical principles. We do not live amidst a chaos of historical circumstance unaffected by anything accessible to the "scientific method" as traditionally conceived. I suspect that the origin of life on earth was virtually inevitable, given the chemical composition of early oceans and atmospheres, and the physical principles of self-organizing systems. Much about the basic form of multicellular organisms must be constrained by rules of construction and good design. The laws of surfaces and volumes, first recognized by Galileo, require that large organisms evolve different shapes from smaller relatives in order to maintain the same relative surface area. Similarly, bilateral symmetry can be expected in mobile organisms built by cellular division. (The Burgess weird wonders are bilaterally symmetrical.)

But these phenomena, rich and extensive though they are, lie too far from the details that interest us about life's history. Invariant laws of nature impact the general forms and functions of organisms; they set the channels in which organic design must evolve. But the channels are so broad relative to the details that fascinate us! The physical channels do not specify arthropods, annelids, mollusks, and vertebrates, but, at most, bilaterally symmetrical organisms based on repeated parts. The boundaries of the channels retreat even further into the distance when we ask the essential questions about our own origin: Why did mammals evolve among vertebrates? Why did primates take to the trees? Why did the tiny twig that produced *Homo sapiens* arise and survive in Africa? When we set our focus upon the level of detail that regulates most common questions about the history of life, contingency dominates and the predictability of general form recedes to an irrelevant background.

Charles Darwin recognized this central distinction between *laws in the background* and *contingency in the details* in a celebrated exchange of letters with the devout Christian evolutionist Asa Gray. Gray, the Harvard botanist, was inclined to support not only Darwin's demonstration of evolution but also his principle of natural selection as its mechanism. But Gray was worried about the implications for Christian faith and the meaning of life. He particularly fretted that Darwin's view left no room for rule by law, and portrayed nature as shaped entirely by blind chance.

Darwin, in his profound reply, acknowledged the existence of general laws that regulate life in a broad sense. These laws, he argued, addressing Gray's chief concern, might even (for all we know) reflect some higher purpose in the universe. But the natural world is full of details, and these form the primary subject matter of biology. Many of these details are "cruel" when measured, inappropriately, by human moral standards. He wrote to Gray: "I cannot persuade myself that a beneficent and omnipotent God would have designedly created the Ichneumonidae with the express intention of their feeding within the living bodies of caterpillars, or that a cat should play with mice." How, then, could the non-morality of details be reconciled with a universe whose general laws might reflect some higher purpose? Darwin replied that the details lay in a realm of contingency undirected by laws that set the channels. The universe, Darwin replied to Gray, runs by law, "with the details, whether good or bad, left to the working out of what we may call chance."

And so, ultimately, the question of questions boils down to the placement of the boundary between predictability under invariant law and the multifarious possibilities of historical contingency. Traditionalists like Walcott would place the boundary so low that all major patterns of life's history fall above the line into the realm of predictability (and, for him, direct manifestation of divine intentions). But I envision a boundary sitting so high that almost every interesting event of life's history falls into the realm of contingency. I regard the new interpretation of the Burgess Shale as nature's finest argument for placing the boundary this high.

This means—and we must face the implication squarely— that the origin of *Homo sapiens*, as a tiny twig on an improbable branch of a contingent limb on a fortunate tree, lies well below the boundary. In Darwin's scheme, we are a detail, not a purpose or embodiment of the whole—"with the details, whether good or bad, left to the working out of what we may call chance." Whether the evolutionary origin of self-conscious intelligence in any form lies above or below the boundary, I simply do not know. All we can say is that our planet has never come close a second time.

For anyone who feels cosmically discouraged at the prospect of being a detail in the realm of contingency, I cite for solace **a wonderful poem by Robert Frost,** dedicated explicitly to this concern: ***Design.*** Frost, on a morning walk, finds an odd conjunction of three white objects with different geometries. This peculiar but fitting combination, he argues, must record some form of intent; it cannot be accidental. But if intent be truly manifest, then what can we make of our universe—for the scene is evil by any standard of human morality. We must take heart in Darwin's proper solution. We are observing a contingent detail, and may yet hope for purpose, or at least neutrality, from the universe in general.

Robert Frost

I found a dimpled spider, fat and white,
On a white heal-all, holding up a moth
Like a white piece of rigid satin cloth—
Assorted characters of death and blight
Mixed ready to begin the morning right,
Like the ingredients of a witches' broth—
A snow-drop spider, a flower like a froth,
And dead wings carried like a paper kite.

What had that flower to do with being white,
The wayside blue and innocent heal-all?
What brought the kindred spider to that height,
Then steered the white moth thither in the night?
What but design of darkness to appall?—
If design govern in a thing so small.†

FIRST DAY OF ISSUE

Homo sapiens, I fear, is a "thing so small" in a vast universe, a wildly improbable evolutionary event well within the realm of contingency. Make of such a conclusion what you will. Some find the prospect depressing; I have always regarded it as exhilarating, and a source of both freedom and consequent moral responsibility.

ARTICLE DESIGN BY PAMELA CANNON

Mah-jongg, dominoes, Pachinko, and Hanafu (flower cards) are all venues for gambling. The exterior of the construction is made up of giant mah-jongg tiles—all modular—constructed of plywood. They are exact replicas of actual tiles. I stacked original, small tiles one upon another one evening at dinner so that they were self-supporting—like a house of cards. The structure had an interior space, so this became the model for the final construction. Each of my tiles is 9″ x 12.″ Some of the original small tiles of ivory are on the floor of the construction, functioning as stepping stones in a Japanese garden. The gravel around them is replaced by silver pachinko balls.

I wanted a distorted/deconstructed interior that reflects (in the many mirrors) anxiety and risk-taking. I also wanted it to look the way a pachinko parlor sounds—loud, with metal balls descending against metal posts and each other in multiples of perhaps five hundred or a thousand at one time, as in a room full of players.

The figure with arms reaching upward located in the rear on the right was originally a carved, wood tourist item—*hotei*, one of the seven deities of good fortune. He is the god of contentment and happiness, but I've transformed him into a happy Yakuza, an underworld criminal in Japan, characterized by full body tattoos. He has two stacks of yen bills in his hands.

The other "chance" (not a game) implied in the title is depicted in the interior space as the office of the Yakuza boss. He is symbolized by the gesturing shadow figure behind the screen. On both sides of the screen are small bottles containing human pinky fingers. If an underling in the Yakuza gang fails to perform an important task or creates an embarrassing situation, he must ritually cut off his own finger as an act of contrition.

Jack Nichelson

THE RED DRAGON: Where There Are More Than Games of Chance
(Electrified, 24"h x 24"w x 24"d plywood construction with mixed media)

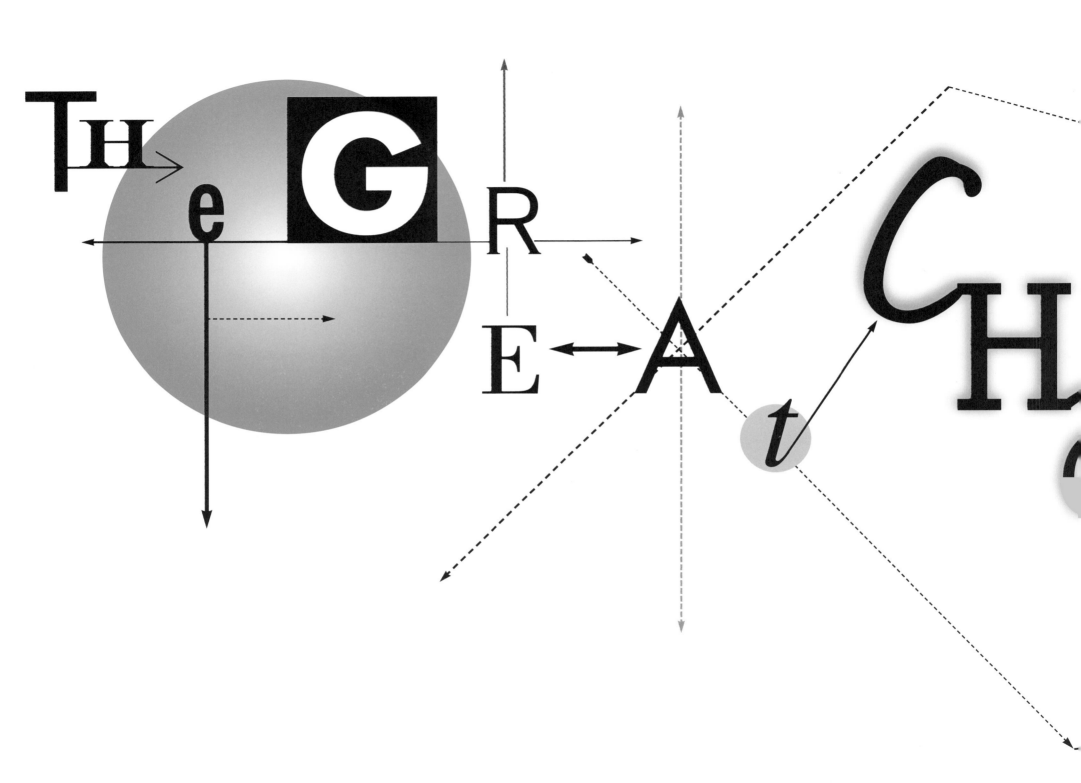

IN

of

Chance

ED BINKOWSKI

Is chance the leer of the devil or the smile on God's secret face? Is it reducible to a physicist's formula or a lucky charm? All our various perceptions of chance may be ordered along a continuum ranging from the malevolent force that dashes our hopes and exults in our fears; through the neutral force that, on balance, has no real effect other than "the cost of doing business" in an inefficient world; to the benign force, one in which we may participate, that exalts our destinies even as it shapes them.

The Cynic's Chance: Perverse Purposelessness

At this end of the chain, there are no accidents, only unfortunate coincidences. The apparent workings of chance are mundane expressions of the obvious, malign plan. Not only does God play dice: He cheats. All but the most naive perceive the pointlessness and isolation of our lives and the illusory nature of "free will." Only the incorrigibly innocent and sentimental fail to appreciate Oscar Wilde's observation: "The good ended happily, and the bad unhappily. That is what Fiction means."

For the devout believer, we are either a demiurge's playthings—"as flies to wanton schoolboys"—or this is a Gnostic universe with the Evil One in ascendancy. Our chances are of only two varieties: slim and none. Our ambitions and hopes are but trial balloons to be shot down, either for transgressing the appropriate limits of humility or for indulging the idle sadism of our betters. Even the most optimistic know we are only impotent pawns on the battleground between the divine force that fuels creativity and the perverse chaotogenic energy that infidels misidentify as entropy, rather than the Enemy.

For the irreligious, at this point on the chain chance is an active and sadistic power that will always win in the end; at least, that is the born loser's protest, the whiner who knows that the deck is stacked against him. It is not enough to rail against the odds; there must be a cosmic conspiracy that has ruined him for attempting to cross an unseen boundary. As in the song "The Dealer" he knows that "You can't win, you can't break even, and you can't get out of the game." The best that can be expected of any of us is a noble, resigned despair: Kierkegaard's "abridgment of hope." Indeed, the only possibility of salvation is to acknowledge that there is no chance of salvation; the man without hope is the man without fear.

The Failure's Chance: Malicious Mischief

One link up on the chain, chance is still an adversary, but one that can be beaten, a foe that is more stubborn than merely mean. The Christian devil is a foil rather than an equal opponent. For the non-believer, Murphy's law rules chance is Mother Nature's revenge, and sooner rather than later. In more animate view of the world, there are Satan's imps and Nature fairies, English pixies and German elves, gremlins to frustrate the pilo and kobolds to tease the miner. We fail because we are undone by literally "little" things. A more constrained vision simply acknowledge "the inherent perversity of physical objects": toast always fall buttered-side down. Even the most high-tech computer geek wi know to blame failure on a "quantum glitch": an unpredictable, unob servable fluctuation of an electron, the ultimate ghost in the machine

Planners talk about the Law of Unintended Consequences: ever solution makes things worse, as in the new highway that increase traffic jams. John Brooks is credited with an eponymous law for not ing that the more people assigned to a project, the later it will be. Th nominal realist will talk about transaction costs and inefficiencies o scale, but the real issue is the one identified by H. L. Mencken: "Ther is no problem, no matter how complex, that does not have a solutio which is simple, obvious and wrong." Chance, like God and the devi is in the details. Jim Thompson, pulp mystery writer, said it best in *Th Killer Inside Me:* "To commit the perfect murder, you need guts, a plan and luck. Practically nobody has luck." The killer is always tripped u by the inconsequential detail; the grit in the gears is a no-longer divine Nemesis. We are not allowed the "luck" to go too far, to trans gress the natural order; instead, chance produces the banana peel, with someone or something just out of sight, laughing at our pratfalls.

The Gambler's Chance: Payback and Talismans —If chance does not reside in Satan, nor in his works, it may still be in his pomps. A totally mindless chance, no longer fueled by the will of an actor or striving for the soul of a believer, might yet be an abstract property of events and objects that maintains an indifferent balance. "The race is not to the swift, nor the battle to the strong, neither yet bread to the wise, nor yet riches to men of understanding, nor yet favor to men of skill, but time and chance happeneth to them all" (Ecclesiastes 9:11). The balance is impersonal, amoral, and totally inflexible.

WHAT GOES AROUND, COMES AROUND; CHANCE ITSELF IS GOVERNED BY RULES.

Unfortunately, the rules are usually not known, so it always pays to wear your lucky shirt, carry your rabbit's foot, and drive fast only when your car has a St. Christopher's medal hanging from the rearview mirror. Seasonal cycles provided the first props against chance, and soon we believed that random events would run through cycles of their own. Is it ever really "time" for the roulette wheel to spin red? Of course; it's come up black the last five times. In statistical analysis, such sequences are called martingales; for obvious reasons, any betting system that uses such reasoning is known as "gambler's ruin."

Viewed from this link on the chain, chance is the great leveler, the second law of thermodynamics writ large, the heat death of the universe—that point when energy is so uniformly distributed that all of existence has been reduced to a monotone hum—presaged by the confusion that overwhelms our intentions on a daily basis. When some happy consequence unexpectedly occurs, we can never be sure what "special" thing made it happen. Our charms and habits are not so much whistling in the dark of a hostile universe but rather attempts to bring a touch of idiosyncratic color to the relentless, flat gray of chance.

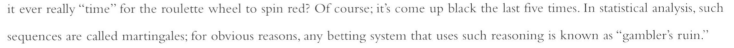

Conformist's Chance: Routine Randomness—

A dried-up "modern" with a withered imagination believes there is no balance, no cycle. Chance has neither memory nor purpose, but is just the expression of a long-range tendency. The romantic may delude himself into thinking that his lottery ticket is a sure winner; the conformist comforts himself with the knowledge that he has the same chance of winning as anyone else. The easiest way to believe in statistics is to become one.

With this view in mind, Damon Runyon improved on the prophet: "The race is not always to the swift, nor the battle to the brave, but that's the way to bet." Chance is an unwelcome but usually insignificant intrusion: play the odds, carry an umbrella, buy insurance, and always wear rubbers. Chance is the work of the actuary, not the Adversary. With more courage than sense we buy lottery tickets and insurance policies, ignorant of the notion that probabilities can apply only to ensembles, not individuals. From this perspective, chance as a threat has been dethroned, almost made dull. Can the ultimate oxymoron be "risk management"?

We tend to treat these probabilities, these tendencies, as poor cousins of causal relationships, embarrassed by the direct lawlike behavior of their betters. Indeed, most of the time we think of probabilities only in terms of what we view (rightly or wrongly) as equally likely events—this coin toss, that throw of the dice. This very inability to distinguish, which provides the strength of mathematics, makes chance seem a rather shabby and ignorant affair.

The Skeptic's Chance: Lack of Information—

At this stage in the chain, chance no longer has any force; indeed, it is defined away altogether. Chance appears to exist only because we do not know enough. The coin *will* come up heads or tails depending on the crosswinds, the height above the floor, the angle of the wrist on the throw, and so on. The only uncertainty attached to the event is the level of information we possess about it. Even if the coin is biased, or has already been thrown, if we have no *a priori* reason to guess one way or the other, we will say that the "chance" of heads is one-half, just the same as for tails. This chance has nothing to do with the coin or the world, but only our limited view of both.

It may be that these limits are irreducible. Heisenberg's much misapplied Uncertainty Principle states that we cannot know with accuracy both a particle's position and its momentum. Still, no one doubts that the particle is real, somewhere, traveling at a particular speed (at least not until we climb the next link in the chain of chance). Within such limits, the world is a knowable machine, and we can be as cautiously optimistic as Sir Thomas Browne: "What song the sirens sang, or what name Achilles chose when he hid among women, though unanswerable questions, are not beyond all conjecture." We may be reduced to guessing, but the game is fair. Entropy will win in the long run, but it will be a long run indeed.

In the early twentieth century it almost seemed as if chance were about to disappear altogether. Better technology and better theories would inevitably dissolve the gray cloud of randomness. But chance was eventually found to be more a wall than a cloud; the only reason science had such success in abusing and ignoring it was that all the easy problems were tackled first.

The Mathematician's Chance: Deterministic Chaos—The most profoundly discouraging insight of modern mathematics is that even completely deterministic systems may not allow predictability; that is, even with a formula, even with the right formula, chance will always win. A simple example is that annoying drip from the faucet. The droplet from the tap gets bigger and bigger until it finally goes kerplop, following simple and well-known laws; it is still impossible in practical terms to predict when it is going to fall. Moreover, the most infinitesimal change in starting conditions is enough to make a radical change in the final outcome; from seemingly indistinguishable causes, radically different effects occur.

As James Gleick puts it in his popular *Chaos:* "In weather, for example, this translates into what is only half-jokingly known as the Butterfly Effect—the notion that a butterfly stirring the air today in Peking can transform storm systems next month in New York." The score is Chance 1, Newton 0. The world is not a predictable machine, even in principle, due to this disproportion in size between cause and effect. Consider a Newtonian pool table: the balls and cue are point masses; the balls travel in perfectly straight lines on a frictionless and perfectly flat table to rebound off the edges with perfect elasticity. We feel that we can write down the path of the ball exactly. But if the position of the ball and the force of the cue are known only within the boundaries of Planck's constant (the limit for the Uncertainty Principle), then the ball's possible paths cover *every* point on the table within seven collisions. It could be anywhere—even if we know everything—so in the end we know nothing.

And yet the perturbations themselves seem to show some form of regularity, of bundling. The mathematicians talk of Feigenbaum numbers that capture the regularities in irregularities and of fractals that measure distance in partial dimensions. New theories and buzz words—chaos, catastrophe, complexity, contingency—emerge, each of which suggests in a different way that we are blind men trying to understand the elephant on which the world rests. (And why do all of those words begin with "c"?) And yet, purpose is beginning to insinuate itself once again as we climb another link in the chain.

COMPLEXITY

The Physicist's Chance: Law Without Law—Guided by statistical thinking, most scientists now reluctantly admit that "chance" is the *only* source of what seems to be regularity; "reality" is just an average. The only laws are statistical laws. "This is the way the world works, probably" is all we can ever say. Chance is not the exception; chance is the rule. Matter, even existence, is just a concentration of higher probabilities. The quantum theorists tell us that the many levels of universes inside the etymologically indivisible atom are filled with particles that are neither here nor there but everywhere and anywhere with a greater or lesser likelihood. We can refer to an electron's probability shell to give our ignorance and incomprehension a name, but are not otherwise enlightened.

Some nervous types will claim that these apparent impossibilities—"incredibilities" might be a better word—simply reflect the inadequacies of the current scientific model, and such timidity must be respected. But the mathematics works *so* well, and the averages are *so* well defined. If the doubters are right, what even greater incomprehensibilities lie behind the apparently self-contradictory self-organization of self-less monads? If the randomness is itself not chance, where can our narrow minds hide?

You can be very sure that your quotidian chair will not dissolve into the nothingness that sustains it, just as you can be sure that all the air in the room will not suddenly "decide" to gather at the other end—but these things *might* happen, no matter how low the probability. This whole insubstantial pageant, faded or not, rests on what statisticians call the law of large numbers. And whose law is this? What kind of law is it that the "numbers" obey? Nobel-laureate physicist John Wheeler described it as: "Law without law! Law beyond law! Particles flouting fixed formulas yet fabricating firm form!" Where is the firm form from? Who is the man behind the curtain?

The Romantic's Chance: The Secret Order—At this end of the chain, there are no accidents, only happy coincidences. The apparent workings of chance express a hidden, benign plan. God's dice are loaded in favor of *this* universe. All but a gifted few fail to perceive the depth and multiplicity of connections that inform and direct every aspect of our lives. Only the most callous and jaded will fail to agree with Fred Astaire's character in *The Gay Divorcee:* **"Chance is the fool's name for Fate!"**

For the religious believer, the devil has returned, except that he has been part of the plan all along. Milton's Satan claims that he is "That Power which erring men call chance." More to the point, Goethe's Mephistopheles reveals his identity: "I am the power that always wills evil yet always works good." The problem of evil remains insoluble, but everything happens for a reason no matter how well that reason is hidden from us.

Even hard science has come full circle. With varying degrees of acceptance, the talk is everywhere of some subterranean connection among all events. Be it quantum mechanics' search for hidden variables, superstring theory (so nakedly literal: those unseen higher-dimensional pieces of twine that hold everything together), Bell's action at a distance, Boehm's implicate order, and even mad Sheldrake's morphogenetic field, all posit a convergence, a secret plan. It is not that the theories aren't working, it's that they're working too well. This *can't* be an accident.

One of the most extreme suggestions inverts the old religious proofs for the existence of God from design arguments. In John Wheeler's introduction to Barrow and Tipler's *The Anthropic Cosmological Principle:*

Meaning is important, is even central. It is not only that man is adapted to the universe. The universe is adapted to man. Imagine a universe in which one or another of the fundamental dimensionless constants of physics is altered by a few percent one way or the other? Man could never come into being in such a universe. That is the central point of the anthropic principle. According to this principle, a life-giving factor lies at the center of the whole machinery and design of the world.

For example, if the strength of gravity were just slightly greater, all matter would coalesce into a single ball; if it were just slightly less, no solid bodies would ever form. Every physical constant is overdetermined to be just so. The inverse square law must be a square, not a cubic function. There are no atheists in observatories. If the cosmologists are right, our belief in a Creator is irrelevant; it is clear that a Creator has more than sufficient faith in us. *Credo quia incredible.*

This pattern is repeated again and again; apparently random and independent descriptions of the universe are all balanced on a razor's edge. We are living in a much "simpler" world than we imagine, with apparent variation largely constrained. **Chance itself is too perfectly random; there is no chance for CHANCE.**

Edward Binkowski, author of *Satellite Information Systems*, is a statistician working in New York City. A former advisor to the Department of Energy, the Oak Ridge National Laboratory, the Census Bureau, and his daughter Alison, he has taught at Cornell Medical School, Fordham Law School, and Hunter College.

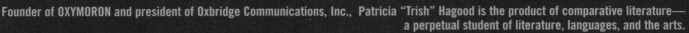

Founder of OXYMORON and president of Oxbridge Communications, Inc., Patricia "Trish" Hagood is the product of comparative literature— a perpetual student of literature, languages, and the arts.

Xenia Argon is a New York City native transplanted to the Boston area. She writes about the local environment, but in an extended sense.

Diskin Clay grew up in Reno, where his horse betting tastes were formed at The Sierra Turf Club. He teaches and writes on Greek literature and philosophy in the Dept. of Classical Studies at Duke University. Summers see him in Greece, Cyprus, Turkey, Paros and Thasos working on archaeological projects.

A witch, teacher, freelance writer/editor, and English Renaissance literature scholar, Barbara Ardinger lives in Long Beach, California, with her cats Schroedinger and Heisenberg. She is the author of *A Woman's Book of Rituals & Celebrations* and *Seeing Solutions*.

Jenifer Nostrand's poetry appears regularly in such magazines as *The Kansas Quarterly, Amelia Magazine*, and *The Greensboro Review*. She was the guest poet in a recent issue of *The Birmingham Poetry Review*.

Stephen Jay Gould is the author of sixteen books, most recently *Full House*, and such international bestsellers as *Dinosaur in a Haystack, Ever Since Darwin, The Panda's Thumb, Bully for Brontosaurus, Wonderful Life*, and *Eight Little Piggies. The Mismeasure of Man* won the American Book Award for Science and the National Book Critics Circle Award. He teaches geology, biology, and the history of science at Harvard University.

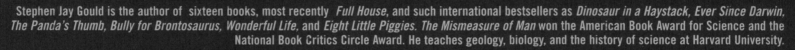

Marcel Tetel is vice president of the Société Internationale des Amis de Montaigne, an Honorary Citizen of Saint-Michel de Montaigne, and a member of the Consulat de la Vinée de Bergerac, sworn to drink only the fine wines of Bergerac.

John Boe is a professional storyteller, award winning essayist, prize winning teacher at U.C. Davis, editor of *Writing on the Edge,* and author of *Life Itself* (Chiron Publications, 1994), which poses such questions as: "If cleanliness is next to godliness, is messiness next to goddessness?"

Rolland Golden, a Folsom (LA) water colorist has had over one hundred one-man shows, including touring exhibits in the U.S.S.R. and southern France. His paintings are in the permanent collections of the Pushkin and New Orleans Museums, among others.

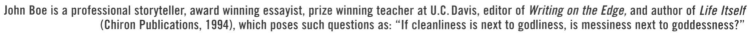

DAVID BELL COMPLETED HIS PH.D. IN FRENCH LITERATURE AT THE JOHNS HOPKINS UNIVERSITY IN BALTIMORE, WHERE HIS EXPOSURE TO POE LORE WAS ASSURED. HIS INTEREST IN NINETEENTH-CENTURY DETECTIVE FICTION (FRENCH AND AMERICAN) WAS THUS A DETERMINED COINCIDENCE. HE TEACHES AT DUKE UNIVERSITY AND WRITES ABOUT THE RELATIONS BETWEEN LITERATURE AND SCIENCE.

KEVIN CLARK IS PROFESSOR OF AMERICAN LITERATURE AND CREATIVE WRITING AT CAL POLY, SAN LUIS OBISPO, CALIFORNIA. HIS POEMS AND CRITICISM HAVE APPEARED IN *THE ANTIOCH REVIEW, BLACK WARRIOR REVIEW, COLLEGE ENGLISH, THE IOWA REVIEW,* AND *THE GEORGIA REVIEW*. HIS TWO CHAPBOOKS ARE *GRANTING THE WOLF* (STATE STREET PRESS, 1984) AND *WIDOW UNDER A NEW MOON* (OWL CREEK PRESS, 1990).

KATHLEEN BARTOLETTI IS A NEW YORK ARTIST AND MEMBER OF THE NATIONAL ARTS CLUB, WHOSE WORK ILLUSTRATES THE THEMES OF FORTUNE, CHANCE, AND RISK. OFTEN A CUPID OR A WOMAN HOLDING A CHILD APPEARS IN THE CENTER OF A WHEEL OF FORTUNE, A DARTBOARD, OR A TARGET. THE WOMAN MAY BE FORTUNA, A FORTUNE TELLER, OR A MADONNA.

DAVE JOHNSON TEACHES AT POETS HOUSE (SOHO), THE NEW YORK PUBLIC LIBRARY, AND TEACHERS AND WRITERS COLLABORATIVE. HIS BOOK OF POETRY, *MARBLE SHOOT* (HUMMINGBIRD PRESS) APPEARED IN 1995.

ANNA BALAKIAN IS THE FIRST BIOGRAPHER OF ANDRÉ BRETON. SHE IS THE FORMER CHAIR OF THE DEPARTMENT OF COMPARATIVE LITERATURE AT NEW YORK UNIVERSITY AND FORMER PRESIDENT OF THE AMERICAN COMPARATIVE LITERATURE ASSN. HER TWO MOST RECENT BOOKS ARE *THE FICTION OF THE POET: FROM MALLARMÉ TO THE POST-SYMBOLIST MODE* (PRINCETON UNIVERSITY PRESS, 1992) AND *THE SNOWFLAKE IN THE BELFRY: DOGMA AND DISQUIETUDE IN THE ACADEMIC ARENA* (INDIANA UNIVERSITY PRESS, 1994).

ROBERT GRUDIN TEACHES LITERATURE AND HUMANITIES AT THE UNIVERSITY OF OREGON. A GUGGENHEIM FELLOW IN 1992-93, HE IS AN AUTHORITY ON THE LITERATURE OF SHAKESPEARE AND HIS PERIOD OF THE RENAISSANCE. IN 1995, HE FOUNDED THE ENDOWMENT FOR CIVIC HUMANISM, A FOUNDATION TO SUPPORT CIVIC SERVICE PROGRAMS IN SCHOOLS AND UNIVERSITIES. HE IS THE AUTHOR OF *ON DIALOGUE: AN ESSAY IN FREE THOUGHT, TIME AND THE ART OF LIVING, THE GRACE OF GREAT THINGS,* AND THE NOVEL *BOOK*.

JULIE TETEL HAS PUBLISHED FIFTEEN ROMANCES. TO DATE, HER PAIRS OF PROTAGONISTS HAVE ALL BEEN HUMAN, BUT THE UPS MAN WILL SURELY TURN OUT TO BE A HIGH-RANKING FBI AGENT WHO WAS IN A FORMER INCARNATION—YOU GUESSED IT!—A WARTY FROG AND WHO HAS THE POTENTIAL TO GET RID OF HIS DNA ALTOGETHER IN ORDER TO BECOME A REALLY HUNKY ANDROID.

RICHARD FOREMAN, PLAYWRIGHT, MACARTHUR FELLOW, AND MANY OTHER FELLOWS, IS A "PIONEER IN END-OF-MILLENNIUM CONTROLLED CHAOS," AND DIRECTOR OF THE ONTOLOGICAL-HYSTERIC THEATER IN NEW YORK CITY.

EFREM WEITZMAN IS A NATIONALLY KNOWN ARTIST-DESIGNER WHO HAS CREATED ARTWORKS THAT CAN BE FOUND ALL OVER THE UNITED STATES IN PUBLIC BUILDINGS, BOTH SECULAR AND RELIGIOUS. HE ALSO OFFERS WORKSHOPS IN THE *I CHING*, STRESS MANAGEMENT, AND SENSORY AWARENESS.

Margaret Boe Birns is an adjunct Assistant Professor at New York University and a Member of the Faculty of The New School. She specializes in nineteenth and twentieth century literature.

Constance Brock - Past: Poems in the *New York Times*; novelette in Paris. Present: Mystery novel in the works. Future: Hope it rolls a pair of perks.

"More Than You Know" is part of a novel-in-progress. Melissa Malouf is a sucker for the old songs. Her new book is called *It Had To Be You*.

William Everdell teaches at St. Ann's School in Brooklyn Heights. His latest book, *The First Moderns: Profiles in the Origin of Twentieth-Century Thought*, will be published by the University of Chicago Press in 1997, not entirely by chance.

Mario Bunge is the Frothingham Professor of Logic and Metaphysics at McGill University. He is the author of more than seventy works including the now classic treatise *Causality*. His latest book is *Finding Philosophy in Social Science* (Yale University Press, 1996).

The artist stands naked and alone at the edge. Monica Kassan.

Lawrence Sklar is William K. Frankena Collegiate Professor and Professor of Philosophy at the University of Michigan. His books include *Space, Time and Spacetime*, and *Physics and Chance*.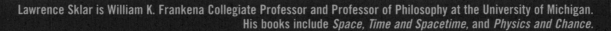

Robert A. Fowkes is Professor Emeritus of German Linguistics at New York University and past president of the International Linguistics Assn. and the St. David's Society of New York. He once taught a course on dragons at NYU.

Caroline Hagood is a freshman at St. Ann's School

Louis Hagood is a psychoanalyst-in-training at the Theodore Reik Institute and runs Oxbridge in his spare time.

Glenn Schaeffer is president of Circus Circus Enterprises, Inc., the gaming industry's largest company, and chairman of the Nevada Resort Assn. He holds two advanced degrees in literature and is a member of Phi Beta Kappa.

Henry C. Pearson is a proud son of Kinston, N.C., a long-time beloved art teacher at The New School, an illustrator and collector of the work of Seamus Heaney, and a geometric painter whose work is in the permanent collections of the major museums.

She saw the truth in a flash. Rosalee Isaly

Bernard Weitzman is a Jungian-trained analyst and a practioner of Vajrayana Buddhism. He is a full-time member of the Psychology Department of The Graduate Faculty at the New School and a practicing psychotherapist in the field of contemplative psychology. "In addition to thinking about our experience, we can also experience our thinking."

Jack Nichelson, artist and Professor of Art (retired) at University of Florida (Gainesville) constructs "boxes" that are microcosms of our social and psychological worlds. Influenced by Kurt Schwitters, religious reliquaries, and Japan, his work transforms cultural debris into modern icons.

John Kadvany is a graduate of Woodrow Wilson High School in Long Beach, California. He is working on *The Extraterritoriality of Imre Lakatos*.

Nicholas Campion is a freelance writer and journalist. He read history at Cambridge, the School of Oriental and African Studies (London), and the London School of Economics, and lectured for many years. He is the author of *The Great Year* (Penguin, 1994), an acclaimed study of cosmology and history.

Estelle Shay is a painter who moves at will among differing visions, seemingly unconnected. The painted frame is introduced as an element linking remote realities that move across time and space. The contrasting styles and techniques suggest the ambiguity of experience.

A self-taught photographer, Duane Michals is represented by the Janis Gallery, and his witty and imaginative work is represented in museum collections around the world. He has published over twenty books. The most recent is Salute, Walt Whitman, (Twelvetrees Press, Santa Fe). This fall, Thames and Hudson (London) will unv. a new coffee table book—The Essential Duane Michals (not "Sensual" as Duane had wished).

Primarily self-taught, Linn Sage prefers the provocative to the preplanned. Like most successful satirists, she is deadly serious and is currently preparing a book, Never Sever the Head. Her work is in the Metropolitan Museum of Art and the International Center of Photography.

Pamela Cannon, graphic designer and
consultant, is a graduate of the School of
Visual Arts in New York.

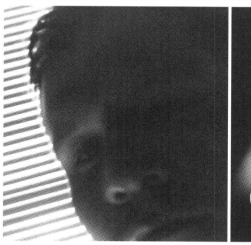

Ken is a graphic designer
They design and art direct things.

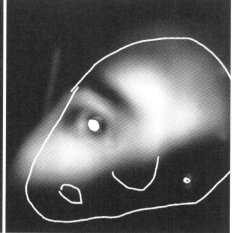

Gerald is an Art director.

KUDZU
By Doug Marlette